The Complete Wilderness Paddler

THE
COMPLETE
WILDERNESS
PADDLER

*by James West Davidson
and John Rugge*

*with illustrations
by Gordon Allen*

VINTAGE BOOKS

A DIVISION OF RANDOM HOUSE · NEW YORK

First Vintage Books Edition, January 1983
Copyright © 1975 by James Davidson and John Rugge
Illustrations Copyright © 1975 by Alfred A. Knopf, Inc.
All rights reserved under International and Pan-American
Copyright Conventions. Published in the United States by
Random House, Inc., New York, and simultaneously in
Canada by Random House of Canada Limited, Toronto.
Originally published by Alfred A. Knopf, Inc. in 1975.

Library of Congress Cataloging in Publication Data
Davidson, James West.
The complete wilderness paddler.
Bibliography: p.
Includes index.
1. Canoe and canoeing. 2. Camping.
I. Rugge, John. II. Title.
[GV789.D38 1983]   797.1'22   82-40021
ISBN 0-394-71153-X (pck.)

Manufactured in the United States of America

Contents

IV THE UPPER STRETCHES

V. THE RIVER CANYON

Introduction

A few years ago, Mr. Huck Finn wrote a book about some escapades of his. Literary critics and other respectable people ("sivilized folk," in Huck's words) didn't think very highly of it. The Concord Library Committee called it "the veriest trash." Luckily there were enough children around who liked it to keep the book alive until the professors caught on and began to read it and take it *very* seriously. Now we hear that some people want to take it out of the public schools because it ain't fit to be read by children.

We mention Huck partly because we admire him a lot, partly because we think we understand him a little, and partly because we are hoping he might help you to understand us. Huck was a fellow who felt "sivilization" closing in too tight around him, so tight that he had to leave for a while. To get away he chose a river, and after his trip was over he wrote a passably good book about his adventures. To quote him somewhat out of context, there was some things which he stretched, but mainly he told the truth.

Of course Huck and us have our differences. It's not too easy to admit to some of them. For example, he went eleven hundred miles down one of the five biggest rivers in the world, whereas we have generally settled for two or three hundred miles on more anonymous tributaries. He made do with improvised equipment which as near as we can tell didn't cost him a nickel, whereas we have depended more than we like on store-bought gear. The big difference, though, is that Huck returned from his travels wise enough to just tell stories, whereas we returned from ours with the audacious and foolhardy idea of writing a handbook for wilderness canoeing.

That is what this book is about. Our aim has been to lay out for you, as simply and clearly as we can, the specific techniques needed for undertaking a canoe trip in the wilds: all the way from finding a wilderness in the first place (which is tougher to do than in Huck's day) to scouting portages, crossing big lakes, and running heavy rapids. We've attempted to be as comprehensive as possible, writing not only for those whose canoeing is limited to weekend jaunts but also for those whose wilderness routes demand expertise in crossing ice-covered lakes, repairing punctured canoes, lining boats through unrunnable rapids, and other such tasks of a full-scale expedition. We have attempted to be comprehensive in detail as well as in scope. Too many hand-

books, we find, are written by experts who gloss over the crucial fine points because they've absorbed them as second nature, or assumed them so obvious as
not to need mentioning. When we tell you about researching the topographical
maps of your river, we focus on specifics, like how contour lines can indicate
before you ever see a river your chance for running a particular set of rapids.
Or in portaging your gear, how carrying your pack *and* a canoe can sometimes
be easier than carrying the canoe alone. Or in running rapids, how leaning way
out of the boat can make it less tippy than crouching low in the center.

We thought for a long time about the best way to collect in one book the
thousand and one skills of the wilderness paddler. It finally occurred to us, as
we were sitting one evening under a rain tarp in the middle of Labrador, that
we ought to just follow as much as we could Huck's plan and tell the story of
one expedition, talking about each of the various canoeing techniques as the
occasion arose. If, for instance, we crossed a large, many-armed lake which
proved especially difficult to navigate, why not use that experience to recount
the basic techniques of canoe compass work, and the solutions we found to
our problems? Or if we sweated out an afternoon trying to hunt up the remaining traces of a twenty-year-old Indian portage, why not stop there and
talk about the various ways to ferret out unmarked routes? The more we
thought about it, the more we liked the idea. A story like that would make a
lot more interesting reading than the usual abstract instruction books of how-
to techniques. And it would bring to mind all the concrete details so useful in
a handbook of wilderness lore: the memory of our friend Peach hauling his stern painter in just a bit too early when we were lining Joe's boat
through a big curler; or the recollection of how four of us nursed a fire to life
after a three-day soaking rain.

Since we happened to be under a tarp in Labrador when we got the idea
for our book, and since the river we were tracking, the Moisie, proved to be
wild enough to put to the test most all our canoeing techniques (not to mention a few we never dreamed of before), we've decided to follow that expedition along in this book. The Moisie River has more lessons to teach than
these pages have space: Rim Canyon, Igloo Rock, the damn alderbushes, to
mention only a few. In due time we'll let the river speak for itself. Right now,
you may want to know something about the four characters who ran that river
and who frequent these pages. You may well ask who we are to be inviting
you to spend time with us on a river—a long river at that. The sad truth is,
we're not much better at producing respectable credentials than Huck was.
John Rugge and Dave Peach are both medical students, but you would never
guess it from the amount of time they are out in the woods. Jim Davidson's
spare hours are taken up with writing about obscure Colonial American min-
isters, since he is in fleet pursuit of a Ph.D. (one of the more curious wonders

of the modern world). Joe Hardy is the only one of us gainfully employed, as an instructor in education at a small college in Vermont.

We could assure you that not even counting our back-lawn tenting experience as six-year-olds, the four of us have logged a combined total of fifty years of canoeing and wilderness experience. But that's most likely a bogus calculation. How would you like to be operated on by forty surgeons with a combined total of twenty years' training?

To try to tell you more about ourselves in the Introduction makes for an awfully big temptation to lie. Since we are, like Huck, trying to write mostly a true book, with only a few stretchers here and there, we figure our best bet is to stop now and let you get on with our guide. We hope the techniques we describe are useful enough and the stories we tell outlandish enough to give you the determination to go out and find your own river to run and your own stories to tell.

Acknowledgments

This book no more belongs to us alone
than does our river or our trip.
It is first and foremost the eminent domain
of those who know the difference between
the way we tell it and the way it was:

JOE *and* PEACH

About halfway down the Moisie, the four of us realized somewhat in amazement that, though we had brought what seemed a tremendous amount of movie film, in actuality it added up to only thirty minutes. The magnitude of our quandary stopped us dead. This trip was going to last 37,440 minutes and we had to figure which thirty deserved to be recorded on film.

We've had the same problem writing this guidebook, only more so. There is no way to distill on these pages a canoeing upbringing—the kind that Rug got from his father or that Jim got working with Joe Reiners, Jr., at Adirondack Swim and Trip Camp; yet this book would never have been written without the benefit of those proper upbringings. There is no way to compress all the experiences, canoe jaunts, and misadventures shared with friends; yet they are very much a part of this guidebook. Walt Corson, Chet Fenton, Brad Prozeller, Ron Turbayne, and Pete Davidson are only a few of the wraiths who stalk these pages: invisible and yet indispensable partners from an unseen world. Finally, there are those from whom we received help in distilling the things we did include. On more than one occasion, Bob and Kelly Nessle of Wilderness Truck, Inc., let us try to tear their boats apart on our canoe-evaluation outings; Peter Hornbeck and Pat Strohmeyer, boatbuilders of Olmstedville, N.Y., gave us valuable advice on how to put them back together again. Other friends have been kind enough to give all or parts of our first draft the benefit of careful readings and helpful criticism. We think particularly of Les Bechdel, Ted Weniger, Alan Fincke, Terry Pell, Dr. Ray Duff, Dr. Fritz Hauser, Dr. Jacques Grunblatt, and very likely also Richmond Brainerd, if we can ever find out where he now lives in Vermont.

Anyone who has even glanced at the rest of this text will know how much in debt we are to Gordy Allen, our talented illustrator, for catching the precision and detail of canoeing strokes as well as the flavor of the North woods. He in turn wishes to thank Bill Hilton for invaluable aid; also Josh and Kerry, semianonymous woodsmen.

Our editor, Angus Cameron, was hopeful enough to think our distillation might work, skeptical enough to keep after us in the interim, and in every way a helpful critic—even to the point of loaning us a spare fishing pole.

Jim Davidson

John Rugge

Smith's Restaurant
North Creek, N.Y.

I. PREPARATIONS

1. Finding a Wilderness

The wilderness exerts its pull on every self-respecting member of the human race, and we've often wondered why. Maybe the thought of all that empty space insults people, the same way that a vacuum upsets the rest of nature. Or maybe it appeals to our better side, to our restless spirit.

The strange thing is, few of us ever take the leap and actually get out into genuine honest-to-God wilderness to see it for ourselves—strange because the block isn't so much physical as mental. Most people, you see, just aren't sufficiently aware of the need to think big; they let the books convince them that the wilderness is somehow a quality of the heart, something *inside* them. Nonsense. The wilderness is plain open space, the sheer physical presence of the earth unwinding without us people.

How big does a wilderness have to be? We're not sure. But how long it will take someone to perceive the wildness depends on the mode of travel. A backpacker can begin to sense distance inside a hundred miles; a canoeist needs a route several times that long. By Land Rover, the Sahara is scarcely big enough. Big enough, that is, to throw a traveller back on himself with no prospect of chancing on a signpost, a fence, or outside help.

For the person who sets out into this country, a full appreciation of wild space will be one of the major accomplishments of his trip. Yet, oddly enough, this perception can also serve as the initial inspiration. Such spaces are only dimly encountered in the confines of the civil world, but they are there. The proof is, Rug would in all likelihood never have found his way to the Moisie canyons had it not been for an encounter with the Boundless back in the foothills of the Berkshires. That was the February when Joe Hardy called from Maine to say he'd found some snowshoes in his uncle's attic, would be passing through Massachusetts that weekend, and how would Rug like to come up from New Haven and do a bit of winter hiking?

Rug said fine, he was willing. They hadn't been camping together for a couple of years, not since their outing on the Souhegan River; but Rug knew Joe as a man with enthusiasm for the outdoors which could surmount even the most unfortunate mishaps—a good thing, since Joe seemed plagued by more than his share. The time on the Souhegan it was the car keys he had tucked in the top of his wet suit at the beginning of the day's run. As Joe descended the river, the keys descended his wet suit, the unfortunate circumstance being that the keys finished their trip to the bottom of the river well before Joe finished his. Rug had fumed all the way through the hitchhike back to the car and even more as they stood in a drizzle watching a smug teen-ager they hired break into the car with a coat hanger. But Joe remained unruffled. "Well, Jawn," he said in his imperturbable Maine accent, "worse could've happened." Rug allowed he was expending a considerable amount of energy trying to imagine *what,* so Joe smiled and said, "Could've been you that lost the keys, and then there'd be no one to blame but yourself."

They laughed about that one again snowshoeing up a small hill in the Berkshires. It was a perfect day for reminiscing: the hike easy and the snow falling lightly. Rug told Joe the story of how he and his dad lost the red canoe through the gorge on the Boreas River and had to hike out six miles. Joe told Rug the one about his brush with death on the ice fields at Rainier. Rug said he already heard it twice before. As the two neared the top of the knoll, the snow flurries picked up and clouded the sky. The wind began blowing in earnest and quickly the snow squall closed over them. Rug and Joe trudged on in silence for several minutes, and then Joe said, almost to himself, "Can you *imagine?*"

"Imagine what?" asked Rug.

"I was just thinking of Hudson. When his crew mutinied and set him off in James Bay in a lifeboat. That was December. Can you imagine it, how Hudson must have felt? Watching his ship sail away, until it was just a speck on the horizon? And then feeling that wind slice across the bay? And sitting there in that little boat and *knowing*—right down to the pit of his stomach—that there was nobody but him and that ship for hundreds of miles?"

Rug was ready with a reply, but right then the two of them cleared the head of the knoll and saw the road through the blur of the storm. Just beyond they could make out a gaudily painted burger stand. The sign said: "North Country Short Orders."

The intrepid snowshoers eyed each other with the same expression of resignation.

"Hudson didn't get let off in December," said Rug somewhat tartly. "The truth is, his ship never made it out in the winter because the Bay had iced over. The crew cut Hudson adrift in a small shallop the next June with about eight others in the crew."

"You mean they actually survived a winter in James Bay?"

"Oh, sure. That's not half so bad as camping on arctic sea ice, and Stefansson did that. James Bay is a picnic compared with arctic sea ice. For that matter, you and me and these snowshoes could handle James Bay, just so we brought a good rifle."

"Thanks, Jawn, but I'd prefer visiting the place when the trade winds are more seasonable."

An offhand comment, as Joe was the first to admit. But somehow it provided the sufficient critical mass for an idea, coming as it did on the heels of all the stories of past camping experiences, the hike through the woods, the memory of Hudson's journey, and then the disappointment of the burger stand. It was the realization that if you wanted to feel the spaces the old explorers had felt, you could not do it messing around in the Berkshires. Joe remembers Rug squinting at him for a moment, and then asking, "What are you doing this summer?" And then hearing himself reply, "Funny, I was just about to ask you the same thing."

So the Moisie Expedition was born. Not that Joe or Rug knew it was the Moisie they would settle on—maybe not even that it was going to be an expedition. But that night back at Rug's father's place in Springfield, they got hold of a yellowed National Geographic Continental, so old it still showed Newfoundland independent of Canada. It also showed the Moisie; and a check with an up-to-date road map indicated there was a railroad which seemed to run—just possibly—close enough to put the river within striking distance.

This is the stage—right at the beginning—where you have to think big. Go straight to a map of the entire continent. The full spread of the Continental gives the right sense of proportions so you can begin to unleash your dreams. Jumping immediately to highly detailed maps of small areas cramps the style and may leave the trip you really want off the edges of your charts. As for us, we unrolled the big map and took a good look at the U.S.A. (that is, the lower forty-eight). And couldn't find a self-respecting wilderness anywhere. At first, we thought our standards might be warped. Not wanting to fall into a hermit's type of inverse snobbery, we checked with Webster. As it turns out, nothing at all was wrong with our intuition. Webster defines wilderness as a "trackless waste of any kind," and while we're not sure what he means by "waste," "trackless" seems like a pretty fair criterion. By Webster's standards as well as our own, even the Grand Canyon of Colorado can't qualify as genuine wilderness these days, what with all of Robert Hatch's gargantuan rubber rafts plying their trade.

Unless you have a better eye than we do, you'll get pretty discouraged about the U.S.A. and turn to Canada and Alaska. You will want to look over large parts of British Columbia, Alberta, the prairie provinces, northern Ontario, and Quebec, because all offer vast expanses of trackless terrain. Better yet, finagle a route through one of the five high-status areas of the outback: Alaska, the Yukon, Labrador, the Barren Grounds, or the high arctic. After all, tell a friend you're planning a canoe trip to Alberta and all you get are yawns. But mention in an offhand manner that you plan to follow a river all the way to the Arctic Ocean, and even the most phlegmatic soul pricks up his ears.

Your dreams, of course, may have to strike a bargain with reality. Even if you're new to wilderness canoeing, you probably realize that it requires a diversity of talents which can be developed only with practice. So you may want to reinstate the lower forty-eight once the initial visions of grandeur pass. Although most of the states are devoid of wilderness in the strictest sense of the word, they do offer plenty of enjoyable and exciting canoeing. Novices would do well to seek out the many brochures which national, state, and provincial parks provide detailing canoe routes open to outdoorsmen. In the meantime, don't let these preliminary voyages limit your vision: like our guidebook, they ought to be viewed as aids for getting you to your ultimate goal. Go ahead and call your shorter trip an expedition, and *let on* (as Tom Sawyer would say) that you're "headed for the Barren Grounds." Which is the truth, give or take a couple of years.

Whether or not you decide on the high-status areas, the Continental map gives the broad sweep that enables you to make comparisons. Locate the rivers or lakes you have traveled in years past, and mentally set them side by side with your new prospect. Is the new river the right length for the amount of time you have to spend? Allow about ten to fifteen miles of river per day of canoeing and don't forget to add in a suitable number of rest days. (This is merely the vaguest rule of thumb to get you started. As we'll see later, any talk about "average" days on a river is generally meaningless.) If your map indicates the altitude of the terrain, you may also be able to get a preliminary idea of the river's gradient. Most of the good wilderness whitewater trips we've taken have averaged a river drop of four to eight feet a mile. The Moisie dropped about 1700 feet in 230 miles. (Once again, these are only rough estimates for your initial guidance.)

Your map can also give you a preliminary clue on another important subject: how you plan to get to your river. Roads, of course, are the first possibility; but keep in mind you have to end your trip as well as start it. Travel with only one car, and you must make arrangements to get back to it when you finish, or have it driven to the other end of the trip. If your party uses two or more cars, you may be able to arrange a shuttle. Another possibility is leaving your vehicle at the mouth of a river and chartering a plane into the back country. If so, plan your arrangements well in advance. Make sure (1) that your pilot will carry canoes (not all of them do); (2) that you know the load capacity of the plane (ditching crucial supplies at the last minute is no way to start a trip); and (3) that you can afford it. Rates are high, and you have to pay the pilot for his mileage both up and back. A third possibility is the railroads. Many of the Canadian branch lines will ship canoes and gear in the baggage car, often for a negligible charge, while you ride in comfort up front. Their routes often run along remote lakes and rivers, and sometimes they are even willing to make nonscheduled stops. Write well in advance for more specific information. (General advice can be had from the Canadian National Railway, Rail Travel Bureau, Montreal, P.Q., Canada.)

Continental maps are excellent for opening possibilities. But your dreaming should be complemented by the other kind of thinking necessary for any wilderness expedition: the art of thinking little. Anyone who plans to canoe a river start to finish has to set his sights both broad and narrow, to combine the wide sweep with the deep detailed scrutiny. By making a decision to head for genuine wilderness, you may well cut yourself off from the packaged advice available for more modest canoeing ventures. Don't get discouraged by an apparent lack of information. The advance guard of Western civilization has spent four hundred years exploring the nooks and crannies of the continent, and chances are your river has had its own share of wanderers and trappers. The trackless waste may have eroded their footprints, but explorers leave their marks elsewhere. Strange as it may seem, your next step toward the wilderness is in the direction of civilization's heart itself: the library.

The larger the library, the better. Suburban collections are eminently practical affairs, stocked mostly with the best sellers and mysteries commonly demanded by the local clientele. City public libraries are better, but often reflect a similar bias. Large metropolises like Boston and New York are excellent prospects. What is needed, you see, is a library grand enough to store trivia and odds and ends: the records which most hardheaded men would label worthless effluvia of the past. Almost every state in the union has one or two of these behemoth libraries—either public repositories or private or state university collections—and you should definitely make use of their resources.

This library research is a lot of work, but worth it in the end. If you stick to the park brochures, you can't expect to stray too far from the beaten track. On the other hand, what brochure ever told the story of Mrs. Leonidas Hubbard's incredible race down a Labrador river, or Storker Storkerson's drift on the Arctic Ocean, or Sam Hearne's trek across the Barren Grounds?

Do a little looking in the library and you'll find them all. And those leads can point you to your own wilderness.

SOME "KEY" BOOKS. Below we mention a number of volumes you may find useful in your search for a river. But recognize them for what they are: only keys to the beginning of your search. Explorers who take the time to write about their own voyages often have read similar accounts and will mention them. For that reason, get into the habit of checking what you have probably hitherto considered the dullest parts of a book: the introductions, acknowledgments, bibliographies, and footnotes. The book's actual text may be the least valuable part—a narrative of a river which for one reason or another you have rejected. The footnotes, on the other hand, might list sources more relevant to your interests.

As you read any of these accounts, take them with the grain of salt any guidebook needs. Evaluate them critically. Are they written by people whose judgment can be trusted? How soon after the voyage were they composed? (A fifty-year-old reminiscence can be pretty hazy; a book based on notes from the trip's journal—or, better yet, the journal itself—is more reliable.) For older accounts, is there a scholarly or expertly annotated edition which describes the explorer's routes using modern place names? Are helpful maps included? If the description is not written by the explorer himself, is the account merely hero worship, or is it written by a knowledgeable and critical authority?

The books here are only a sprinkling of the many available, but we've tried to cover the various "high status" areas of wilderness we mentioned. We move in a direction roughly east to west.

For Labrador, you might want to read *A Woman's Way Through Unknown Labrador* by Mrs. Leonidas Hubbard, Jr., and *The Long Labrador Trail* by Dillon Wallace. Wallace and Mrs. Hubbard's husband originally set out in 1903 to canoe to Ungava Bay via the George River. They never even got to the George, and Hubbard starved in the attempt. When Wallace made it out, Mrs. Hubbard apparently blamed him for Leonidas' death and resolved to make the journey properly herself. Wallace retaliated with his own expedition and the race for the mouth of the George was on. We're not telling who won, but Mrs. Hubbard made the trip in style, as the photographs of her at tentside in long skirts demonstrate. *A Woman's Way* also contains the journal of Leonidas' original trip, an extremely moving record. The poor wretches kept struggling from pond to pond trying to find the George, but took one wrong turn after another, growing weaker every day. Rug's father remembers *his* father telling him as a boy (over the newspaper) that Hubbard's fatal mistake was taking rifles instead of a shotgun and birdshot.

Hudson Bay has been one of the central Canadian outposts in the move west, and many a good river flows into its wide waters. A brochure which describes this area is "Canoe Routes to Hudson's Bay," available from the Canadian Department of the Interior, Ottawa, Canada. A more historical approach to the region is through the records of the still flourishing Hudson's Bay Company. The company was instrumental in pioneering routes across the entire continent, and several histories are available on the subject: Robert Watson, *The Hudson's Bay Company,* Robert E. Pinkerton, *Hudson's Bay Company,* and Douglas MacKay, *The Honourable Company.* The Bay Company is one of those institutions which has squirreled away volumes of records, some of which have been published by the Hudson's Bay Record Society, London, and others by the Champlain Society, Toronto. Equally interesting accounts of the fur trade can be found in the journals of the individual trappers. A good example is Alexander Henry's *Travels and Adventures in Canada and the Indian Territories.* On the other hand, *Maude Watt: Angel of Hudson's Bay* is a prime example of the secondhand biography to avoid: the kind that puts a pretty face on adventure without any sensitivity for lines of character.

Hudson Bay served as a jumping-off spot for trips west across the Barren Grounds. One interesting account of early travels in the area is Samuel Hearne's *Journey from Prince of Wales's Fort in Hudson's Bay to the Northern Ocean.* Hearne tried three times from 1769 to 1772 to find the legendary Indian copper mines on the river of that name flowing into the Arctic Ocean. He finally made it on foot to the Coppermine, where at Bloody Falls his Indian guides murdered the local Eskimos. Hearne is uncommonly literate for a man who spent long years in the middle of nowhere. Here, for instance, is his description of Moses Norton, the half-breed Bay Company commander who called the tune at Prince of Wales Fort:

[Mr. Norton] kept for his own use five or six of the finest Indian girls which he could select; and notwithstanding his own uncommon propensity to the fair sex, took every means in his power to prevent any European from having intercourse with the women of the country; for which purpose he proceeded to the most ridiculous length. To his own friends and country he was so partial, that he set more value on, and shewed more respect to one of their favourite dogs, than he ever did to his first officer. Among his miserable and ignorant countrymen [the Indians] he passed for a proficient in physic, and always kept a box of poison, to administer to those who refused him their wives or daughters. . . . As he advanced in years his jealousy increased, and he actually poisoned two of his women because he thought them partial to other objects more suitable to their ages. . . .

An inflammation in his bowels occasioned his death on the 29th of December 1773; and though he died in the most excruciating pain, he retained his jealousy to the last; for a few minutes before he expired, happening to see an officer laying hold of the hand of one of his women who was standing by the fire, he bellowed out, in as loud a voice as his situation would admit, "God d—n you for a b—h, if I live I'll knock out your brains." A few minutes after making this elegant apostrophe, he expired in the greatest agonies that can possibly be conceived.

A much later inhabitant of the Barren Grounds is the subject of *The Legend of John Hornby* by George Whalley. Hornby was not an explorer by any stretch of the imagination. He never discovered anything, never prospected, never became a peace officer, never even killed a man to anybody's knowledge. Hornby is remembered solely for his feats of prowess. He once ran a hundred miles from Edmonton to Athabasca Landing in twenty-four hours to win a shot of whiskey, which he never cared for and didn't drink. He was known to prefer portaging his outfit 200–300 pounds a trip. He enjoyed early-morning walks barefoot through the snow and kept the sleeping quarters in his cabin (that is to say, the floor) at a breezy five degrees below. Now you tell us: Why would a Scot, even a second son, head for the Barren Grounds, drift around and invite starvation again and again, until finally in the winter of 1927 . . . he starved?

Moving farther west, try Alexander Mackenzie's *Voyages from Montreal, on the River St. Lawrence, through the continent of North America, to the frozen and Pacific Oceans.* Mackenzie was attempting to open a route to the Pacific for (who else?) the Hudson's Bay Company. He followed the big river which now bears his name and ended a little farther north than he bargained. The trip, made in 1789, was generally uneventful; the original text is tough sledding, but several editions are available in updated English. Remember that Mackenzie was a businessman first, explorer second, and writer third. A nice contrast to this is *Dangerous River* by R. M. Patterson, an account of two men who went up the South Nahanni River for a year in the 1930's to prospect and trap. This book is all the better for its unpretentiousness. It doesn't build to any big climax, but does give an excellent feel for what it means to live with a river. It's a mix of near disasters, old tales, and quiet satisfactions.

If you're thinking of an all-out trip through regions of the high arctic (or even if you're not), you'll want to read Vilhjalmur Stefansson's *The Friendly Arctic.* Stefansson believed, at a time when nobody else did, that northern icebound seas were not "arctic deserts" devoid of all life, and that explorers could live off the drifting pack ice if only they knew the proper hunting techniques. To prove it, he and two companions, Ole Andreason and Storker Storkerson, set off in 1913 to drift and sled their way north from Alaska. The drama is superb, especially when Stefansson, dressed in skins, returns to land and fails to be recognized by members of his pickup party because they had given him up for dead as soon as he left sight of the mainland. Throughout the book, Stefansson stresses how easy it is to live off the land, but don't be fooled. Read carefully and notice how much expertise and experience he brings to living off the country. Try it yourself without that savvy and you could wind up very dead.

SOME PERIODICALS WORTH CONSULTING. In addition to the old standbys like *Field and Stream,* a new breed of magazines like *Backpacker* and *Outside* are emerging with a greater emphasis on backpacking, canoeing, and ecology. Occasionally conservation-oriented magazines like *Audubon* feature an out-of-the-way canoeing article. Of greater interest for whitewater enthusiasts are the publications put out by the buffs themselves. The American Whitewater Affiliation publishes *American Whitewater* every other month, and occasionally wilderness trips are described therein. These accounts supply more details about the quality of the whitewater than most travel journals. The American Canoe Association publishes *Canoe,* also a bimonthly. Running through back issues of these two magazines may be more difficult since fewer libraries collect them. You may want to subscribe yourself for future reference. (For the AWA, write Box 4895, Federal Way, WA 98003; for *Canoe,* write Highland Mill, Camden, ME 04843.) *The Beaver* is a magazine published four times a year by the Hudson's Bay Company (write the Company, 77 Main Street, Winnipeg, Canada R3C 2R1) which covers the lore, history, and present development of the Canadian North. It details older expeditions more often than modern treks, but as we've seen, these can be valuable accounts. *The Beaver* also regularly features reviews of current books about the North.

In addition to the books detailing past expeditions, there is a growing literature of guidebooks to specific rivers in the United States and Canada. We have listed some of them in Appendix III. Before trusting any of them, it is a good idea to check out the reviews of them in the canoe journals, especially in *American Whitewater,* since the accuracy of these guides varies considerably.

Your library research will take some time—several months, perhaps—to sift through materials, follow up leads, wait for interlibrary loans. As work on this front progresses, be alert for other promising leads. Among other sources, consider:

BOAT AND CAMPING SHOWS; WHITEWATER RACES. Boat shows consist primarily of those big 80-horsepower Mercs suitable for dual-carb water skiers. But a big enough show—or the camping exhibitions—may have a lead or two. Rug visited one in New York and got useful literature on canoeing in the Barren Grounds. Whitewater races, of course, are more fun than boat shows; while there, keep your eyes open for boats that look like wilderness veterans. The organizers of the race may be able to point out some of the old hands who could help you. Movies of whitewater trips are often shown in the evenings, and these too may supply contacts. You might also try printing on your own boat the rivers you've canoed, to attract the notice of similar-minded wilderness boaters.

NATIVES. The peripheries of wilderness areas are sparsely settled but nonetheless can yield helpful information. There are, of course, many wilderness guides who make a living by taking people through the country; but unless you plan to use their services, they are best avoided. And their services don't come cheap. In some areas, Indians still hunt the territory. Getting their advice before you arrive can be difficult, but it's at least worth stopping at any nearby reservation when you finally begin your trip. We were able to spend a day in Sept-Iles, Quebec, talking with a man who had canoed the large lakes approaching the Moisie River. Although he had never passed over the watershed, he knew others who had and pointed out a portage which shortened our route considerably.

One way to contact local woodsmen without actually making the trip north is through the churches and missions spread across frontier areas. Ask one of your home-town churches for the address of its denomination's national headquarters. (Try the Episcopalians or Roman Catholics first for Canadian rivers.) Then write the central organization care of their board of missions and inquire if a priest or minister resides near the outpost you're interested in. If so, write him asking for information about your river; or lacking that, ask him to put you in touch with someone more knowledgeable. Clergy whose congregations include families spread through the interior often know the country fairly well.

Another link with the interior is the medical personnel who serve remote areas. Some provinces have their own medical extension services (Ontario is among them) and for further information on such operations, try writing the Canadian Department of National Health and Welfare, Ottawa, Canada. Rug discovered, quite by accident, that private medical societies can be helpful. He ran into the offices of the Grenfell Society in late May while passing through Boston on a dehydrated-food trip. Sir William Grenfell, it turned out, was a hale and hardy young physician who founded a medical mission in Labrador at the turn of the century. (So hale and hardy, in fact, he ultimately wrote two autobiographies—the second one updating the first because he lived much longer than he had expected.) The successors of Grenfell in Boston were only too happy to help out by calling a friend, the mayor of Sept-Iles, to find out whether the ice had gone out of the lakes and rivers yet.

SOME FINAL ADVICE. Any information you gain from these sources must be evaluated the same way as the written accounts. Some, even a lot of it, may be misinformation. How close is your informant to the facts he is giving you? Our mayor of Sept-Iles had plenty of advice, but part of it turned out to be inaccurate, since he was talking about country several hundred miles to the north. The Indian we talked to proved more trustworthy, especially regarding the areas he himself had canoed and could point out on our maps. Remember also to take canoeing experience into account. Nonpaddlers often have wild misconceptions about what water is runnable and what is not. For that matter, so do many canoeists.

In the end, it's better to cast a wide net and sort out the reliable from the unreliable rather than start with little or no information. Sure, you'll make some mistakes and draw more than a few blanks. Rug thought he was being ingenious by writing the Chief Factor, Hudson's Bay Company, Sept-Iles. He wondered why he got no reply and then discovered on arrival in Sept-Iles (to his great embarrassment) that writing "the Bay" in a city that large was like asking for information about the woods from the local A & P.

So don't be discouraged if this hit-or-miss technique works imperfectly. It's the same one the old voyagers used: asking around, reading up, and finally departing with the hope that they could learn whatever they didn't know by the time they got wherever they were going. It took three centuries to get Western man from one side of the continent to the other. Be happy if it only takes you three months to settle on your own wilderness; and don't give up just because it's more like three years before you manage to free your calendar for the ultimate expedition.

2. Troubleshooting a River

There wasn't much more Rug and Joe could do with that National Geographic Continental up in Springfield, except speculate and dream. But once home Rug begged a typewriter from another med student and fired off a series of letters. The first two were addressed to the Quebec Department of Parks and the Department of Tourism, Fish and Game, both inquiring about the Moisie as a possible canoe trip. The third was the most important: addressed to the Canada Map Office. Rug was writing for topographical maps which could supply him with crucial information about the river he had chosen.

That should be your next step too. Topographical maps are available from both the United States and Canadian governments. Get U.S. topos for lands east of the Mississippi by writing the U.S. Geological Survey, Distribution Section, 1200 South Eads Street, Arlington, Va. 22202. Maps of land west of the Mississippi can be had from the U.S. Geological Survey, Federal Center, Denver, Colo. 80225. Most areas of the United States have been mapped at either a scale of 1:62,500 (a mile equals an inch) or at 1:24,000 (a mile equals about two and a half inches). Either scale will provide an adequately detailed picture of the country you will be traveling. For Canadian trips, write the Canada Map Office, 615 Booth Street, Ottawa, Ont. K1A 0E9. Maps are available from them at scales of 1:250,000 (one mile equals a quarter inch) and 1:50,000 (one mile equals an inch and a quarter), although the latter does not yet cover all parts of the country. Both governments will supply free indexes of the maps they have, so your first step is to get the relevant indexes and then order the specific areas you need. We understand that you can obtain the same maps in sets for all the outstanding wilderness areas and canoe routes in North America from the Wilderness Sports Catalog, P.O. Box 85, Chapel Turn Road, Eagle Valley, New York 10974.

Delivery may take as much as a month. Bide your time, and meanwhile don't be surprised if you begin to hear, as Rug did, from the other correspondents:

Gouvernement du Québec
Ministère du Tourisme,
De la Chasse et de la Peche

Dear Mr. Rugge:

This is reference to your inquiries about a canoeing voyage on the Moisie River. We regret to inform you that this will be impossible. Sections of the river are owned by private fishing clubs.

We are sending under separate cover our pamphlets entitled "Sportfishing in Quebec" and "Quebec, Oui, M'sieu."

Please enjoy your stay in Quebec.

Yours truly,

(signed)   FAY CHOUBLANC
Special Assistant

And shortly thereafter:

Gouvernement du Québec
Ministère du Parcs

Dear Mr. Rugge:

Thank you for your request about the Moisie River. We regret to say the river is not canoeable because of its extremely dangerous nature. There are, however, many fine lakes and rivers which afford excellent boating, of which we are sure you will find many to your liking.

We are enclosing a number of pamphlets describing our system of provincial parks and fine opportunities for canoeing.

Sincerely yours,

(signed)   CAL DE SACQUE
Public Information Officer

Not what you would call encouraging; but Rug rightly took the rejections with a grain of salt. Granted, the river was dangerous, and the Department of Parks probably smart to say so. After all, they had no idea who was writing them about canoeing. But one man's poison is another man's meat and Rug decided to let his own verdict await further investigation. As for the idea that private camps monopolized the river, Joe pegged it as one of those myths perpetuated by a bureaucrat whose closest approach to a river was via pictures in Folder 45B Quebec, Oui, M'sieu. As it turned out, the suspicion was well founded.

A week later, Rug received the 1:250,000-scale maps of the Moisie, and he could begin to make his own evaluations. His immediate concern—as yours will be—was to determine whether there were any indications that the river was *not* a reasonable choice. Some issues to consider:

CAN THE RIVER BE REACHED EASILY? If you can afford to hire a plane to fly you to the headwaters, the answer is obviously yes. If, like us, you're depending on other means of transport, you may find that the railroad or highway takes you relatively near the headwaters, but not exactly where you were hoping. Now you have the maps to see if there is any way of canoeing to the watershed of your particular river. If you have our kind of luck, a large lake and one portage will be enough to get you into the next drainage basin. But often the geography entails a journey through chains of smaller ponds, or a drag and haul up a tiny tributary. Remember to check carefully the miles of portages your route requires. Those spaces on the map look minuscule at one inch to four miles, and it is easy to overestimate your tolerance for long carries. Wilderness portages without trails are entirely different from the clearly marked and well-traveled versions found on canoe routes in provincial parks and the like. If you happen to hit an open meadow, that's easy sailing. But making a left turn with the canoe on your head in a thicket of jack pine is another story.

CHECKING THE RIVER ITSELF. The 4:1 maps provide a good idea of the general character of the river. What sort did you have in mind? If your whitewater canoeing experience is limited, you are likely to prefer rivers whose gradient is gradual, with most of the drops coming at falls that are more easily portaged around. Many rivers provide this kind of canoeing: sometimes widening out into long thin lakes, other times plummeting over rocky cascades, but for the most part moving contentedly along. If you are more inclined to whitewater, then you will be watching the maps for the slashes marked with an "R" for rapids. But there are conditions which even the most experienced whitewater canoeist would want to avoid.

For example, in the two sections of rivers taken from maps with a scale of four miles to the inch (see illustration), both have rapids indicated. Yet one of them holds out the possibility of a pleasant and exciting run, while the other gives you good reason to eliminate the river from consideration immediately. Take a look at the two and see if you can figure out which river is which—and why.

Now if you are smart you will have figured out that we are being a bit unfair. Although you should be able to take a good guess at telling which river invites catastrophe, we haven't provided all the information you need to be positive. The contour lines are the key to the situation, and we haven't told you that the contour interval is 200 feet.

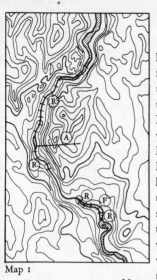

Map 1

Map 2

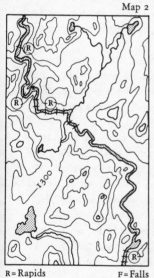

R = Rapids   F = Falls

But maybe we're going a bit too fast. If you haven't used topographical maps before, some information about contour lines is in order. They are the brown lines on the maps and provide you with the elevation of the terrain you are crossing. In Map 2 you'll notice that one line is labeled "1300," which means that every point of land along that line is 1300 feet above sea level. In effect, these lines make the map three-dimensional by translating the height and shape of geographical features into signs that can be used on a two-dimensional map. If you wanted to, you could translate them back into more easily recognizable pictures without too much trouble. Notice that on Map 1 we have drawn a line, A, through some of the contours. The map shows us what the contours would look like directly from above; but we can translate these into the view you would get looking at the river from the side, at ground level. If we took a knife and sliced a cross section of the land along line A, the horizontal picture would be something like what you see in our diagram on the following page. Of course, you don't have to make this translation every time you interpret the map. Even if you haven't used contour lines before, you can see that lines squeezed close together indicate a steep slope, while those spaced farther apart signal a flatter area.

Now you are ready to cast a more critical eye at the two sections of river. It is evident first of all that River 1 is walled in by steep sides, some of them 1000 feet high. In fact, at some spots the contour lines crowd together so closely that they cannot be squeezed in, and are instead broken off —an indication of vertical cliffs. Of course, steep sides or even high cliffs do not automatically rule out a river from consideration, but they *may* eliminate all reasonable chances for portaging at that point. About the steepest slope that a man can walk upright is 50 degrees from horizontal, which looks on the page like so: / . Any steeper and you'd better grab for handholds. If you've got a strong back, plenty of time, and the disposition of a Dall sheep, you might try hiking a slope like this with a backpack, but you'll never manhandle seventy-five pounds and seventeen feet of boat up a 1000-foot precipice. If you plan to do River 1, you are committing yourself to running the rapids through the cliff section or to shipwreck in the effort.

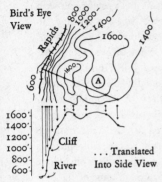

Bird's Eye View

Rapids

... Translated Into Side View

Cliff

River

So let's take a close look at the river itself and assess our prospects. A few miles below where the steep walls close in at 600 feet, the river drops through six miles of rapids, indicated by the thirteen hatch marks and the label "Rapids." In the next eight miles, the run is punctuated by intermittent rapids and one marked falls (F). How much solid information do we have about these fourteen miles of whitewater? Plenty. First of all, the obvious. There is one drop—that falls—which is absolutely and positively unrunnable. We have never seen a falls or "chute" indicated on a Canadian topo that did not deserve the name. On the other hand, many cascades that we called falls, the map makers unjustly demoted to rapids, and some rapids that we paid the courtesy of a portage did not even receive any mention on our charts.

More important than the hatch marks and written labels is the slope of the river. If you look closely at Map 1, you will find three contour lines crossing the river. The river drops 200 feet in about two miles near the top, then 200 more in about the next four miles. Below, the gradient appears less but a falls and still more rapids are indicated.

A drop of 100 feet per mile is a slope of about 2 degrees from horizontal. Drawn out, you can hardly perceive the incline. Hiking a slope like that is a positive pleasure; but water travels differently from the walker. Water slides and pushes and piles up on itself at the smallest excuse. Give a stream of water—any stream—a vertical drop of two inches and it will bubble and slurp. Give it 100 feet in a mile and it will crash and roar and spell catastrophe for open boats. Even 50 feet in a mile bodes an impossible drop for open boats in most rivers.* Between 10 and 50 feet, you and the river have to negotiate. Important factors are the water level, the steadiness of the drop, the configuration of the river bottom, and the age of the river's boulders —information not available from the topo map.

Just one additional clue about River 1 is given to us, and that is its changing width. You will notice that the river narrows measurably in the

---

* The smaller the river, the steeper the gradient may become while still remaining runnable. The steepest set we've ever run in open boats is a two-mile stretch with the first half averaging 80 feet per mile and the second 95 feet per mile. It was an extremely narrow river and one hell of a ride.

first rapids, and below is squeezed into a single line by the converging cliffs. We figure that closing in the banks of a river has much the same effect as raising the water level where the river maintains its regular width. And we've seen rivers whose boulders have been shuffled by the spring riptide. In a narrows, just like in spring runoff, the waves grow taller and (what's worse) steeper, until they curl back on themselves, collide with the next wave hurrying to catch up, and burst into a violent mix of dark bubbles and whitewater.

By now you should have a pretty clear picture of River 1. After flowing through moderately hilly country, it is abruptly closed in by steep valley walls 500 or 600 feet high. The first couple of rapids may be negotiable, but then the river descends in a series of cascades several hundred more feet, and the walls grow at both their bottom and top to 1000 feet. The next few rapids appear to be portageable on the left but soon the unwary canoeist is likely to come to a rapids with a sheer cliff on the left and no way to cross the river. Or there may be a place or two with cliffs on both sides and after running that spot no way to retreat upstream. If this run sounds dramatic, try getting into the situation yourself and see how dramatic you feel.

On the other hand, you may be the type who comes across a river like this and can't get it out of your head. You may persuade yourself that there is likely even room to portage along the banks *between* the edge of the river and its cliffs. We have to admit that you might be right, and if you can't settle for less than a complete answer, there is one further option available. You can order copies of the original photo from which the topo maps were made, from the Map Distribution Office in Ottawa or the U.S. Geological Survey, Washington, D.C. But until you can demonstrate that your route is humanly possible, don't try it on a lark. It's hard to play the gallant adventurer if some disgruntled Mountie has to interrupt his weekend to fetch you.

Once you have a feel for River 1, Map 2 is an easy exercise. The total descent in over twelve miles of river is less than 200 feet. If some of the rapids drop at sharp ledges or are too shallow or prove otherwise impassable, there is no evidence of any obstruction (cliffs, tributaries, swamps, long mileage) which would prevent an easy portage. As it turns out, the set is a frisky but by no means dangerous run.

In many areas of Canada, small-scale 4:1 maps are still the only ones available, and you will have to depend on them. In other areas you can purchase larger-scale maps of a mile to an inch and a quarter. In return for slightly more paperweight to cover the same mileage, the $1:1\frac{1}{4}$ maps provide much more detail. From the inside of a canoe, that means you can count on identifying more landmarks from the map with less chance of confusing one for another.

On one trip Jim took a few years ago, the only available map was a

small-scale one. It clearly showed the Rivière à la Perche, which had to be traveled upstream to get to the next watershed, and he and his friends pushed along their route as the map indicated (dotted line). The stream was rocky and narrow (often not more than ten feet wide and sometimes considerably less). The dragging and hauling seemed to go on interminably. But estimating mileage was next to impossible because of the uneven and slow progress. Only as the sun was beginning to set and the group arrived at an open pond with a marsh at one end were they able to tell that they had taken the wrong turn and ended at point A, up the wrong tributary. A year later Jim and his friends returned to the trouble spot with more detailed maps, and discovered that the proper turn could be found only if one knew *exactly* where to look for it. It was not the main tributary, and it diverged from the other branch in a reedy, nondescript corner of one of the few places where the stream widened slightly and became a swamp.

So if the more detailed maps are available for the area you plan to visit, by all means order them. The extra information they supply can often save you traveling time, and may suggest interesting side trips as you canoe down the river.

In order to show you what a difference they make, and at the same time

give you an idea of how they can be most effectively used, we've reproduced here one section of the Moisie exactly to scale as it is seen on both large- and small-scale maps. Your first step in using either one is to take a pencil and draw in arrows at the points where each new contour line crosses the river. As we have seen, the distances between them serve as tip-offs to potential trouble spots.

On the less-detailed map, the contour interval is 100 feet. If you squint hard enough or use a magnifying glass, you will discover one line crosses the river near the top set of rapids, and the next one about three miles below, just downstream of the

junction with the other river. That means the elevation drops 100 feet in three miles for an average of 33 feet per mile. That kind of gradient is reasonable for running rapids. But there is no law saying that a river has to drop at a steady gradient between two contour lines. Judging by the percentages, there is probably a law the other way. In either case, the small map with its 100-foot contour intervals doesn't offer fine enough resolution to give any reliable information.

The detailed map tells the story better. With intervals of 50 feet, we can

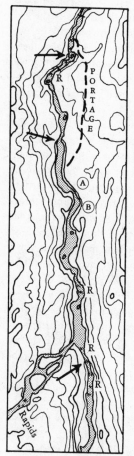

see a drop of that amount in the first mile. That's bad enough, but notice that the only rapids marked on that stretch are in the first third of a mile, which could very well mean the river drops most of its 50 feet in that first section—at the rate of nearly 50 feet for a *third* of a mile, or 150 feet a mile! It's a sure bet for a portage—and a gruesome one it turned out to be. The river plummeted through a spectacular set of cascades, descending steeply past the island bend and tilting sharply all the way to the next island. Peach and Rug meticulously followed the craggy shoreline around its left side (facing downstream) and discovered, much to their dismay, that during high water more unrunnable rapids—not marked on the map—continued on and off for the next three quarters of a mile.* By the time they had scouted a portage route around behind a hill and we had gotten canoes and gear around, six hours had elapsed.

As you can see, there is no guarantee you will *not* encounter a rapids just because none is marked on the map—especially when traveling in high water or over a relatively steep river gradient. Continuing on, the bottleneck at point A forced us to line the boats; and to our surprise we found more rapids at point B—which fortunately turned out to be runnable. No such luck, however, with the rapids half a mile above the entrance of the other river. After we had dragged and lined our canoes past those ledges and falls, it was time to look for a campsite. We couldn't have found a more scenic spot than the bluff we chose overlooking that tributary, which (you will notice if you look carefully) joins the Moisie with a spectacular 200-foot plunge in the last half mile.

---

* When we refer to the "left" or "right" banks of rivers, it is always from the point of view facing downstream, not necessarily the same as it looks from reading the map.

All in all, our day produced discouragingly little in the way of mileage: ten hours from breakfast to dinner, and four miles to show for it. But we learned a few lessons about reading maps that you may find useful. To wit:

Maps are good for telling what you won't be able to run, but not so good about what you can run. It was easy enough to predict trouble in that six-hour-portage area; but the rapids between the next two contour lines, where the drop averaged only 25 feet per mile, could not be judged one way or another from the map. In the end, some rapids will be unrunable even when the circumstances seem good on the charts, because there is no way to indicate whether the drop is over an abrupt ledge or down a more gentle pitch.* In *general* (provided the average gradient seems reasonable) the chances of running a rapids are greater if the river is wider and the rapids continue for a longer stretch.

There is no such thing as an "average" day of river canoeing. On lakes, it is easy enough to plan roughly on an average mileage in your timetable (barring high winds on very large lakes or a surfeit of long portages). But an "average" day on the river could be either the four miles we made on the stretch above or the forty-five we did on a lower section, where the current and rapids helped us. In estimating your journey's timetable, remember that portages can take a long time. You will have to scout first; then (on long trips at least) take two carries to bring the gear and canoes through. And be generous in guessing about how many rapids you'll have to carry around; if the Moisie is any indication, your worst fears will be surpassed.

Don't lose your sense of scale if you are traveling through canyon

country. This is easy enough to do when looking at topographic maps where contour line after contour line presses close in upon the river. But after examining these maps, don't underrate the problems of a portage with "merely" two or three contour lines next to the shoreline. That's quite a bit of climbing if you have to cross them; and a 100-foot sheer cliff wall is just as impassable to canoes as a 1000-foot one.

Make sure you check the contour interval on each map. Watch the 4:1 maps in particular, where the interval is liable to change from one chart to the next. Rug nearly had a heart attack one late spring morning when he discovered that the contour interval in canyon coun-

---

* Actually, the U.S. Geological Survey publishes river-profile maps for a small number of rivers. These charts, available only for rivers marked in blue on the state U.S.G.S. indices, will indicate the precise nature of the gradient. These are very valuable. As Colin Fletcher would say, sometime we'll have to look one up.

try was 200 feet, as opposed to the 100-foot difference on the topos which detailed the earlier parts of the river. That meant that the 800-foot cliffs had grown to 1600-foot mammoths, and even worse, the river's gradient had doubled. You can see what a surprise you would be in for if rapids you thought were descending at about 35 to 40 feet a mile all of a sudden became 70 to 80 feet. A potential run is transformed almost certainly into a portage.

Remember that the season of the year can make a big difference in rapids. The amount of water flowing through a river system at any one time is controlled by many factors: the size of the watershed, the steepness of the drainage, the time of year, and recent weather conditions. Since many whitewater rivers are relatively small and have steep banks, they are best run in the spring, when melting snow swells rapids to runnable levels. But on the large river systems of the North and West, running is likely to be possible throughout the summer. Even so, conditions will vary greatly for the same river from June to August. As a general rule, assume that portages will be fewer, or at least easier, later in the season. At that time, many rapids which were unrunnable at high water will be safe to shoot; ones that were earlier a tough challenge may disappear altogether. On the narrower upper stretches of the river, the opposite may be true: nice rapids in spring runoff can become rock gardens where dragging or carrying is a must.

Pace your trip. A close study of the maps may reveal a day's spectacular side trip, maybe another dramatic falls on one of the river's tributaries or a high hill which affords an overview of the whole river valley. Then too, your advance research may show several back-to-back stretches with tough portages, and you might schedule a day of rest to break up the hard labor. Of course, this kind of planning does not commit you to a detailed timetable that must be followed religiously. Some people bridle at the thought of even the least bit of advance scheduling. "This is a wilderness trip," they complain. "You're supposed to get away from the regimented life of civilization in order to relax and do as you please." All well and good. But if you take fifteen days' worth of food and discover after ten that you've covered only 50 of your 250 miles, then watch yourself get cornered into an exhausting routine. Up at dawn, paddling by seven, two raisins and a biscuit for lunch, more paddling against the sun, and daydreams about those unhurried days at the office.

If you've been following our guidelines closely, chances are you'll now be able to map out your own prospective trip intelligently. Those grandiose visions of you and your friends marching across Webster's trackless waste are on their way to becoming reality. But if you haven't had many actual chances to practice map-reading skills, we've provided on the following pages a few test situations along with our own interpretations and actual experiences.

Topographical Problems

Reading maps is in most cases a matter of simple common sense, but it is common sense of the sort which demands an aggressive examination of all the features on your charts. Like the amazing deductions of Sherlock Holmes, once you know what to look for, the conclusions are elementary, but first you have to develop Holmes's eye for detail. Hence the drills.

The map at left shows a section of the river you are planning to canoe. Scale: 1:50,000, or an inch and a quarter to the mile. Contour interval: 50 feet.

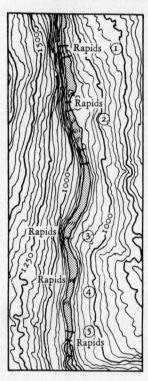

1. In which direction is the river running? How can you tell?

2. How high is the steep section of the bank on the right side of the river at Rapids 1?

3. What is the elevation of the river at the bottom of the map?

4. Mark the contour lines and estimate the average drop in feet per mile for each of them.

5. Give your estimates for the probability of running each of the rapids. Assume you have moderate ability in whitewater and can handle most situations runnable in *open* boats.

6. If you think any rapids will require portaging, evaluate the terrain to see if one side seems better than the other.

7. How many hours or days would you estimate (roughly) it would take to cover this section of river?

ANSWERS

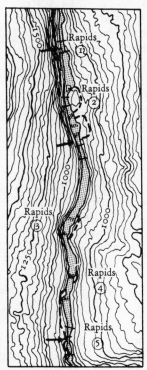

1. The river runs from the top of the map toward the bottom. The contour lines which cross the river are (almost) invariably in the shape of a V or U, and the closed end always points upstream. This is because the stream is at a lower elevation than its banks, and in order for the line to cross the river at the same height, it must "travel" upstream until the river's level is at the same altitude.

2. The steep part of the bank rises about 500 feet before the gradient eases off.

3. The 750-foot contour line crosses the river just at the bottom of the map.

4. Arrows mark the three contour lines which cross the river. There is a drop of over 50 feet per mile between the first two and a little over 25 between the second and third.

5. Because of the large drop, sets 1 and 2 would have to be assumed unrunnable. Actually, we found we *were* able to run the first set, but only with extreme caution—and you certainly could not count on that. The second was another set of violent ledges and falls, mixed with unrunnable rapids. Since the gradient on Rapids 3, 4, and 5 is not so steep, we might have some hope of running them, although 5 should raise our suspicions because the river narrows so much there. In fact, we found they were all rocky ledges whose sharp and bouldery drops necessitated portages. This is a good example of our point that although maps can definitely reveal bad trouble spots, they can never guarantee good running.

6. The portages we took are indicated by the dotted lines. Obviously, you would eliminate the right bank of the river because of its steepness, unless there turned out to be enough room to portage right at the river's edge before the steep wall began. This, of course, the map would not show. We portaged around behind the hill on the left side of the second set after discovering an old Indian trail which avoided the more rocky terrain next

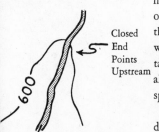

Closed
End
Points
Upstream

to the river. That hill, which is "only" one contour line on the map, was definitely worth skirting when carrying canoes. The third set of rapids also appears to have a steeper slope on the right, making the left side preferable. The maps give no hint of which side is better on Rapids 4 and 5. When we got to it, we chose left on 4 and decided afterward we were wrong; for 5 we carried right.

7. This stretch of river took us most of one day to cover. We got a late start (around eleven o'clock) just above the first set and didn't finish the last portage until seven in the evening. The portage behind the hill could have been done quicker except for a mix-up when Peach hauled his canoe to one side of the hill while Jim carried his to the other; but that is just the sort of thing that will happen from time to time.

If you feel unhappy because you predicted that some of those lower rapids might be runnable, think how we felt predicting the same thing—the difference being we were there and had to carry our mistakes around all day in the bushes.

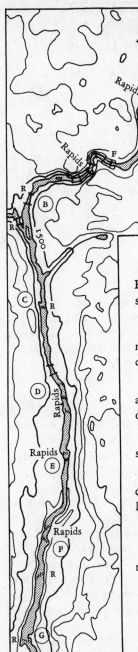

Here's another section of the river, same scale, same contour intervals.

1. The river divides in two at the top of the map. Which side of the large island would you choose to take? Why?

2. Which side of the falls would you carry around? Why? What's your guess about the other rapids?

3. What about the rapids just after the two sections of the river reunite (A)?

4. Which side of the next falls would you carry around? Why? What about the rapids below the falls to the next island?

5. Sets B through G?

6. Estimate the time it would take to cover this section of the river.

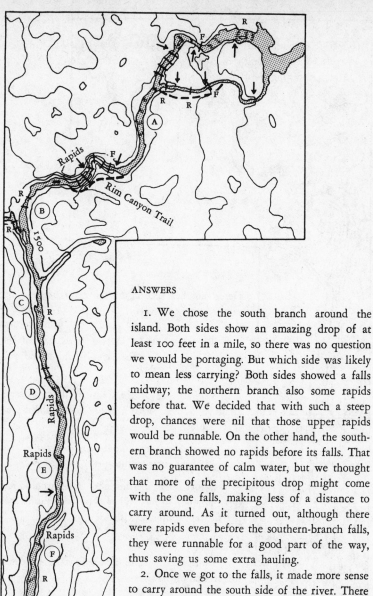

ANSWERS

1. We chose the south branch around the island. Both sides show an amazing drop of at least 100 feet in a mile, so there was no question we would be portaging. But which side was likely to mean less carrying? Both sides showed a falls midway; the northern branch also some rapids before that. We decided that with such a steep drop, chances were nil that those upper rapids would be runnable. On the other hand, the southern branch showed no rapids before its falls. That was no guarantee of calm water, but we thought that more of the precipitous drop might come with the one falls, making less of a distance to carry around. As it turned out, although there were rapids even before the southern-branch falls, they were runnable for a good part of the way, thus saving us some extra hauling.

2. Once we got to the falls, it made more sense to carry around the south side of the river. There was no guarantee we would be able to get off that island at the lower end, with rapids marked on either side.

3. When the river reunites and heads south (A), the gradient approaches 40 feet a mile. A

slope like that could either be runnable or not, but several indicators point to an optimistic assessment. First, rapids are marked almost continually along that stretch, meaning the descent is spread over as much of the distance as possible. Secondly, the new contour line begins at the next marked falls. Since falls marked on topo maps are usually substantial drops, let's estimate this one to be at least 10 or 15 feet high. This estimate reduces the likely drop on the upper stretch to something more on the order of 25 or 30 feet per mile. Thirdly, there are no bottlenecks indicated; the river is wide and straight. We were cautiously hopeful, and, as it turned out, also right. In high water they could be run close to shore with several places requiring careful scouting; in low water they would be no problem.

4. For the next falls, the obvious choice is a portage to the left because the rapids below are certainly unrunnable with that drop of almost 100 feet per mile. The route on the left side cuts across the inside of the river bend for a shorter carrying distance. This portage is a good example of how easy it is to overlook one or two contour lines. Although nothing like the lower river, this falls plunged through its own impressive 100-foot gorge. We called the spot Rim Canyon Trail because our portage route followed a caribou path along the edge of the cliff. The descent down to the river was so steep that carrying the canoes on our heads was out of the question—we had to slide them down, letting the bushes do the cushioning.

5. You have undoubtedly noticed that the gradient now lessens to about 15 feet a mile, with rapids here and there among flat stretches. In high-water conditions, the bottleneck at B had to be lined. The set at D looks long, wide, and gradual, whereas some of the other spots (particularly C and G) look suspiciously like ledges. However, with such a slight gradient, you can afford to be cautiously optimistic. We were able to run all of them— a pleasant surprise.

6. Estimating times: You should expect slow going from the two precipitous drops. We spent most of one afternoon getting around the big island and camped three quarters of the way over the portage. The next day we got only to the end of Rim Canyon Trail, though a few hours were spent hiking around the gorge to take in the dramatic cascades. The current pushed us along the next day and we covered about fifteen miles to the next falls, well past the bottom of this map.

3. Seedtime

Spring was coming, no doubt about it, as spring always comes to New England: with a healthy smattering of bluster, gentility, and guile. First there are the gusty winds portending change, shaking out the cold humors of winter; then the sudden warmth stirring the buds, spreading a gentle ease across the land. The spring thaw that pulls the crocus from its shelter likewise coaxes out the human spirit, but the guile of the season soon follows with its sharp frost and another snow squall. Advance and retreat, advance and retreat, until finally a soft spring rain soaks deep enough to purge the earth of its last shivers. At first glance, the guile may seem cruel: a sore disappointment to try the hopes of an early spring. But New Englanders have learned better. They know the sharp storms heighten the taste of the coming season, and serve only to transform what would have seemed a gentle sweetness into a searing, implacable call to break loose for another year.

So it was a great time for recruiting, and Rug knew it. So should you. The good recruiter plays the same game that spring does: advance and retreat, advance and retreat. Give your prospect a combination of weal and woe, fair weather and foul, and he or she is sure to come around. The fair weather makes your proposal attractive, but the stormy side is what makes it irresistible. That doesn't make sense, but then again, neither does spring; and you'll have to admit, spring works.

Bide your time in those late-winter days: laying plans, spying out the land, narrowing down your list of prospects until finally you find the right friend, the right day, and the right time. Rug set his sights on Dave Peach, a med student who had done some winter camping in Vermont and also canoed a good deal in the summer. Rug knew little more about his prospect than these rudimentary facts. He had talked to Peach personally on only one occasion, and that was about a particularly difficult qualifying exam scheduled for the following week. "Ah," Peach had said in his offhand manner, "either you've paid attention and know the stuff, or you haven't and you don't," and directly left town for another weekend in Vermont. Rug liked that kind of approach, and respected it even more when he heard how well Peach did on the exam. A man who was healthy enough to face a six-hour qualifier by camping in a snowbank might be just the sort who could be talked into spending part of his vacation carrying canoes over six-hour portages. Provided, of course, that the underlying scheme was crazy and grand enough to warrant such labor.

That was the way Rug reasoned anyway, and hence placed himself strategically not far from the row of medical-school mailboxes that Peach inevitably frequented at the end of the day. Sure enough, not more than five minutes behind schedule, Rug's prospect emerged from the clinic doors and ambled down the hallway, blissfully unaware of his status as marked man. Rug bent over his own sheaf of mail and redoubled his frown of concentration.

"Hi, John," said Peach, fitting his key into the mailbox.

"Oh, hello, Dave," said Rug, and looked up from his letters. "What's new?" Neither Rug nor Peach knew the other well enough to be on a last-name basis.

"Ah. Aches and pains."

"Well, the warm weather is here anyway. What are you planning for this summer?" Rug knew full well that Peach was considering a canoeing venture through Parc Vérendrye in Quebec, but listened patiently anyway as Peach ran through a catalogue of lakes, streams, and bogs which comprised the proposed route. Then, as the two of them walked down the rest of the corridor and out into the mild spring air, Rug dropped his own bait.

"Vérendrye's a nice little park," he said. "I'm leaving in June on a canoe trip myself. Thirty days. We start in Labrador, paddle across a high plateau, and then bushwhack to a river that flows south several hundred miles into the St. Lawrence."

Dirty Rug's casualness was intended as counterpoint to his high-toned ambitions. He said "thirty days" to establish the scale of the trip; then rolled out that magic name, Labrador. What provincial park can compete! No matter that few woodsmen, maybe not even Peach himself that day, could point to Labrador on the globe. Wherever it is on the maps, it is wild, it is vast, and it is Far North.

Peach looked at Rug and said, "Labrador, huh."

"But the main thing is the canyon."

"Canyon, huh."

"Yeah," said Rug. "The river cuts a canyon for itself that stretches out about a hundred miles. It's pretty deep too. Eight hundred feet at the beginning, and more like eighteen hundred downstream. The Indians used to run some furs up it, but not many whites have tried it. The best I can make out, nobody at all has done it by canoe for twenty years. You know, you might be just the guy we've been looking for. We still don't have a fourth man for the trip. What do you think?"

And that was it. With two big images—the high Labrador plateau and a deep canyon little known apart from the old Indian fur trade—Rug managed to lay out the Moisie proposition. But before Peach could swallow and begin a reply, Rug dug down for his pocket watch, frowned and hurried off, leaving Peach alone and defenseless—trapped between his own expanding thoughts and the seductive breeze of the late afternoon.

After making your initial proposal, it's best to lay low for a while. Don't mention your trip again for days, even weeks. But after a suitable wait, arrange to have your friend over for a leisurely dinner. Keep the conversation before the meal casual, but make sure your friend comes out to the hibachi to help you sear the steaks. After the meal, start your campaign in earnest. Enlarge on some of the central themes you've already touched on, such as the plateau and the canyon. Have an abundance of detail to document your description of the trip. Use old photographs, show topo maps, dig out that account by the trapper who poled up the river in 1853. At the same time, play up what you do *not* know about the trip. Freely admit you have no idea exactly how bad those rapids are. After all, as Rug told Peach, nobody's been there to take a look at them in twenty years or more. If your recruit is worth his salt, he will take the trip just to check them out himself.

You have to expect—even encourage—your prospect to voice all his doubts, worries and objections. There are at least a thousand reasons not to take a major wilderness trip, and anybody who can't think of a few big ones is not concentrating. When your man springs those that bother him most, don't panic, and most important of all, don't meet them with the salve of an easy answer. That's the last thing he wants to hear.

Let's take an example. What if your friend admits that portaging with all that gear over rough trailless country gives him pause? Don't reassure him that the Indians did it twice a year with hundreds of pounds of furs. Don't pull out statistics on lightweight canoeing designs. Better to roll your eyes heavenward and make it clear that not one in a thousand would attempt the ordeal you face. Let him know that you share his apprehensions, that you fear it will be worse than he's yet imagined. This tactic will drive your new recruit crazy as he realizes, too late, his predicament. Caught unawares, he has stumbled into a freewheeling poker game where the chips are fear and doubt with all cards wild. He has anted one of his worst fears but the dealer has raised the stakes and still chosen to stay in the game. Desperately, the greenhorn will play another card and show his next fear.

As dealer, you should be ready to evaluate each new apprehension on the spot. If it has some legitimate basis in reality (such as whirlpools, bears, bugs), deal from the bottom of the deck. Show him your dread is bigger than his, and at the same time demonstrate your unshaken resolve to go it anyway. Eventually your friend will come to understand the trip in its finest epic proportions. To nurture such an understanding is the grandest and subtlest purpose of your evening's presentation.

Depending on the character of your prospect, the dinner may be only the first of several earnest confabulations. But the time will eventually come when you need to elicit a straightforward, honest declaration of intentions. Is your friend in or out? The crunch is, there is only one sure method to get a straight answer, and that is to ask a straight question. For example, "Well, Dave, are you in or out?"

Put this closing question to your prospect but once. If he says to count him out, leave it at that. If he says he's not sure, tell him to let you know by next Tuesday because thirteen other pals are waiting to hear from you. Do not return to your former huckster style and attempt to sell him on the trip again. You are not peddling your old Volkswagen. Truth to tell, you're out of the sales game altogether. On behalf of the trip, you are seeking an outright claim on your friend's soul. To join a major expedition is to assume the risks and to accept responsibility for the well-being of every member. Membership means bondage to and for all others on the trip; once in the wilderness, each person's bond to another is unbreakable except by separation or death and irreplaceable by any means. Devious stratagems and even a few stretchers to help your recruit understand your early plans are fair enough, but each person's decision to join has to be his or her last individual act. Once this choice has been made, all responsibilities are shared and all decisions negotiated.

If your new team member is inexperienced, he may not be fully aware of the meaning of his decision. He may think he is simply giving his word, not his soul. Considering all things, that's a natural enough mistake, and you will be right to want to correct it. The best way out is to take Rug's approach and hand your recruit a shopping list entitled "Outfit," with an earnest request for suggestions and revisions. Then get him to spend hard cash on wilderness provender. Twenty-four pounds of Civil Defense biscuits and a dozen bottles of bug dope will serve your purpose better than any sermon on Loyalty and the Expedition.

4. Outfit

March, April, May: these are months when the ordinary life of the expeditioner seems to run along peacefully, the everyday routines of the civil world providing their usual surface of continuity. Yet the plans of a wilderness trip inevitably set in motion undercurrents that are no less powerful for being quiet and mostly unobserved. The infrequent get-together or odd postcard swells into a steady stream of letters, inquiries, and order slips. The occasion for all this intercourse is a methodical assembly of ten thousand details—the coordination, purchase, and packing of the needs of a completely self-sustaining party.

It all begins with a list. For the only guarantee of a complete outfit is the time and thought you put into the master compendium of gear and supplies. Its composition is detail work, but you have to treat it as an all-important project. This list is your philosophy of the good life, and unlike the philosophers, you are going to live by it.

Canoeing Gear

Burlington, Vt.
March 8

Hi, Johnny!

I don't know about you but I've been taking the Moisie to heart. I got an offer the other day for a teaching job over the summer, but am stalling until we can decide whether the trip is feasible or just a harebrained scheme. Have you heard from Canada yet?

It's a funny thing but I picked up a book off a cart at the library the other day. I don't remember why it caught my eye, but it was about a Canadian trapper and one chapter told how he canoed 200 miles *up* the Moisie in 1853. Only thing is, I put it back on the cart to get to my seminar and when I came back the book and the cart were gone. If I remember right, his name was Halsey Chatsworth, though it may have been Chelsea Haltsworth. Does either strike a bell with you?

Anyway, let me know if you are still thinking about spending the summer like some kind of river rat.

JOE

New Haven
March 15

Dear Joe,

What do you mean harebrained scheme? Of course it's harebrained. I just got the official word from Quebec, which is it can't be done: the river's too rough.

So I think it's pretty clear we had better make it a four-man party. Right now that looks like no great problem. For our third man I'm working on a guy in my class by the name of Dave Peach. I don't know him that well, but he's done a lot of canoeing and has a lean and hungry look about him. (Never mind what Shakespeare says, for a trip like this, we need guys with lean and hungry looks.)

The fourth man we owe to *Chatsworth: The Genius of England's Prophecy,* who turns out to be a poet. You see, I was rummaging through the Yale catalogue looking for your lost trapper, went to check out this reference, and got sidetracked into the Map Room, where I thought to look up some topos of the Moisie. I was wasting my time trying to locate the 50,000-scale maps and was told by a young fellow that their collection included only the 1:250,000, some of which he located for me. At first I assumed he was the librarian's assistant, but he turned out to be a whitewater man hunting up trips for a canoeing camp in the Adirondacks. Says he is a historian by trade but canoeist by vocation. He took an awful long look at the Moisie, especially where the river pulls in the contour lines at the canyon. He says it's totally out of the question about his going along, he's got this commitment to work for the camp, plus a big dissertation to finish, so on and so forth. You know the type. Soon as I get those 1:50,000 quads from the Canada Map Office, I'll have him over for a cookout. He doesn't stand a chance against the maps and my old buffalo-steak routine.

What really concerns me now is that we haven't even begun to put together an outfit. I'm sending along a preliminary checklist and have initialed the equipment I already have. Be sure to go over it carefully and let me know what I've forgotten.

A couple things I'm having trouble finding, but you may have better luck in the surplus stores around Burlington. I figure we need about 12 or 14 one-oz. bottles of fly dope and if you can also pick up a couple large tins of Civil Defense biscuits, it would be a help.

Keep in touch,

RUG

P.S. I just noticed one minor omission on the equipment list—CANOES. Where are we going to get them? I can't see wasting all that money on rentals.

Rug meandered a bit in getting to the point, but once there, he went right to the central issue. A canoe trip requires a canoe. The first question is how to get ahold of one.

Our answer is buy your own. That's the advice of fanatics, but even if your wallet rides as light on your hip as ours usually does, it makes good sense. Last time we checked, rentals were five or ten dollars a day, and often more for whitewater boats. On a twenty-five-day trip, that's a lot of money that could better be spent in a permanent investment. If you're serious about canoeing, dig down deep into that wallet or check book and go looking for the perfect canoe.

We should warn you in advance, you won't find it. Not because modern technology is unequal to the task or because design theory needs further refinement, but simply because canoes must do a number of things well. The perfect canoe should track straight on the big lakes and yet turn sharply in whitewater. It should ride light in the carrying yoke and hold up in pounding against the rocks. It should boast enough freeboard to turn back all standing waves but hunker so low that it never catches the wind—except for tail winds, of course. Designs have been evolved which can deal well with any one of these conditions, but the shape of a boat which permits excellence in one area retards performance in another. It's essential, then, to understand how the various lines of a canoe contribute to its performance.

DESIGN. First considerations belong to overall dimensions. Sleek competition slalom canoes measure as short as 13 feet 1 inch, while war canoes stretch out to 22 even 24 feet. Between these extremes for the warrior classes lie the usual lengths for peacetime canoeing: the 15- to 18-footers. Until you compare the performance of these, it is hard to imagine the difference one foot of canoe makes. But it is tangible. Since every canoe regardless of size has to have two ends, any extra length is in effect added to the middle,

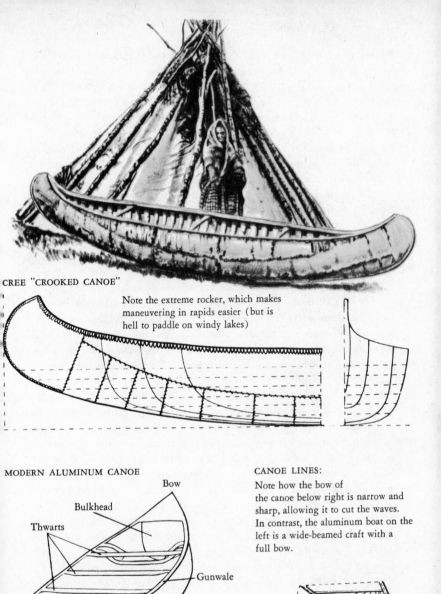

CREE "CROOKED CANOE"

Note the extreme rocker, which makes maneuvering in rapids easier (but is hell to paddle on windy lakes)

MODERN ALUMINUM CANOE

Bow

Bulkhead

Thwarts

Gunwale

Freeboard

Draft

Stern

Painter

CANOE LINES:

Note how the bow of the canoe below right is narrow and sharp, allowing it to cut the waves. In contrast, the aluminum boat on the left is a wide-beamed craft with a full bow.

where a canoe is bulkiest. Thus the midsection of an 18-foot canoe is quite roomy, but in the 15- or 16-footer, it's more akin to the equator—a convenient geographical fiction without real dimensions or storage space. More important, the bulky middle floats a canoe by displacing volume. The buoyancy gained by one foot of canoe is sufficient to see a 17-footer through many rapids which would swamp her shorter sisters. On the other hand, the price of length is maneuverability, for the obvious reason that there is more boat to maneuver. And a long canoe is not only heavier on the portage trail, it's also more awkward and unwieldy.

All in all, it's no accident the 17-footers are the most popular among general canoeists. For smooth-water trips or running single, a 16-foot or even a 15-foot boat may be preferable; for expeditions out of range of settlements for a month or more, you might consider the merits of an 18-footer. Otherwise, a 17-footer will serve gallantly. Which is to say that for every time you want a shorter canoe there will be a time you need one longer.

A canoe's width gives substance and volume to its length, and the same problem of how much is too much nags the prospective buyer. A beam of about 36 inches works reasonably well for a 17-foot model, but a 15-footer of the same width will perform differently, for fairly obvious reasons. A canoe cuts through the water something like a wedge: the sharper the angle, the less resistance and the easier it is to paddle. By subtracting from a boat's length without also decreasing width, the leading angle of the wedge becomes broader and resistance increases. Many of the shorter boats on the market tend to be too tubby, perhaps because of the popular notion that a wide beam lends needed stability to a canoe. A wide canoe is certainly slower to list, but not necessarily more seaworthy. In rough water, steadiness is achieved more by paddling technique than by inherent design. More on this point later, but for now believe us: tippiness (within limits) is irrelevant to a fair evaluation of canoe design. In the parlance of the trade, a boat is not "tippy" but is "tender," and tenderness is a sign of life.

Depth, the third dimension, is a crucial consideration for open (that is, uncovered) canoes. Raising the sides is a time-honored defense that works to fend off uninvited waves. Many canoes on the market are too low amidships for open running. As a rule, count out any boat with a midship depth of less than 12 inches; and depending on the other design characteristics of the boat, you may need as much as 15 inches.

The absolute specifications of length, beam, and depth lend a somewhat misleading aura of exactitude to a discussion of canoe design. More important are the curves that shape the flow of its lines. There is, for example, the contour of the bottom. Should it be a V, round, or flat? The fastest flatwater canoes have sharp V bottoms to cut knifelike through the water. As always, single-minded breeding leads to undesirable side effects. In this case, the more extreme versions turn only slowly and they draw a ridiculous amount of water—six inches and more. Flat-bottomed canoes, which have gained near-monopoly status among the leading manufacturers, take the opposite tack. At the cost of speed and ease of straightaway paddling, they have the virtues of a shallow draft (two to three inches with two men aboard), better maneuverability, and more cargo space. The flat bottom, like the wide beam, is said to count for stability—another half truth. The shape of a canoe's bottom, you see, goes far to determine the shape of its bilge (the curve from the bottom to the sides). A canoe with a flat bottom has to wrap a sharp bilge curve; and the sharper the bilge, the harder it is to lean when you want and the tippier the canoe becomes when it does roll to its side. Just when you could appreciate a little steadiness.

Rocker, the line described by the keel in lateral view, is another curve that contributes to a canoe's personality. Lots of rocker allows the boat to pivot easily on its middle and thus gives quick response on tight turns. But it also encourages fickle meandering when you are most trying for a straight course across a lake. Extreme rocker was the distinguishing feature of the birchbarks used by the Indians who traveled the Moisie. Dubbed "crooked canoes" by the early Frenchmen, they look like an accident of astigmatism.

The keel itself contributes to a boat's directional stability. By sailboat standards, a canoe keel is not much—only a half-inch strip running fore to aft on the bottom of the boat. Yet unobtrusive as it may seem in drydock, that strip contributes over one hundred square inches of resistance to sideways drift in the water. Many canoeists prefer to compromise between directional stability on lakes and pivoting ability in whitewater by getting a canoe equipped with a shallow "shoe" keel which offers less resistance. Either kind gives structural reinforcement to the hull and protects the boat against sharp impacts from below.

More difficult to describe or evaluate is the contour of a bow (or stern) at the waterline. Designers have taxed their ingenuity providing lines and curves which flare in endlessly hopeful combinations. A full bow works best for climbing the steep upslopes of waves; but in calm water, that same bow plows ahead instead of gently gliding through. Conversely, while a sharper bow cuts a seam to allow smooth quick passage on the flats, in heavy waves it cuts out a wedge of water, which gravity dumps in the bowman's lap.

In the end, putting these design considerations together to evaluate one particular canoe is not always easy. If you can borrow or rent a variety of models to field-test on a river run, do so. Otherwise, for wilderness cruising, try to strike a balance in design between a maneuverable high-floating boat for big whitewater and a sharper-lined model which will hold its course over the long distance of flatwater paddling. By knowing the several characteristics which militate in either of these two directions, you can evaluate the trade-offs involved. A Grumman 17-footer, for instance, has a midship depth of only 12 inches, but it is blunt-ended and flat-bottomed, so will do well enough in bigger water. The Old Town 17-foot ABS has 15 inches of depth and needs it, since the bow has a sharp front line which cuts through waves much more than the Grumman.

MATERIALS. By all rights the optimal design deserves the best material, which should be durable, lightweight, attractive, cheap, and easy to work. The original experiments were carried out with tree trunks and birch bark. A few craftsmen still make these picturesque boats, but their scarcity and fragility eliminate them from consideration for whitewater.* Almost as rare these days are the cedar smooth-skins. In bygone times Yankee and Canadian woodworkers built canoes with planking so perfectly joined their boats required only varnish and buff to seal them watertight. The most painstaking of these men shunned even the use of steam to shape their boards; instead they searched the forests for roots of the needed arc so that the grain actually created the curves of the canoe. Surviving specimens of this breed deserve the respect and gentleness you might extend to a favorite old uncle, the kind you know to be at once sinewy and frail.

Wood-and-canvas canoes still remain on the market. The natural grace of the long cedar planks sweeping beneath the stout crisscross of ribs can be irresistible. These planks, however, only abut one another and waterproofing is provided by a tight skin of heavy canvas (about 25 pounds) impregnated with filler and paint. In an encounter a few years ago between an unnoticed boulder and a brand-new canoe of Canadian origins, Rug and his father learned that the canvas can cover a multitude of sins. Having broken the boat in half, the Rugs were treated to a look at the inner anatomy, only to find that all the planks were only 12 to 14 inches long, the short ends being hidden underneath the ribs. For once failing to catch the irony, Old Rug called it "scrapwood" and spent the whole hike out composing scathing letters to the manufacturer, though none ever found their way to paper.

* For more information on the history and construction of these old beauties, see *The Bark Canoes and Skin Boats of North America,* by Edwin Tappan Adney and Howard I. Chapelle, available from the Superintendent of Documents, U.S. Government Printing Office, Washington, D.C. 20402. Adney devoted sixty years to studying Indian canoes with the last of the surviving craftsmen. Chapelle has collated Adney's work, contributed his own painstaking diagrams, and collected some remarkable old photographs in a beautiful book that invites the rediscovery of forgotten skills. If you're actually interested in buying such a boat or in seeing one under construction, contact Henri Vaillancourt, Box 199, Greenville, N.H. 03048.

There are more serious objections to the wood-and-canvas canoes, especially for general wilderness use. Being a work of long and dedicated human labor, they have become quite expensive, running a thousand dollars and up.* And despite their aesthetic charm, wooden canoes still suffer from being wooden. Even when recently varnished, a canvas canoe absorbs water and gains weight. Well-maintained canoes may add only a few pounds but the weathered veterans can grow a terrifying 30 or 40 pounds. The approaching obsolescence of wood and canvas for whitewater can be laid mainly, however, to the development of materials that are pound for pound vastly stronger and more resilient.

One offsetting advantage of canvas canoes is that they have been built in an enormous variety of designs. In addition to the many different models that larger companies offered before the contraction of the market forced cutbacks, every independent canoe maker was his own free-lance artist. To a sensitive eye, the finished product reveals the intentions of the craftsman, the job he was building his boat to do, even the very river he would run. If you happen on a canoe whose intentions match your own and are not able to pass it up, it would be worth your while to strip the canvas and replace it with a covering of fiber glass. There are enough subtleties of technique to require another guidebook† or the help of an experienced friend, but the whole project can be done in three or four afternoons for a hundred dollars. The result is a canoe with a bottom impervious to water, stronger by half, hardly at all heavier than the original, and coarser in its lines by only a few millimeters.

Since fiber glass is relatively inexpensive and easy to mold, many of the newest and most exciting designs make use of it. Almost all whitewater racing boats, for example, are glass, and wilderness paddlers should also consider it. One advantage in particular stands out: easy to mold means easy to fix. Even on the riverbank, a fiber-glass canoe is just about infinitely repairable. If you have a kit of cloth and resin and can find the pieces of your boat, you should be able to put it back together again. (See page 237–8.) Because fiber glass is so workable, it also provides the simplest way to break into the boatbuilding business. In addition to the big canoe factories,

* On occasion, one may be lucky enough to pick up a second-, third-, or umpteen-hand canvas boat for a pittance. Rug, by a careful indication of just enough lack of interest, has bought used livery canoes for five and ten dollars.

† We recommend Charles Walbridge, *Boatbuilder's Manual,* published by Wild-water Designs, Inc., Penllyn Pike and Morris Road, Penllyn, Pa. 19422. This manual outlines the variety of fiber glass, plastics, and plasticoids that are available for boat-building and teaches step by step the construction of covered canoes and kayaks. Maurice Lannon, *Polyester and Fiberglass and Information on Some Other Plastics* (Gem-O'Lite Plastics Corp., 5525 Cahuenga Blvd., North Hollywood, Calif., 91601) is less up to date than Walbridge but does deal with re-covering wood boats.

there is a whole cottage industry of one- and two-man operations producing whitewater boats. Some of these turn out shoddy work; others, by avoiding the overhead of big business and by doing hand lay-ups, make the finest fiber-glass canoes going. Since there is such a wide range of designs and quality, you would be well advised to know a few fundamentals of the technology.

Fiber glass is glass which has been extruded as tiny fibers and subsequently woven together as a cloth. In this form, fiber glass is extremely strong for its weight but obviously lacks rigidity. Builders of fiber-glass boats take this cloth (or such related synthetics as polypropylene, nylon, Dynel, Diolen, S-glass, and PRD), shape it around a mold, and impregnate it with a liquid resin (either epoxy or polyester) which subsequently hardens. Color is provided either by adding pigment to the resin or by putting a gel coat on the outside of the hull, which gives the boat a smooth-finished appearance and hides any blemishes underneath.

The best construction provides flexible strength. By flexibility we mean the quality to give in or bend with the compression impact of hitting a rock in whitewater; by strength, the resilience to pop back and retain the hull shape. Many of the best craftsmen try to find the ideal balance of competing virtues by sandwiching layers of fiber-glass cloth (which gives needed rigidity and the smoothest wear) with inner layers of a synthetic (which provides greater flexibility). The weave of the cloth is equally important. Matting, a compress of loosely packed fibers, results in a heavy, brittle boat; a coarse basket weave, called roving, is stronger, but finely woven cloth is superior by far. Cloth and resin should be combined in proper proportions —that is, the least possible resin that will thoroughly saturate the cloth.

How can the prospective buyer know a good fiber-glass canoe from a slipshod one? The reputation of the builder can be a helpful guide, but remember that commercial success does not necessarily indicate commercial value. Some of the most popular fiber-glass canoes, at least among the resorts, are notorious for poor construction. The best bet is to buy a canoe the same way you would buy a car. Ask some questions, look it over, and kick the tires. What is the lay-up? Avoid machine-sprayed mat at all costs; it is identified by red tracer fibers which can usually be seen on the inside of the canoe. How many layers of cloth are used and what kind? If synthetics are alternated with fiber glass, look carefully for evidence of delaminations. These can be most easily seen near the ends of the boat or over any wear spots on a used boat. Look carefully for air bubbles on the inside of the hull; they should have been sanded out. Also check for whitish areas that may indicate resin-starved cloth. Equally detrimental is resin flooding, which adds to weight without contributing real strength. The best sign of such oversaturation is the puddling of resin on the bottom of the inside hull. Is the gel coat thick and the color deep? It may make for a nice finish, but like all cosmetics, gel coats don't add strength to the boat. Other factors are more important. As for the hull itself: site along its curves to see how uniform and smooth the surface is. A worn or improperly prepared mold will turn out a boat with ripples, bumps, or asymmetrical curves. After inspecting the boat, lean on it firmly. It should flex with moderate pressure (about 75 pounds) and return to its normal contour spontaneously. If you hear cracking or see splintering, the boat is too brittle.

Before fiber glass was invented, aluminum was the standard choice for tough whitewater runs, and the old standby still has its advantages. As with fiber glass, aluminum canoes are reasonably cheap, and pound for pound they are a good deal stronger. There is just no material that will hold up like aluminum to the thousand and one indignities a boat has to suffer on wilderness trips. The standard canoe manuals detail the proper ways to get in and out of a boat: don't bridge the canoe, don't dock it in rocky spots where the waves pound, don't drag it along the ground, so on and so forth. You won't hear this lecture from us. Too many times, we've been grateful for a safe harbor no matter how much it pounded. In true wilderness away from groomed trails, you may well find yourself dragging your boat upstream or lowering it over steep rock precipices, despite the horrible rending sounds. Times like these, and there are plenty of them, an aluminum boat is unsurpassable.

The main drawback of aluminum is that its metallic surface tends to grab rocks. This is no small source of trouble if the current happens to grab the other end of the boat; in fast water, the result is a sure broach (where the canoe swings broadside with the current) and a possible capsize. A coat of wax, we are told, will help. Another small modification we would suggest on factory boats is a coat of paint for the bow deck. That little triangle of shiny metal may otherwise reflect the glare of the sun into the bowman's eyes. Whitewater canoeists who are sloppy in boulder gardens will find that these canoes double as aluminum drums. The noise makes it difficult to hide your mistakes from the rest of your party, but the fish no doubt appreciate the warning of the boat's approach. Aluminum boats that capsize often take more punishment than fiber-glass models, but once pretzeled or severely torn, repair becomes almost impossible. Quick rescue work can do a lot to prevent such a tragedy, however, and it's amazing what punishment aluminums *can* take. More than once, we have wrapped aluminum around a rock and pried it free to discover the bottom of the boat pushed up to the center thwart. It is acceptable technique to stop, prop the ends of the canoe on a couple of logs, step into the middle and jump around, and then continue the trip as if nothing had happened.

When shopping aluminum, check for a number of features. Since these boats depend a great deal on rigidity for their strength, there should be at least three thwarts (in addition to the seats) on 17-foot models. Make sure they are sturdy and firmly attached to the boat—especially the middle thwart, which carries the canoe's weight on portages. A poorly attached middle thwart will come loose in the middle of a trip because of the jouncing motion of hiking, and it is somewhat of a letdown to have seventy-five pounds suddenly land on your crown. Also check for strong seat attachments. Although rescue operations should never rely on them for pulling a submerged boat free of the current, there are times when you have no choice. And weak seats will pull right out of the boat, leaving you with more problems than when you started the rescue.

One of the newest materials to appear in the shape of a canoe is something known as ABS foam. ABS (Acrylonitrile Butadiene Styrene) is a hard-rubber product which is supplied to boating manufacturers in double sheets with a foam layer sandwiched in between. The sheets are heated and vacuum-molded into the desired hull shape. The canoe makers who use ABS (Old Town, granddaddy of them all, is among them) claim a number of advantages for their products: the main ones being that the flotation is supplied by the foam sandwich construction instead of in bulkheads fore and aft, and that the material is the toughest stuff ever to hit whitewater.

We have put several brands through their paces, and the ABS definitely gets high marks. It is the slipperiest of canoe materials, which makes it a gloriously quiet boat in flatwater and considerate of minor mistakes in the rapids. Shallowly submerged rocks which aluminum would grab, the ABS slides over with nary a murmur. In big water, ABS comes out looking even better. One bad Sunday on the Boreas, we ran a few involuntary field tests and our capsized boats came through drops we're sure would have demolished any other canoe. The virtue of ABS here is not only its strength but its flexibility and slipperiness. Even when a sunken boat gets broadsides, it will not catch on as many rocks; and when it does, the boat flexes, slides, gives, bounces off and on down the river.

So ABS is definitely a good material. But it does have some problems. One is that you pay for what you get. Prices are generally 200 to 250 dollars higher than aluminum and fiber-glass models. Another drawback is that the sandwich flotation is only barely adequate; in heavy water, prepare to have your boat disappear from sight for long stretches. Some manufacturers remedy this problem by putting extra flotation in, occasionally by making the seats of Styrofoam. In this case, make sure there's enough room to stow your feet underneath in kneeling position, and that you can extricate them easily in case of a capsize. One brand we tried failed this test, though it must be admitted Jim has monstrously big feet. The seats may also be comfortably contoured—a thoughtful provision—but make sure they also have drainage holes (or drill them yourself). Otherwise puddles of water collect on rainy days. Another drawback is that although ABS is superbly durable in heavy-water capsizes, it does not hold up as well as aluminum in the continual dragging and scraping of shallow stream work. Sharp rocks slip past quietly, but they take their toll with a sliver of the ABS.

One final note of caution: the slippery material on the outside is just as slippery on the inside. In tough rapids, where paddlers must be firmly braced in their canoe, the problem can be solved by installing friction pads for the seat, knees, and feet. The rubber from inner-tube tires works well. Cut it to shape, apply contact cement, and smooth in place.

In addition to ABS, two other materials have been introduced to the canoeing market, polyethylene and Du Pont's Kevlar 49. In performance, polyethylene boats are most similar to ABS: the material does not like sharp lines, and it is slippery and flexible—even more flexible than ABS. Thus polyethylene canoes are difficult to destroy in a capsize. This flexibility, how-ever, also means that the bottom of a boat will tend to "oilcan," or ripple, as the canoe glides through the water. To minimize this flexing, which reduces a hull's efficiency, some manufacturers add an ungainly interior keel to rein-force the polyethylene. Coleman Marine Products, through aggressive market-ing and low prices, has made its polyethylene general-purpose canoe the Model T of the industry.

On the high end of the price scale, Kevlar boats are made of a cloth like fiber glass, except that the fabric is much more durable and lightweight (police use it in bullet proof jackets). Where a 17-foot polyethylene boat may weigh 80 pounds and ABS and aluminum weigh 70-75, a Kevlar model will run only 55 to 60 pounds, a significant advantage of the wilderness portage trail. Like fiber glass, Kevlar's sharp lines permit some of the sweetest and most responsive designs on the market. Expect to pay $1200 and more for the premium.

Details of construction are important on all boats. After examining the seats, flotation and thwarts, check for painter attachments. Ideally, lines should be placed at both stems at the waterline. An eyebolt or even a drill hole centered on the deck is an acceptable second choice. A range of colors for the canoe is available; our experience leads us to prefer yellow. Try climb-ing out of a rapids some late afternoon and look downstream for an overturned green canoe immersed in green river water somewhere between overhanging green forests, and you will understand why.

ACCESSORIES. The same considerations of design and material implicit in the selection of a canoe apply to its propeller, the paddle. The hand-carved Montagnais model that Peach found on our portage trail to the Moisie is only four feet long and just three and a half inches wide at the blade. We can't be sure if this design is the outcome of Indian taste or the result of the stunted local spruce. In either case, modern civilization has come up with some considerable improvements.

The standard blade width of most commercial lines is six or seven inches. Whitewater men need a bigger bite to match the power of their carrying currents and generally settle on eight, nine, or ten inches. The usual rule for determining paddle length is "nose to toes." Like most others, this rule deserves a couple of exceptions: very tall and very short canoeists should observe moderation. Jim, who is six foot six, prefers a paddle six or seven inches short of the bean pole to which he is entitled. Also, all else being equal, the sternman requires a slightly longer paddle than the bow because he sits a bit higher off the water. The one other crucial feature to consider is the design of the handle. For whitewater, a T-grip gives the wrist precise control over the angle of blade to current, as well as commanding leverage to change it as needed.

Frankly, the four of us are at loggerheads as to whether an ideal paddle exists or whether different designs suit different conditions. Jim and Peach stuck with the T-gripped wide blades no matter what the occasion, but Rug and Joe preferred round-handled, shorter, slimmer models for lake country. They claimed that a lighter paddle allowed a man to stretch out into a more comfortable, lanky, all-day pace. In the end, the argument is moot, since wilderness travel demands that every paddler carry an extra as insurance against breakage or loss.

The prospect of a break brings us back to the problem of wood. Old Town makes a splendid spruce paddle, though none with a T-handle. Clément of Three Rivers, Quebec, offers a complete line of laminated paddles that are perhaps the most beautiful ever made commercially. Unfortunately, wooden edges tend to burr in the unavoidable crunch of poling off the bottom and fending off rocks, and laminated paddles are prone to split, especially in the second season after a dry winter. Copper bang plates and fiber-glass splints help to correct these deficiencies, but the repairs detract from the very qualities that give wood its original appeal—light weight and aesthetic charm.

Synthetic materials have once again been pressed into service. Grumman makes an aluminum paddle that functions perfectly well but has not gained wide popularity, perhaps because it more resembles the tool of an industrial mechanic than the wing of a free spirit. Fiber-glass paddles come in all varieties and can be highly recommended. They are quite indestructible in normal use, which includes everything except rolling loaded canoes over them. (No need to pick out the heavier models, some of which are real arm breakers.) If you buy a paddle from an amateur builder, be certain it will float and heft it to make sure that its weight is roughly balanced between blade and shaft. A disagreeable quality of fiber glass is that it provides a cold grip in chilly waters. A nice compromise lies in the paddle with a fiberglass blade and wooden shaft.

Vest Type
Segmented
Closed-Cell Foam

Closed Cell
Foam
Vest Type

Horsecollar
Life Jacket

As indispensable as the paddle is a good life preserver. Only the rank novice, one who has not felt the river work over his own body, fails to take the term with dread literalness: *life preserver*. The waist belt, fine for water skiers waiting for motorboat rescue, is totally inadequate for the fully clothed wilderness canoeist who picks his trouble spots for their very remoteness. Several adequate designs are available. The standard, popular, and cheap horseshoe collar has the advantage of (usually) floating the occupant head up and nose out. But a word of caution if you buy one: The flotation consists of kapok sealed in plastic compartments. If these are punctured (as they can be simply from pressure if used as a cushion around the campsite) they soon become waterlogged and more dangerous to wear than going without. This defect is remedied in the medium-price preservers, which consist of closed-cell foam (PVC or polyvinyl chloride) cased in nylon shells. Various designs, both horseshoe collar and wraparound vests, are available. The wraparound models don't restrict paddling movement as much as the horseshoe collars, and will double as windbreak, camp cushion, backrest, and bedtime pillow. They are less sure to float an unconscious person face up, but in the foam and froth of heavy rapids, the extra flotation around the back gives needed support (as well as protection from rocks). The closed-cell foam preservers are also available in a segmented vest style. A break in the segments just below the rib cage makes these vests easily adaptable to kayaking with a spray skirt and closed deck.

One appeal of these jackets seems to be that they are more stylish and more comfortable by virtue of being less bulky. But bulk is what provides buoyancy! A typical segmented model jacket gives about ten and a half pounds of flotation compared to twenty pounds by a larger horseshoe in kapok.* Unfortunately, there is no reliable guide as to how much flotation is enough. In canoeing competitions, the International Canoe Federation requires that, if life jackets are necessary at all, they must provide at least 13.2 pounds of buoyancy. The Mellon Institute, according to Carl Trost, ran tests on twenty-two individuals and demonstrated that the lifting force necessary to hold the head above water ranged from zero during inspiration to twelve pounds during expiration, so thirteen pounds seems to be a good ball-park figure. Nonetheless, some people float better than others (depending on weight, surface area, lipid content, lung capacity, center of buoyancy, and center of gravity), and different people may require different jackets. Great height, large bones, little fat, and heavy clothing are all indications for the more buoyant vests. In very rough whitewater, still additional buoyancy is helpful; on occasion we have been enough intimidated by a river to wear two preservers, one over the other.

Whitewater helmets are mandatory equipment for covered canoes and kayaks, optional for open wilderness boats. When a covered boat capsizes, the occupants remain in place. If their technique is good enough, they Eskimo-roll back to an upright position and continue paddling downriver. While upside down, however, their boat has gained a couple of three-foot keels, and the paddlers' heads are on the receiving end of any hard knocks. One good bump and your canoeing career is at an end. Hence the helmets. In an open boat, since you leave the ship as it keels over, your head remains upright and in less need of protection. But if you feel more secure with a hel-

* We are borrowing information from Carl Trost's excellent article "Life Jackets?" in *American Whitewater*, Spring 1972.

met, take it along. They're available in various models; be sure to get one that offers protection around the temples.

Canoe covers for open boats (usually homemade of canvas and snaps) are not practical accessories for a wilderness trip. They do enable you to run rapids that would swamp an open boat, but they are extra weight on the portages, time-consuming to put on and off, and fragile in the misfortune of a capsize. Permanent covers, as provided by the fiber-glass banana boats, meet all these objections but create new ones. They contain less storage space, and their low thwarts force the paddler into a deep kneel that cuts off effective communication between the lower legs and the rest of the body. Like kayaks, they offer exciting sport on short outings; and some boaters report using them for trips as long as a week to ten days. But for long wilderness runs we prefer the traditional designs. If you do decide to go covered, you will need to outfit these tender boats with thigh straps and toe blocks. Useful in any kind of a canoe are knee pads, available at canoe outlets or garden stores.

Instead of covers, we take bailers. Cut the bottom out of a Clorox plastic bottle, attach a ten-foot cord to the handle, and tie the other end to the stern seat.

Painters are essential. For lake or lazy-stream canoeing, a short line of eight feet may suffice: just enough for easy docking. In wilderness areas where portage trails are infrequent, the technique of lining boats along a rapid's edge demands good strong lines, both bow and stern. Use at least quarter-inch braided nylon (1100-lb. test). The thinner $\frac{5}{32}$-inch width may have enough strength for the job (700-lb. test) but is tough on the hands when hauling free a submerged boat. Even worse, it is downright dangerous in a capsize, since it can become entangled with your feet when you are bobbing down the rapids. Jim's brother Pete found this out once in a capsize adventure in the Quebec woods. Fortunately for him, the sunken canoe did not nosedive for the deep undercurrents (as can happen in heavy rapids) nor did it rake him through any rock gardens. He was very lucky.

The proper length of painters presents another problem. Some rapids may require as much as fifty feet of rope to do a good lining job. But the extra length is unwieldy and can be dangerous during a capsize. Twenty-five feet is satisfactory for most lining and safer in a spill. You may want to bring a couple of extra fifty-foot lengths for difficult situations.

On a wilderness trip, first aid for the canoe is as important as doctoring supplies for your own ills. The key item in the kit is a roll of waterproof silver "duct" tape which takes care of minor leaks. It's available from outdoor suppliers and hardware stores. Also handy is a roll of moderately strong wire to repair a seat that comes unattached, or some extra nuts and bolts for securing thwarts whose rivets have come loose. For fiber-glass boats, take along extra fiber-glass cloth, a can of resin with its little bottle of hardener, and a brush—all available at marinas. (See page 237.) Familiarize yourself with the properties of the mixture before you leave—how the amount of hardener affects the "setup" time of the resin, for example.

Tied to Thwart

Blanket

Binder

Tautline Hitches

MFN 851

One final word about what special equipment is necessary to transport a canoe from home to river by car: None. Actually, we have no serious objection to canoe racks—they are moderately priced and most are easy enough to clamp on. Our only point is that they are not necessary unless for some reason you need to extend your car roof to carry two canoes side by side (perhaps so you can place a third canoe on top of them).

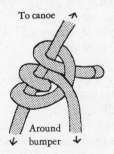

To canoe

Around bumper

For one canoe, we find it about as easy to tie directly onto the roof. First lay a blanket and then center the canoe on it. Next tie a rope around each edge of the bow and stern seats. Bring each rope up, over, and around the canoe and secure it to the opposite corner of your car's bumper. A good knot to use is the rolling hitch or tautline, the same as for tying tent stakes. Once tied you can tighten at will without any backsliding. The coup de grâce is to place a binder around the ropes just under the canoe. Draw the binder tight, but don't try for high C: you might end with a canoe-sized groove in your roof. This arrangement secures a canoe adequately for all but turnpike driving in a high wind. For high-speed travel, just tie another rope to the center thwart at one gunwale, bring it through the car, and up to the opposite gunwale. In addition to gaining a short clothesline for the return trip, you will have clamped down a canoe that no natural force can budge.

Food

Burlington, Vt.
April 7

John,

I officially cut my mooring lines twice today, so I figured I ought to give you fair warning: there's no turning back now. The first one was this morning when I told the Dean I couldn't teach at summer session. The second was this afternoon when I consummated the Big Deal and got myself a canoe! I've been working on Dennis down at the marina and he finally came through with a healthy discount. I told him I would nag him all spring otherwise, that we were all dyed-in-the-wool river rats, I would sell my grandmother down to New Orleans next time he asked me for a favor, etc. So if you've managed to snag your friend Peach with his 17-footer, we're all set on maritime locomotion.

Like I said on the phone, I will be glad to look into whatever natural foods you want on the menu. Just tell me how many meals and I'll figure quantities and report on price. I think some of the unbleached flours, cornbreads, etc., may be worth taking in place of the supermarket stuff. I also have to disagree about peanut butter. The natural spread is TEN TIMES better than the homogenized A & P variety. I think we should take a vote among the group—and I cast my ballot for spending the extra \$\$. If we're going to have peanut butter for lunch for a month it had jolly well better be *good* peanut butter.

JOE

P.S. Now that I think about it, maybe it was Chauncy *Choats*worth.

The history of nothern exploration is full of disasters by slow starvation. We think of Captain Bernard and Charles Thomsen of the Stefansson expedition. Mistakenly believing the overdue Stefansson to be lost, Barnard and Thompson set out as a search party and were themselves overtaken by arctic storms. With luck and perseverance, they struggled to a remote cache left by the expedition earlier in the year. Finding a small amount of flour and an abundance of sugar and tea, the two men headed back into the blizzard with the flour, but they left behind the sugar in the evident belief that it was only a condiment without nutritional value. Months later Stefansson found his "rescuers" frozen under a snowbank.

Fortunately, common ignorance about nutrition has given way to common knowledge. And today the woodsman can enter the woods with a good deal more varied menu. In 1905 Dillon Wallace listed the provisions he and his companions took to cross Labrador by canoe: "298 pounds of pork; 300 pounds of flour; 45 pounds of cornmeal; 40 pounds of lentils; 28 pounds of rice; 25 pounds of erbswurst; 10 pounds of prunes; a few packages of dried vegetables; some beef bouillon tablets; 6 pounds of baking powder; 16 pounds of tea; 6 pounds of coffee, 15 pounds of sugar; 14 pounds of salt; a small amount of saccharine and crystallose; and 150 pounds of pemmican." Last year we set out across the same country with vegetable soup, pork chops, applesauce, and gingerbread. Outdoor stores and backpacking food manufacturers are doing a booming business these days. The newcomer will rightly be impressed (1) by the range of the selections and (2) by their cost. (Jim called it outrageous and gastronomical.) Before turning over your bankbook, take another side trip to the two or three largest supermarkets in your vicinity. Many of the lightweight specialty items for campers are also tucked away on the shelf at the A & P. The suburbanite's Redi-Make sliced potatoes with onions are the same as Trailblazers Campfire Hashbrowns except in name and price. On the other hand, between Mountain House freeze-dried chicken stew and Kraft's chicken noodle dinner there is all the difference between a chicken and his cackle, and the chicken is sometimes worth the extra price.

The key is to recognize the difference between dry food, dehydrated food, and freeze-dried food. Rice, instant pudding, and spaghetti are examples of dry food. They are naturally water-free and even though the sport shops are glad to sell them to you with a fancy name, you'll be wise to patronize the supermarket. Dehydrated food is prepared by various techniques of hot-air drying until 95 percent or more of the originally contained water is removed. Many foodstuffs—potatoes, fruits, milk, coffee, even maple syrup and spaghetti sauce—can be successfully dehydrated at no great sacrifice of taste. When carried out on a large scale, great economies become possible; by a collusion of nature and the teamsters, powdered milk is actually cheaper than fresh. An increasing number of dehydrated foods are stocked at the grocery. Now and then, the unwary woodsman may get hooked on a specialty item available only at the sports shops (dried apple slices, for example) and he has to pay the extra price.

Other foods, especially meats and vegetables, suffer during dehydration because their cellular structure is destroyed beyond the recognition of either microscope or palate. Freeze drying preserves both the organic microstructure and the original savor. Despite the teamsters, the process offers no practical advantages to the housewife (coffee is the exception) and thus backpackers have to divide the expense among themselves. With a little diligent inquiry, a party planning a long trip can find a distributor who will sell in bulk for a modest savings. This also permits the packing of meals in quantities to suit a human appetite instead of relying on those packets that serve four hypothetical midgets.

In planning a menu, try to achieve a working mix of flexibility, variety, and simplicity. Wilderness cookbooks presently available have enough exotic recipes to keep a chef of the wild slaving in the kitchen morning to night, and we don't aim to add to them. Personal tastes vary greatly, so we note here only a few essential points on each meal.

Breakfasts should be divided between short-order and drawn-out affairs. On a rainy day, there's plenty of time to fuss over the perfect fire to fry the perfect flapjack. On the other hand, cold cereal (by which we mean Familia or Granola, not the fluff from Battle Creek) allows a fast start for late sleepers or enables early risers to make a big lake crossing before the midmorning head wind blows up. (Make your own Granola, by the way; the store-bought stuff is outrageously expensive. We used the recipe provided in the *Last Whole Earth Catalog*.) Oatmeal or other hot cereals provide a filling bulk for meals which are otherwise skimpy (such as freeze-dried scrambled eggs). Canned bacon is good, if you don't waste the grease. Spam, which tastes abominable when cooked within four walls, comes out much better over the open fire. We always added Tang and cocoa to round off the meals.

The hallmark of our ideal lunch is simplicity. Set in the middle of long paddles and exhausting portages, it becomes the one time of maximum replenishment and rest, hence a study in motionless gluttony. Lunch should be large in quantity, trivial in preparation, high in caloric value, and as far as we're concerned, constant as the rising sun. Lunch came straight from the pack: Civil Defense biscuits, peanut butter, and cheese (cloth-wrapped, low-moisture); some honey or jelly; chocolate-chip bits (semisweet melt less easily); lemonade to wash it down. But above all, that peanut butter—Deaf Smith's oily, nutty concoction made a convert even out of Rug. On the printed page, it sounds monotonous, but we never tired of it.

For supper, our habit is to rotate through four or five favorite meals. This provides enough diversity but still makes planning and purchasing food for a long trip no more difficult than for a four- or five-day jaunt. Spaghetti, dehydrated sauce, plus hard-cased sausage (all store-bought) made a filling meal. Other main dishes used freeze-dried beef as the core of the meal, served as burger patties with mashies and gravy or as stew ingredients with many combinations of noodles and vegetables. The same can be done with chicken stews and tuna helpers from the supermarket. Supplement the main course with biscuits, vegetables, fruits. For cold desserts, try instant puddings or Jell-O cheesecakes; for the baking fire, chocolate cake, brownies, or ginger-bread. Just make sure the store-bought mixes do not require the addition of eggs; and remember to include powdered milk if needed.

When it comes to the final calculation of exact quantities, difficult questions arise. How many pounds of raisins to allot four men for twenty-five days? How much peanut butter is there in a hundred man-meals? How many "packets for four" do you really need for four? We choose to calculate by calories. The average American consumes 2700 of them a day and gets a little paunchy. On a trip as rugged as the Moisie, you need more like 4000 to hold your weight. Protein and carbohydrates have identical caloric value; each gives four calories per gram or just over 1800 calories per pound. Fats, on the other hand, tally at nine calories per gram or over 4000 calories per pound, making them by far the most efficient way to carry energy. Take corn oil and add it generously to pancakes and biscuits; use plenty of margarine and peanut butter; save the grease from bacon for beans, hashbrowns, or some such. But don't overdo—a fat diet higher than 40 percent is unpalatable except in arctic climes; very high proportions will lead to metabolic derangements akin to those of starvation itself.

Detailed calorie calculations are made with the help of one of the many available books which list brand-name foods with their calories. (They are "weight loss" books, but you'll find yourself using them for figuring ways to add calories to the meals.) Your ultimate shopping list grows out of the exacting process of looking up every item on your menu and juggling calories and quantities until each day's calorie count adds up to about 4000 or whatever number fits your trip.* It's more of that nuts-and-bolts work, but you will learn a few things: that cornmeal tops cake flour 485 calories to 350; that homemade Granola beats General Mills's cornflakes cup for cup 650 to 81; that overcooked spaghetti loses 20 percent of its food value to the brine; that 1500 calories for lunch seems enormous . . . until, weeks later, you stretch out on a midriver rock and reach for old Deaf Smith.

---

* Sticklers remind us that ideal caloric intake varies with body weight and other environmental factors. True enough, but we don't want to carry science too far. Counting calories is not meant to complicate menu making but to simplify the calculation of how much food is enough and guide the shopper to the most nutritious foods.

Clothing

Dear Joe,

Apologies for being slow about your last letter. The past two weeks at the hospital have left me pretty shorthanded on time. Things are cooking, though—it's always interesting coming home to see what's in the day's mail. Last week the quads finally arrived from the Map Office; also a note from Stow Lite saying they do sell their freeze-dried hamburger patties in tins of 32, which should save us some cash. Oh yes, and also that pamphlet "Quebec, Oui, M'sieu," which of course is absolutely no help.

Peach is in. I put the screws to him, told him I had to know by the end of the week. In typical style, he said he would think about it and tell me. Then he says nothing for three days until he arrives at the house wearing this big blue Lord Baden-Powell hat—the wide brim, chin strap, and everything. "Well," he says, "I just made the most important purchase for the trip." As if there was never any question of his going. I told him that in my book good wool long johns ranked higher than a hat. (By the way, I got a pair of wool navy surplus pants for only $12. They are great for canoeing, with the wide bottoms. If you want me to get you a pair, send me your waist size—allow a little large, wool shrinks.)

Hope to get you a tentative menu plan soon. I will get Peach and Jim over for this. Jim says he is very doubtful that he can go, but votes for the natural peanut butter. So we've got our four men. I think it will be a good group, but it is imperative we get together for a shakedown cruise so we can test out our paddling techniques. How about the second or third weekend in May on the Hudson? The gorge section may be a little high—we'll have to see how the water level is. But then, we need some good tough sets for practice. As to the departure date on the real trip, June 5 is our target. Let me know quick if that's not good.

I'll tell you, I am really getting itchy. I don't care if the Quebec Department of Parks says the river's been sold to the King of France. Moisie, Oui, M'sieu!

RUG

Clothes are worn for two basic reasons: to keep you warm and to keep you dry. There are other motives (like wanting to make a conspicuous display of plumage), but for the time being we mean to treat only the first two.

ON KEEPING WARM. Cold-weather campers ordinarily carry an assortment of cotton, felt, wool, leather, nylon, down, and rubber. The key fabric for the canoeist is wool.

Wool is by no stretch of the imagination an ideal invention, except perhaps for the sheep. It is heavy, expensive, hard to get, and scratchy. We wouldn't recommend it to anybody except for two facts: (1) it is warm dry and (2) it is warm wet. Because the canoeist is in for both dry times and quick soaks, often at unpredictable intervals, the advantage is obvious. Wool works so well because it efficiently traps the heat generated by the body's metabolism. Protection against the cold comes not from the cloth itself but from what is trapped inside the cloth: empty space. Wool fibers hold body heat by forming a honeycomb, a network of inner cells—and it does this better than cotton. In a burst of scientific zeal, Peach confirmed this hypothesis by subjecting both fabrics to the lens of the microscope. He discovered that the cotton is woven into a square patchwork that lies low in flat sheets to form large communicating air spaces. Wool is woven according to the same pattern but it doesn't obey. Instead of lining up in straight rows, the strands of wool spin into coils of rope that kink and twirl into tight knots. The inside spaces are tiny and cramped, wedged between flying girders and penetrated everywhere by a web of wandering, lost threads. When wet, they retain this kinky resilience, and hence also the warmth.

Other materials have their place in the canoeist's wardrobe. A rubber (neoprene) wet suit is the only absolute protection for the chill of spring ice water. Unfortunately, the wet suit is very heavy for most wilderness travel. It also tends to tire the paddler by binding at the shoulder and crotch, and is vulnerable to puncture by branches and twigs. Nonetheless, for canoeing rapids at a water temperature below 45 degrees or so, a wet suit can be a lifesaver. (See page 236.) Nylon-backed suits are preferable, and $\frac{3}{16}$-inch neoprene is naturally warmer than $\frac{1}{8}$-inch. In water that is only chilly, just take along the booties for sheer comfort. Down and even feathers provide much more warmth pound for pound than wool when they are dry. The original owners (the birds) use oil glands and patient strokes to keep the down fluffy in wet weather, but nylon shells do not protect so well. After a capsize or a hard rain, down parkas reduce to leaden clumps that require days of hot sun to restore, just the kind of weather you are unlikely to get if you need the down in the first place. Don't misunderstand us about nylon covers, though: they serve well as a buffer against the wind. Wool is hardly warmer than cotton until you cover it with an airtight shell. Since whatever is watertight is airtight, a rain jacket can be pressed into service even on sunny days.

As a rule, several layers of thin clothing are more versatile than one bulky article. By the same reasoning, a jacket that zips or buttons for fine thermostatic control beats a sweater or slipover shell.

Heat loss from any part of the body makes the whole body cold. The obvious implication, as the temperature drops, is not just to add layers but to cover up more parts. In terms of body surface area, the trunk accounts for about 40 percent of the organism. Since it is centrally located and easy to wrap, it gets first priority. A man can survive a frozen toe or leg, but once the body's central heating drops below about 75 degrees, all hope is gone. On the other hand, the extremities certainly should not be ignored and seldom are. But remember that the fifth extremity, the head and neck, is as large in surface area as an entire arm. Jim met a CIA man once who told him that heat-sensitive, infrared photographs were able to spot backpackers coming down the Ho Chi Minh trail by the noose-shaped rings appearing around their necks. What better reminder for a hat and turtleneck?

THE INS AND OUTS OF STAYING DRY. You can get wet in the woods either from the outside or from the inside. Outside, water is everywhere trying to get inside. Alas, water is also inside trying to get out. Not even counting perspiration, a man loses about a quart of water a day by evaporation, drop by microdrop. (Under an operating microscope at a magnification of 250X, you can see the tiny droplets suddenly pop up all over the skin and then just as quickly vanish.) When a person opens up his sweat glands as well, he can put out more than a gallon a day.

For some time, man has been inventing ways to keep his surface dry. In a canoe and on the portage trail, his choices still boil down to a poncho, a rain suit, or a cagoule. Backpackers know that a poncho can keep them dry and double as well for a ground cloth or tarp-tent. But its makeshift sleeves are real trouble in a canoe, since they leave a perfect sluiceway for rainwater whenever the elbow is raised above the shoulder. In a rainstorm, that amounts to a funnel of water for every paddle stroke. A rain suit, with separate coat and pants, can be drawn tight at the neck, wrists, and ankles to seal the wearer absolutely from the watery outside. Those were the advantages in Rug's mind when he picked up three suits on sale just before meeting Jim and Peach for menu planning.

"We're all set for rain," said Rug, flourishing the three fluorescent-orange plastic cases, each the size of a business envelope. "What a steal!"

"I'm not laying any bets on who got robbed," said Jim.

"Well, just hold on while I demonstrate." Unfolding the pleated plastic like fine stationery, Rug gingerly worked his way into the pants and jacket. Then he zipped up the front, snapped the wristlets and anklets, and smiled benevolently. "Looks pretty good to me."

"Can you bend over without binding?" asked Jim.

Rug did several cautious front and back bends, then a pivot or two from the waist. "No problem," he said, beginning to unzip.

"You look a little flushed," said Peach.

"Well, it's hot up here."

"Funny. It feels O.K. to me. Looks like you're kind of damp too."

"Damp!" said Jim. "You're *drenched* under there. How much did these sauna baths cost you?"

Now it was Rug's turn to smile. "One dollar and ninety-eight cents. That's the best thing about them."

In the end, Rug managed to pawn off his presents on Peach and Joe, but Jim chose to buy a cagoule, which is a rain shirt with a long waist extending to about midcalf. Advocates of the cagoule concede the leg below the knee to the elements in return for improved circulation. Jim says he thinks of the cagoule as a chimney with air from the bottom providing sufficient draft to keep the central fire dry and warm. Its disadvantages are the lack of a zipper down the front, the necessity of adopting a somewhat ungainly gait when descending steep slopes (the long shirt can catch on the boot heel), and the possible dangers of entanglement during a capsize. We suggest you either shuck your cagoule when running a tough set, or else tie a cord around the waist to keep it from flopping around too much during a swim.

Jim's cagoule cost twenty-seven dollars, and the difference in price between that and the dollar-ninety-eight specials was due to fabric, not design. The best rain gear is made of urethane-treated, rip-stop nylon, which is waterproof, tough, and lightweight to boot. The best constructions will minimize sewn-through seams, where water leaks in no matter how tiny the needlework. Carrying a tube of seam sealant (available at outdoor stores) can help. Dollar-ninety-eight specials are made of plastic alone. They are waterproof but nothing-else-proof, and the wearer soon cultivates a healthy paranoia for even frail twigs. Joe got discouraged on our first rainy portage when one incautious stride between boulders split his pants up the middle. After that he refused to wear them anywhere outside the canoe. Rug, with grasshopper nerves, managed to get his suit through the trip with only half a roll of plastic tape. Forewarned is forearmed.

FOOTGEAR. From time to time, the canoeist involuntarily turns swimmer or, in other circumstances, a wader of streams. These activities impose stern demands on his footwear. He needs a lightweight shoe with a flexible sole that will cushion and grip the rocky stream bottoms, and to our mind that spells sneakers. Low-cuts, although easier to slip into, are also likely to be pulled off the foot by a fast current. The high-top basketball style stays on and also protects the ankle against underwater scrapes. If you plan to wear these over wet-suit booties, you may need a size or two larger than what you usually wear. Be wary about improvising with an old pair of sneaks that have stretched to the proper size through dilapidation. We have worn out even new pairs in fifteen days of whitewater.

Once away from the riverbank, a man's feet make a different set of demands. His toes ache for a dry sock, his sneaker blisters weep for relief, and under seventy pounds of duffels, his ankles demand some genuine support. Hiking boots are well worth bringing along. All the advice given to the backpacker (and it is too abundantly available to bear repeating) holds for the wilderness canoeist with only a few qualifications. Because a hiker's bog or mudhole is too often the canoeist's portage route, you will want to choose boots with a closed, sewn-in tongue. Higher (8–10-inch) tops cut down the intake of swamp water as well. Or you may want to choose, as Jim did, the shoepac invented by L. L. Bean in 1912. A combination of rubber shoe and leather uppers, its advantages in boggy country are obvious. Those who perspire freely may find the rubber bottom too sweaty; those who seek firmer arch support should buy Bean's removable arch with the steel shank. The rubber soles provide traction inferior to the Vibram lugs of the hiking boot, and so are at a disadvantage in steep or slippery terrain.

FIELD TESTING. Whatever your final choices for a personal outfit, buy early and take a weekend outing or two to discover how wise your selections have been. Then is the time to discover that your new shirt shrunk two sizes instead of one, that it lacks a breast-pocket flap, and that the tail is too short. On our shakedown cruise, Rug learned about pants pockets. His army pants had the type that were oversewn, carpenter style, on the legs. The design may work for an infantry on the march, but around a campfire the pocket rides up and contents roll out.

Only after numerous outings does one learn the full complement of details which contribute to a comfortable stay in the woods, the odd points of construction which make a trip run smoothly. Each man develops his own idiosyncrasies and preferences in choice of wardrobe, and you'll do the same. Nonetheless, we've sketched four clotheshorses decked out in their own fancies just to give you an idea of how function and style blend to create the dyed-in-the-wool wilderness canoe veteran.

PEACH

LORD BADEN-POWELL HAT:
Wide Brim. By the end of
the trip, more wrinkles,
less starch.

BINOCULARS:
Not essential
but handy

Peach wore a nylon
racing type swimsuit
under trousers.
Nylon dries quickly.

SUNGLASSES:
Polarized, cuts glare in
late afternoon rapids

NAVY SURPLUS
WOOL TROUSERS:
Bell bottoms make easy off
over boots, also roll up easier
for stream wading.

NECKERCHIEF:
Cuts heat loss, soak
in bug oil for insect
protection

WOOL LONG JOHNS:
Hard to get these days.
Not as scratchy as cracked
up to be.

JOE

Sewn in tongue
for mud holes

SNO-PROOF:
or some such
dressing to
recondition boots
after too many
bogs

SOCKS:
Always wool

GLOVES:
Handy as
potholders,
bug protection

Closed cell
foam preserver
doubles as
seat cushion

Glasses strap essential in capsizes. Bring extra pair of glasses if blind without them.

TURTLENECK: Cuts down on important area of heat loss in cold weather. Also protects against bugs.

JIM

CAGOULE: Cut full for good ventilation. Expensive

T-GRIP PADDLE HANDLE: Better control in whitewater

ROPE: Tie the cagoule when running rapids (in case of capsize) or just tuck into pants

CLOSED CELL FOAM PRESERVER: Good insulation on cold, windy days

RUG

WOOL FELT CRUSHER: Add chin strap for windy days

STRING TIED TO BELT LOOP: One each for match case and compass carried in pocket

UNTUCKED: Need longer shirt-tail

Flap and button

MID-CALF WOOL SOCKS: Pull up over pant legs when black flies are out in force

HI-TOP SNEAKS: For wading, dragging. You may need to get a size or two larger if worn over booties.

WET SUIT BOOTIES: If you anticipate wading icy streams. Only Rug anticipated.

BEAN BOOTS: Good for portaging in wet country. Jim barely fit into size 14.

Camp Gear

New Haven
May 31

Joe,

A quick note, as we have been thrown a curve ball. I was up
Boston way to finish off the food shopping and ran into a bush pilot
who flies in Labrador for a medical/missionary organization. He told
me as of a week ago when he was up there, the planes hadn't changed
over from skis to pontoons yet! That is to say, it's been an amazingly
late winter and they're still not out of it. Naturally I was more than
curious and pressed him for information. He said he knew the mayor
of Sept-Iles and so gave him a phone call. Mayor said at this point,
the upper 150 miles of the river is still frozen. So is most of
Ashuanipi, especially the nothern end, though some of the middle of
the south end is thawed. He was pretty pessimistic about our making
the trip. If those guys go in there before July first, he said—and I
quote—they're not coming back out any way except the railroad.
Now I realize you can't hold entirely by what he says, but I think a
postponement is in order. Jim votes for about the 25th, which would
put us to the river around July 1 or so; I think we can handle a departure the 20th. Peach leans my way.

Let me know your views right away (call if you like). I got the
train schedules the other day: only two trips a week north, Tuesdays
and Fridays, so we have to calculate that in too.

Otherwise I feel good. I thought the shakedown cruise went
well, although I *do* owe you an apology for Mosquito Falls. I really
hadn't been through there since four years ago, and that was summer
when the water was low. The minute I saw it I knew that you guys
in the open boats didn't have a prayer in those haystacks. But it was
even funnier to watch you come around the bend and see the expressions on your faces as you figured out what the hell you were
getting into. Even from below I could hear Dad give a holler; but
of course he should have suspected trouble in high water. I'll tell you,
both boats went over smooth as a couple of ducks: *plup, plup!* We
needed the capsize and salvage practice anyway.

Let me hear from you quick
RUG

Wilderness canoeing demands a fair diversity of talents. At odd moments
the canoeist is a walker, backpacker, scaler of cliffs, surveyor, camper, and
all-around beast of burden. Luckily, experts abound in all these specialties
and so do guidebooks. For both the fundamentals and the fine points, we

recommend them to you.* Our intention here is not to repeat what they have so thoroughly covered, but to provide a canoeist's slant on the standard outfit. We have also included an appendix (Appendix II) which covers the smaller items.

SHELTER. Even hard-traveling paddlers spend about half their time in camp and that includes (if possible) the worst of the weather. Good shelter is a high priority. Among wilderness types, there is a split between tenters and tarpers, the former preferring a cozy, dry, bug-free refuge, and the latter arguing for the stretching room and work space as well as the tarp's versatility. Our solution is to take both. Backpackers and old flints may call it luxury and worse; we call it the canoeist's prerogative. Canoeable rivers virtually guarantee rain and bug country, and a river party can well afford the few extra pounds of double protection against the elements and the insects.

Many excellent tents meet the requirements of the wilderness canoeist. Nylon is both strong and lightweight; to keep absolutely dry you need a basic construction of breathable nylon (to prevent condensation) plus an overlying urethane-treated, waterproof fly. The tent should be tightly netted to be absolutely mosquito-proof. Make sure your shelter erects easily—otherwise setting up becomes a daily chore. We took two-person tents on the Moisie, but these days prefer to bring at least one four-person model. During a three-day gale, the larger tent is less claustrophobic: five or six people can squeeze in to chat during the day. Dome tents, while good in high winds, have a circular floor plan which turns out to be cramped if several tall people are vying for the full diameter of the circle. One of the cheapest, most practical tents on the market is the venerable Eureka 4-person Timberlane. Ours has given us yeomen service for years.

For a tarp, we recommend 4-mil polyethylene, a nine-by-twelve cut, which is just big enough to house four people, their packs, dry firewood, one edge of the fire itself, and almost all the smoke. This sheeting has no grommets, so you may want some Visklamps, ball-and-garter gadgets that serve

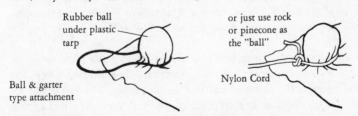

Rubber ball under plastic tarp

or just use rock or pinecone as the "ball"

Ball & garter type attachment

Nylon Cord

---

* We have in mind Colin Fletcher, *The Complete Walker;* Harvey Manning, *Backpacking, One Step at a Time;* Royal Robbins, *Basic Rockcraft;* Harvey Manning, ed., *Mountaineering: The Freedom of the Hills;* Bjorn Kjellstrom, *Be an Expert with Map and Compass.*

as removable, adjustable handles anywhere you need them. Or just rely on any golf-ball-sized rock or pinecone to do the job.

SLEEPING. For many years goose-down sleeping bags have been touted as the incomparable standard of the backpacking trade—lightweight, most easily compressible. That is certainly true, and we used goose-down bags on our Moisie expedition. Since that time, the demand for goose down has sky-rocketed along with the price. Given this situation, some less scrupulous manufacturers have adulterated their down with less expensive—and less efficient—feathers. Since these adulterated bags are impossible to detect short of ripping them open, it makes sense to buy only from a reputable outfitter.

But in our opinion, today's wilderness paddlers should forego down in favor of its cheaper rivals, the polyester fibers such as PolarGuard or Hollofil II. If a down bag becomes soaked in a capsize, it must be handled gingerly to avoid tearing the inner baffling systems. Furthermore, down dries slowly and is useless when wet. By contrast, polyester absorbs less than one percent moisture, retaining both its loft and insulating qualities even after immersion. The bags do not pack quite as well, but the difference is negligible. For canoeists, who must endure the persistent damp of three-day gales as well as the threat of a capsize, polyester is the way to go.

The loft from down or Fiberfill provides good insulation when it lies on top of you; but the body compresses the lower layer of the sleeping bag, so further insulation is desirable for cold nights. Two solutions are possible: an air mattress or a foam pad. Both have their advantages and disadvantages. Air mattresses pack smaller, but take time to inflate and deflate every day. The cheap plastic ones spring leaks all too easily, and are unreliable for long trips; the rubber and canvas models are rather heavy. Nylon types are the choice, about ten dollars. Take a patch kit. If you are canoeing in warm-weather country, the mattress can of course double as sun deck for floating around at a rest-day river campsite. Foam pads are bulkier, but insulate better and do not deflate on you in the middle of the night. For canoeing, the closed-cell type of foam (Volarafoam, Ensolite, Thermobar) is a necessity; the open-celled type absorbs water like a sponge—which is what it is.

FIRE AND COOKING. In truly wild country, the campfire is a pleasure not yet sinful. Necessary equipment is limited to a dry match, a little know-how, and a wood cutter. Collapsible saws that fold sharp teeth into a hollow handle are widely available and make short work of six- and even nine-inch logs. But travelers through wet, wooded country (unless they carry a stove) will find an ax all but indispensable for starting a fire after a long spell of rain. Hatchets and other miniatures are poor substitutes, indeed worse than no substitute at all. Not only are they not up to the job of bringing down big wood, they also force the user to flail at his target with brute strength instead of relying on the long easy strokes of the full-sized ax. We suggest at least a 2½-to-3-pound head and a 28-inch handle. If this advice sounds extreme and such an ax feels a bit unwieldy, it is best to leave all choppers at home. Forests far from civilization and help are no place to experiment with a strange weapon.

Those who enjoy instant fires may prefer to bring a stove. Our choice is the Optimus 111B (identical to the Primus 111B); although heavier than many models, it has a larger and faster cooking fire plus pump priming, which insures easy starting even in very cold weather. Whatever stove you choose, get to know it while still at home. Practice lighting it in the cold and in the wind. Every model has its own way of being cantankerous. Take it apart, mix up the pieces, and reconstruct it. By this time you will have memorized all the paraphernalia that goes with it: aluminum fuel bottle, plastic funnel, nozzle cleaner, and assorted filters, handles, and droppers.

The size of a cooking kit (aluminum, three or four nesting billies) will depend on the number in your party, but remember that spaghetti needs a good-sized pot to boil in, and that two frying pans, one slightly larger than the other, serve well as a small Dutch oven. Strong bail handles are a plus, because your large pots may do double duty as sea anchors, or be lined over a cliff to the river thirty feet below for hauling up water. (Be gentle doing this: bent bottoms heat unevenly and are devils to clean.) Artful cooking requires only a few other tools; we've listed them in Appendix II.

FISHING. Our fishing gear on the Moisie was as primitive as our technique was crude: a few spoons and a length of thirty-pound line that we wound around a stick and trailed behind the canoe. We caught some fish and were pleased enough to put the details down on paper for this book. Then we sent our account off to an outdoorsman who has spent odd parts of the last thirty-five years paddling the northern fringe of this continent looking for good water holes to drop his line. He was impressed all right. "What opportunities you guys missed on your trip," he wrote back. "To think that you were on one of the great Atlantic salmon rivers of the world and didn't know it. Had I been along you would have had some great meals and I would have had some great fishing." We mulled this one over and decided he was the man to give advice about fishing on a canoe trip, not us. So we wrote him again, asked for specifics, and now pass on his reply:

"Paddlers who are already accomplished fishermen will need no special advice, but for others like you who want to go one up from an alder pole, a spinning outfit is no doubt the best choice. A little practice is usually enough to get the lure out and the fish in, something that cannot be said for either the fly rod or the bait-casting rod.

"Spinning rods are available in four-piece form which makes for easy stowing. Even a three-piece rod is more convenient than a two-piecer. A bass outfit is what's called for; perhaps a heavy bass outfit. The reel, fitted to rod weight (i.e., you don't want a heavy salt-water reel for a bass rod), can be either an open-face or a closed-face spin-casting reel. Experts usually prefer the open-face reel, but the tyro, especially if he uses monofilament line, may find the spin-casting reel more foolproof. With the open-face reel, the line sometimes tangles behind the reel spool. To prevent this, or at least to make it less likely, tie on a swivel or two at the end of the line and affix the lure to the lower swivel (equipped with a safety-pin rig). If you use a mono-filament line and it does get twisted, you can straighten it by letting it run off the reel behind the canoe with no lure attached. By trailing the line for a mile or two you will shed the kinks.

"You guys made the mistake of using thirty-pound-test line. An eighteen-pound-test, or even a twelve or fifteen, is quite adequate. And of course, you can get more line on the same-size spool with the lighter-test, something that comes in handy when you foul up and have to break off line. By the way, when filling the spool of the reel, be sure to put a pencil through the spindle on which the line comes so you don't twist the line in reeling it onto the spool. Fill the reel spool to within a quarter inch of the lip of the spool.

"As to lures, the daredevil-type spoon, in red and white or black and white, seems to appeal to a wider variety of species than any other type. Get a number of these spoons in perhaps three sizes and supplement them, if you wish, by a few floating and diving plugs. This outfit will serve you well whether the rivers and lakes you fish are bass, walleye, great northern pike areas or whether your territory lies on the brook trout, lake trout, land-locked salmon water.

"Big pools below riffles or falls when fishing in the river, and shoal edges, narrows, and the drop-offs into deeper waters when fishing in lakes, are areas for casting when you have no knowledge of more subtle particulars about fish location. If you are fishing great northern pike territory, you might put a short length of braided-wire leader on the end of the line and ahead of the lure, but be sure to put on a couple of swivels. Sometimes the spoon spins and thus twists a monofilament line into exasperating loops that are the bane of the novice angler.

"A landing net with a good-sized mouth is handy, but if packing one is difficult (there are collapsible nets) you can beach most fish. Be careful about getting a great northern into the canoe with you: it has a mouth full of teeth and in its thrashing about can sometimes slash wrists or ankles.

"Fried fish is good, but those who have subsisted for long periods of time on chiefly a fish diet say that one gets less bored with fish if it is boiled, or better yet, poached in a small amount of water. Fish prepared this way is good cold, especially if someone has brought along a container of mayonnaise.

Bay leaf in the poaching water adds a bit to the taste and no one can object to including bay leaf or other herbs (such as chervil) in the outfit, at least on the count of weight.

"Tight lines!"

Packing

Written transcripts are not available, but it is a matter of record that the Bell System of Southern New England carried a local New Haven call at 1:10 A.M. on June 14, the substance of which we have reconstructed to the best of recollection.

RUG: Hello.

JIM: Well, I took your message at face value. I hope I didn't wake you, but I only got in from a party just now.

RUG: I figured you might be up late.

JIM: What's up?

RUG: Do you think you could get your gear packed in time to leave by five this morning?

JIM: You're kidding.

RUG: I'm not kidding.

JIM: That's less than four hours away!

RUG: I called our friend in Sept-Iles today—the Grenfell man—and he says the train crews are threatening to strike over some fringe benefits in their contract, as of next Monday. For how long is anybody's guess. That means the last train we can take north is this Friday, which means we have to stow gear there Thursday, which means we have to leave here at dawn, get to Burlington and pack food during the day, and leave by sundown for Sept-Iles. How much time will it take to get your stuff together?

JIM: I haven't even bought movie film yet.

RUG: I phoned Joe and told him to get it for you. Anything else you need bought, make a list—I'm phoning him at six this morning and he'll shop while we're driving up.

JIM: What about Peach?

RUG: He's coming to my place at five. We'll meet you in front of your apartment no later than five-thirty.

JIM: That's only a couple hours from now!

RUG: You're repeating yourself.

JIM: Well, it takes a few minutes for the whole thing to sink in, that's all. I haven't even got the polaroid filter for the camera. Or my pair of work gloves.

RUG: Make a list. I'm getting to bed. At least one of us needs to be awake enough to drive tomorrow.

JIM: Come to think of it, I also need another pair of wool socks. You think they've got size fourteen in Burlington?

RUG: I'll see you tomorrow at five thirty.

Packing for a wilderness whitewater trip is a specialized art. It requires precautions which neither the backpacker nor the flatwater canoeist need take; and for long trips of several weeks or a month, it demands a more precise organization of gear to prevent chaos from erupting every time the duffels are ransacked for the evening's meal. Three areas in particular need close attention: packing gear so it will carry well both on land and on water; waterproofing adequately; and organizing food and camp gear efficiently.

CARRYING: LAND AND WATER. One of the first points to establish is how large you can allow your outfit to grow. Backpackers don't have much freedom of choice here, since human legs can't carry much more than seventy pounds and call it sport. A canoe increases carrying capacity. The standard 17-footer will freight a maximum load of 1000 to 1200 pounds, but to be honest, we wouldn't care to leave the dock with half a ton in the boat. The reason for this is a matter of buoyancy rather than freeboard. The model we used on the Moisie kept about six inches of freeboard with an 800-pound load. Six inches, we admit, may sound like a lot of breathing space, especially to anyone used to running rapids where the mere surface tension on water cresting the gunwale can spell the difference between a swamp and a clean run. But 800 pounds gives the canoe all the buoyancy of a barge: it feels dead in the water, won't turn, won't maneuver, swamps and sinks with a few quarts of splash. Something basic in the design drowns and dies along with it, a secret of engineering carried to the grave by an ancient Indian craftsman.

Figure it yourself: Most uncovered canoes are about twelve inches deep, keel to gunwale. Simple arithmetic shows that six inches of freeboard means six inches of draft. Empirical hydraulic physics, a science learned from the seat of a canoe, teaches that the merest wave, say a seven-inch ripple, will splash over the side. Build up the sides another two inches and you gain two inches of freeboard. Now you can crash through seven-inch ripples, but beware the nine-inchers, for they can sink you. As you can see, building up the sides leaves unchanged the canoe's draft and buoyancy, which *can* be improved by lightening the load to 500 pounds. Now your boat will draft only about four inches to allow eight inches of freeboard (just as if you had built up the sides two inches); but more important, it will begin to behave like a canoe: bucking up in the waves, and riding out three-foot whitecaps. Something in that unknown Indian comes to life again.

Of course, the other consideration limiting the size of your outfit is that the canoeist is a part-time backpacker. Divide the weight of your total load (including canoes) by 75, and divide that by the number of people on the trip to calculate how many pack trips are needed per portage. Then remember that the first trip is half tolerable because you are fresh and the last trip is half tolerable because it's the last, but that there's nothing tolerable about any trips in between. You'll want to shoot the guy who planned them, especially if he's you. For a month on the Moisie we settled on an outside limit of 100 pounds per man plus canoes (and ended up taking 110).

Once the load limits are established, you must decide what to use for packs. Centuries of hauling gear by canoe have provided many charming and rustic alternatives. There is the traditional Maine pack basket whose sturdy design keeps bulky and hard objects packed without deforming the contours of a man's back. The Duluth bag is a more common sight along Canadian waterways, its shoulder straps augmented by a head band to relieve the back and shoulder muscles. Other canoeists even forgo the shoulder straps and use only a leather headband, a tumpline, to carry the entire weight. In this arrangement the tumpline straps are secured to the goods being hauled (be it a large sack of flour, a lumberjack's wanigan, or even a canoe) and the load is hefted onto the back. After a few portages (the skeptic would say a few years), the woodsman develops a prodigious set of neck muscles.

All these means of shipping and hauling have their place, 90 percent of which these days is in the museum. It's not that the old methods don't work. Canoeists have used them successfully for many years, and under certain conditions (trips where you have few portages, or where you actually do plan to carry around huge sacks of flour or wanigans) they serve well enough. But backpacking manufacturers (A. I. Kelty prime among them) have taken the old Trapper Nelson frame and developed it into a sophisticated system which beats all the old rigs for carrying heavy loads with a minimum of discomfort. The most important advances are now standard features on the models of most leading makers of outdoor equipment: lightweight, tubular construction (usually of aluminum), padded shoulder straps (the firmer pads like Kelty's are better), a contoured frame (to fit the curves of a human back), and most importantly, a padded hip belt that can be drawn up snug to lift the weight of the load onto the pelvis and off the shoulders.

Frames like these are expensive, but worth the price (about two or three times as expensive as either the pack basket or the Duluth bag). Cheaper frames are available, but under heavy loads the squishy shoulder pads are of no use, and the back bands loosen up to leave the unpleasant impress of the metal frame along the contours of your kidneys. On the other hand, the canoeist will do equally well to avoid the top-of-the-line models designed for mountaineers. The extension bar often makes the frame too long for convenient stowage amidships, and the new "sway-free suspension" hip-belt systems, ice-ax carriers, and crampon fixtures are unneeded extras.

Pack bags attach to these frames by various combinations of rivets, wires, and clevis pins, none of which has any notable advantage over any others. The three-quarter-length sacks (with room to strap the sleeping bag on below) will do fine. Many options are available dividing the pack into compartments horizontally or vertically. Pigeonholing has its attractions, but every partition creates corners and cuts out effective carrying capacity. We recommend an open sack for the sake of flexibility. Side pockets are an advantage, since they serve to store needed ready-access items like rain gear and little knickknacks (toilet articles, suntan lotion, spoon, drinking cup). The extra pocket sometimes provided along the top flap of the sack is less useful because it can increase the pack profile enough to give problems fitting it under the thwarts of some canoes. Unwieldy loading, in fact, is the major disadvantage of using the modern pack frame for canoeing. This is especially true with 15-foot boats where the space between thwarts is tight for full-length frames. But with a little ingenuity, two packs can be fit in; and with the 17-foot ABS boats which have only a center thwart, you can stow four full-sized Keltys without difficulty.

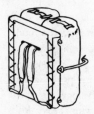 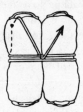  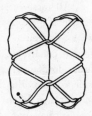

On trips lasting ten days or less, one pack per person will usually suffice. For longer expeditions, extras are needed. If you're like us, you can't afford the luxury of two expensive Keltys, and will have to compromise. For each canoe, we brought along an extra pack frame plus two canvas duffelbags, and roped the duffels to the frame for carrying. Cheap frames can be had from some army surplus stores: British army types are of aluminum with a welter of straps (three for attaching the load, plus hip, chest, shoulder, and forehead straps!). American frames of plywood are also available. Duffel bags with full-length heavy-duty (#10) zippers are more convenient than those which open only at the end. Better yet are two zippers which meet in the middle. (Caution: weak zippers will split open when a duffel is packed too tightly.) On British frames, the duffels can be strapped on; for the plywood models, use nylon cord and a diamond hitch.

The ideal packing arrangement of this full load is the two duffels lashed for the day to their frames (zippers up for access) and stowed in front of the center thwart; the regular pack bags stored (frames toward the floor) behind the center thwart. (Or reverse the positions if the weights vary and a switch helps the boat's trim in the water.) Our canoes could not fit two Keltys side by side, so we removed the duffels from the frame and stowed one fore and the other aft of center. This meant relashing them at each portage, but that was done in about two minutes.

As a rule of thumb, figure that four packs plus four duffels will take four men in two 17-foot canoes on a trip as long as a month. A larger party will need less than a full extra duffel per man, since there are more people to share the carrying of common gear.

WATERPROOFING. Adequate waterproofing is one of the major keys to staying happy on a wilderness whitewater trip. Ideally, careful scouting and good running techniques should prevent capsizes of a loaded boat; but mistakes and miscalculations can't be ruled out. You want your gear packed so that if it does go over with the boat, it will be as dry as it started even if the canoe bounces submerged down several miles of rapids.

Newcomers to the sport are likely to underestimate what it takes to make a pack rapids-proof. They see a stuff bag advertised as waterproof and buy it for their sleeping bag, or see the same quality claimed for their pack bag and take no further precautions. When gear is advertised as "waterproof," it means that the fabric itself will not admit water. That does nothing to prevent the river from sneaking in the openings at the end of the stuff bag or the top of the pack. Gear might not fare too badly if the packs were merely floating in moderately calm water; Colin Fletcher notes (in *The Complete Walker*) that his preparations for swimming the Colorado with pack entailed merely wrapping his valuables in a tarp, keeping them high in the pack, and tying an air mattress around the frame for flotation. But his pack was floating to begin with; in a spill, yours will be securely tied into the canoe and forcibly held underwater. His could avoid the moderate rapids' force by floating over the waves; yours will feel the driving currents search out every nook, cranny, and seam which allows entrance. A sleeping bag packed in a stuff bag will be soaked by the end of the ride; much of the food in an unprotected pack will be soggy and unpalatable.

So make a fetish out of waterproofing. Begin with the sleeping bag: the item of all items which must remain dry. We generally buy the stouter-model plastic laundry bags (3-mil thickness) for adequate protection—flimsier models and trash-can liners tear all too easily. At twenty-five cents a bag, two bags are not an outlandish investment; use at least one, plus a stuff bag to protect the plastic from abrasions. When you stuff the sleeping bag, keep any zippers that might tear the plastic turned inward and squeeze out all extraneous air. Then twist shut the opening several turns and tuck the twist in tight along the lining of the stuff bag. Too much air on the inside means that when you cinch the bag tight against the frame with your tie-on straps, the air will pop the inner plastic bag and allow water to leak back in at a later date. (If you use two bags, twist and tuck each one separately. That makes two seals the water has to penetrate.) From time to time during the trip, check the plastic bags for abrasion punctures and cover them—even the small ones—with tape.

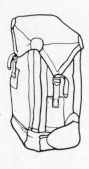

The same arrangements apply for clothes and food bags: either two of the durable laundry bags or else one plus an army surplus rubberized duffel, again to protect the inner bag from abrasions. Surplus outlets sometimes carry rubber "wet packs" (illustrated at left) which are completely water-tight and useful for weekend trips, though a bit heavy for longer expeditions. But these products of an earlier era have been superseded by specially designed cargo bags made of 20-mil vinyl, available from canoe and outdoor shops. The vinyl holds up very well so long as it is kept away from the heat and sparks of the campfire; the best system of closure we've seen is Old Town's use of Velcro strips. Available in several sizes, some manufacturers' models even offer an ingenious double-wall system that cushions as well as waterproofs fragile objects like cameras.

In the end, only sad experience is likely to convince you just how easily water can penetrate the smallest holes. Joe, as we'll see, learned the hard way on our trip; and on another, Jim sealed his spare film cartridges in four or five plastic layers only to find that during a capsize water had penetrated through pinholes and loose closures to all but the final layer.

PACKING EFFICIENTLY. A three-week trip to the backcountry means a total of sixty-three meals to carry, and only an organized packing system will stave off the arguments at each meal about who has the dried peas and where the gingerbread is kept. Much of this organization work is drudgery, but it's inevitably done in the final hours before departure, and the antici-pation of the trip outweighs the boredom of minute details.

Food, once assembled, must be stripped of all superfluous packaging. At first, it won't seem like you're saving much to toss away the cardboard box around two aluminum-foil packets of dried soup. But at the end of the repacking process you'll have collected a garageful of litter. So discard the cardboard shells of pudding, pancake mix, gingerbread, Bisquick; where necessary, repack in plastic bags. As much as possible, prepare the food for cooking in advance. Throw the pinch of salt the oatmeal calls for right in the plastic bag; measure out the powdered milk needed for the pudding and pack it with the mix. Keep the remaining instructions for preparation either in the plastic bag or written on the outside with Magic Marker—along with proper identification of the powder within. (Lemonade looks a lot like vanilla pudding in the twilight of a late camp.) Honey, peanut butter, Tang, and other foods which come in glass jars need to be repacked in either plastic bags (for powders) or plastic jars (for jams, margarine, etc.). If you do carry glass jars, tape them all around the outside to prevent shattering if they break. And don't try to put peanut butter or honey in plastic bags—getting it out is hell. Two of our plastic jars had to be ditched at the last moment in favor of bags because their lids refused to screw on tightly; the mess we made finally eating that honey left our paddles sticky the rest of the afternoon.

Once your food is stripped down and repacked, you have to organize it. Since your goal is to insure that the fewest number of packs have to be disturbed at each meal, it makes sense to put all of one meal together. Those who have planned a menu day by day may want to pack their meals in paper lunchbags, and label them S-1, B-3 (first supper, third breakfast), and so on. Those who prefer flexibility may simply note "spaghetti dinner," etc., on the outside of the bag. To further simplify, have one person take one kind of meal (all the breakfasts, for instance) so that less confusion arises about who has what in their packs.

Distribute the food into piles roughly equal in weight, one for each member of the trip. With four people, one person can take the breakfasts, one the lunches, and one the dinners, with the last man taking the condiments used at almost every meal (margarine, sugar, salt, tea, coffee, lard). On trips short enough to require only one pack per person the food is best packed first, roughly in the order of the way it will be used on the trip. Pack in vertical piles rather than horizontal ones: if you have all the beverages, desserts, and suppers, you don't want to have to dig down four layers each time cheesecake is called for. The clothes bag, which is smaller and lighter, then goes on top of the food pack, and can be removed easily whenever needed. Sleeping bag, foam pad, and tent are packed on the frame underneath the pack. For trips where extra duffels are needed, pack the food in the packs rather than in the duffels. We started doing it the other way, with our light clothes in the packs and two sixty-pound food duffels making a hundred-and-twenty-pound load on the cheap frames! Along with the clothes, pack the bulky items in the duffel: cook set, ax, saw, stove.

All this sounds simple when described on paper, but those four massive piles never fail to intimidate. And when they push the scales past the limit allowed in your original calculations, prepare to fight fiercely for your own definition of what is essential for a month in the wilderness. We did. Up in the back shed of a small farmhouse outside of Burlington, each of us proclaimed his own philosophy of the Good Life with fervent tenacity. Rug would pack the cook set together; unpack it; pack it again, heft it, and mutter; then toss the two frying-pan handles into the corner. Jim would cast a doleful glance in that direction. Surely the frying-pan handles ought to stay; basics like frying-pan handles. But we got the pot gripper, says Rug. Pot gripper'll handle anything. Well, if you ask me, says Jim, I'd keep the frying-pan handles. Toss the reflector oven out if you want— that's what I call useless baggage. But Joe doesn't. Toss the reflector oven? You lose the best cooking facility you've got. Might as well abolish the art of wilderness baking! Just save a little weight by ditching the candles.

Candles! says Rug. You ever try to prepare a meal late at night without candles? If we don't get this stuff divvied up soon, we're going to be *packing* by candlelight. Let's keep the utility gear and do without lemonade at half our lunches. Well, says Peach, it's one thing not to *see* well, and another not to *eat* well. That's quick energy and good calories you're passing up. Someday you're going to *want* lemonade out in those woods, and there'll be nothing to do but sit there and gnaw candles. If I was you, I'd toss out about ten or eleven of those bottles of bug dope. You got enough packed to take a bath!

Then the sun gets lower and reminds us we've got a train to catch. Rug wins his full complement of bug dope, though Jim and Peach insist on cutting back their shares. Joe gets his reflector oven and successfully cuts the number of candles in half. Peach ups the lemonade lunch rations to three quarters. Jim thinks he saves his frying-pan handles, but underestimates Rug's sleight of hand. How all the baggage gets packed into Old Rug's '67 Plymouth and Joe's '65 Chevy is something we never established precisely. You'll never establish it either, when you finally get the last duffel wedged and the bow and stern tautlines snug. You'll be watching the sun dip below the trees, wondering how late the local Mounties' office will be open so you can leave word of your plans and a deadline for them to come looking for you. You'll be checking the tires, making the calculations yet once again of how many hours of driving to get to the northern train station—assuming you don't have a flat or drop a transmission. And you'll finally get off—almost before the dusk settles on the home country for good.

Somewhere out on the far side of Quebec city—out on the far side of the night for that matter—Peach managed to catch up to Rug, who was spelling Joe at the wheel of his Chevy. Peach blinked the brights of Old Rug's Plymouth, found to his surprise they worked this time, and pulled Rug over. Jim rolled down the window and Peach leaned over for a conference.

"I know it's late and all," said Peach, "and nobody on the road, and Quebec drivers are hell on wheels anyway, but this speedometer's been clocking almost ninety catching up to you."

Rug laughed. "I forgot to tell you. Dad's been meaning to have that speedometer fixed for three months now. It reads too high. I've been watching this one and we've been doing only sixty or seventy."

"Ah, Jawn," said Joe, now awake from his catnap. "I forgot to tell *you*. I've got a pair of oversize tires on this machine. My speedometer reads considerably *under* what you're doing."

"What time is it anyway?" asked Jim.

Nobody seemed to know. Joe's watch had stopped, and Peach's was in the side pocket of his pack. So we drove on toward the train station and the river, trusting to figure things by the seat of our pants. We didn't know how fast we were going or exactly what time it was, but that was O.K. It was roughly the way we were planning to spend the next month anyway.

II. BIG-LAKE COUNTRY

5. Ice

Expeditions, like rivers, have an ideal type to which the actualities are supposed to conform. The ideal expedition builds gradually from the moment of conception on through the preparations, and proceeds to a preliminary climax at the time of departure from home base. The actual wilderness journey repeats the pattern with a methodical, straightforward start into territories unknown, a crescendo of discovery as the new land unfolds, and finally, the unexpected kink, quirk, or accident which puts to the extreme test both physical stamina and inner fiber.

Now, we're not saying the ideal expedition doesn't exist somewhere, along with truth, beauty, and the other ideals. But from the shore of Ashuanipi Lake, none of those types was remotely within shouting distance—especially the one about the straightforward start into territories unknown.

June 16 it is, only five days from the summer solstice, and five of us are standing at water's edge looking at a thick layer of ice which stretches all the way to the flat line of the horizon. Four of the five you know, and can imagine the sort of uneasy feelings settling midway between the heart and stomach. Harry Semutiuk you don't know, and so can't imagine his feelings, but they are every bit as pessimistic as ours—maybe even more so. Harry is one of the two permanent residents of Oreway, Labrador, and has been for the past eighteen years; consequently he thrives on pessimism, lives for it, and conveys it by the quart in a stream of conversation characterized by a certain matter-of-fact relish.

"Ye'll never get out," he says. "The cracks haven't even begun yet. Just a few of them out there, and none of them wide at all. Not a one of them. It'll be a week before she goes—at least that. I wuddn't be surprised if it was more, with the weather we're getting. It snowed this morning, ye know."

Joe says politely he didn't know and wonders if it might be possible to make a path across the ice.

"Ye'll ruin yere boats. Those blocks of ice'll bang them right up, and crunch 'em around. Even if ye did have the cracks . . . well, ye can't do it.

There's the wind. I went out once two years ago in the spring breakup. I had a clear path, ye see, right out there into Hungry Bay. But when I come back with my fish, the wind was blowin' the ice all about and the channel was gone. I had to shove my way through with the motor, and it ruined the prop. All the wind had shifted the ice. Ye don't have a motor, see, and what if ye did? It just ruins the prop all to hell. I had to put in a new one. Ye'll never make it without a good prop."

If Harry hopes to intimidate us, he is doing an admirable job. As he walks off to the radio shack, we are left to study the few cracks and debate the merits of premeditated suicide. There is always the return train to Sept-Iles, but we are damned if we've come nine hundred miles to be told we need a good prop to cross a lake.

All of this, you can see, hardly fits into the ideal type of an expedition. Chances are, your own trip will begin on a sunny day, water warm enough for swimming. But you may set your sights on the Far North, where ice crossings are possible any time of year. Or you may be an early starter; Rug once paddled through a week of snowstorms in West Virginia. Nothing is impossible on a bona fide expedition, and since our own trip started on ice, we figure you might benefit from knowing how to cross it.

The absolute best way to get over ice is to wait it out; the next best is to go around it. Lakes and ponds open up according to a timetable that is regulated by many different factors, including altitude, exposure to the sun, the size of feeder streams, depth of the bottom, and the incoming weather. Many lakes shed their winter cover weeks before their neighbors; unfortunately this information is usually more tantalizing than helpful to the ice-locked canoeist. What is important to know is that, especially on larger lakes, the mouths of tributaries, the smaller bays, and the shorelines in general are the first to melt. Furthermore, a steady prevailing wind will clear the lee side of a lake while it blows the pack ice into great heaping piles on the windward shore.

All these calculations led us to embark on a route different from the one we had originally plotted. We had counted on heading almost due west, but our first three-mile crossing was still an ice field. There is real danger in crossing large expanses of shifting ice. Harry may have been a pessimist, but he was right that wind-driven blocks of ice move around like bulldozers. Midway across a big lake is no place to learn about the science of demolition. The next most direct route was to the south, but last week's nor'wester had shut it tight. Although the shoreline to the north meant the longest detour, there the lake narrowed past several islands and broke into some smaller bays. Fortunately, this route proved safe and, in three days of travel by improvised canoe sled, we made it to Kapitagas Channel, a distance that would have required six hours of summer paddling.

Along the way, we encountered many varieties of ice. We mention the major types so you'll know how to handle them.

SOLID ICE, FEW CRACKS. Although almost every bay had a few pools of open water, some were still covered by a thick table of ice a foot or more deep. In that case, it was usually easiest to make a beeline for the next point instead of following the curve of the bay. Near shore you are likely to find a covering of snow, which should be avoided. Snow acts to insulate the ground below it in cold weather, and thus the ice may be less trustworthy in those spots; in addition, it is next to impossible to drag canoes across it. Farther out, the ice is harder and more slippery.

As you paddle from the pool of water to the block of ice, get up speed and as the nose of the canoe hits, lean far backward. The nose slides up and the bowman hops out quickly, the stern still paddling to keep up momentum. *One foot, however, always stays in the boat,* so that if the ice unexpectedly gives way, your weight can be shifted back to safety. The sternman likewise hops out when his end is on ice, and both men push the canoe along scooter style until the next pool of water is reached. The more the momentum is kept up by continual pushing, the less energy is wasted. Progress is easier if you can find some minor cracks to use as a sort of trolley track for the keel. In a few places where the ice was unquestionably solid, Joe and Rug made a harness out of their bow painter and hauled the canoe like an Eskimo dog team. Do this *only* when you are utterly sure about the ice—a mistake could have fatal consequences.

BLACK ICE. Large solid layers of ice do not melt the way you might expect. Instead of the water eroding away the bottom and the sun melting the top until the layer gets thinner and thinner, the ice breaks down vertically— that is, it becomes a honeycomb of water and ice daggers. Since the water penetrates it, the color of the ice becomes dark, and on a sunny day, whole fields of ice will glisten like black diamonds. In terms of traveling by canoe, this ice allows fast progress when the daggers are tightly packed and are not greatly decomposed. Push along with one foot out of the boat just as with the solid ice. Expect to break through more often, however, because you will be hitting spots where the honeycombing has broken the ice into a much looser conglomerate. In some places, the canoe can be "paddle-poled" along, with the ice providing enough resistance to give the blade leverage, but not enough to stop the bow from breaking through.

SLUSH. The logical progression in melting occurs when the daggers break apart and rot into good old-fashioned slush. This is the one ice formation that can hopelessly mire a canoe. Though too thin to give your paddle good leverage, the stuff thickens up ahead of the bow. Before long, it becomes impossible to paddle your canoe any further and equally impossible to get out and push. A combination of a foot of slush on top of a more solid layer of ice below makes for the same kind of quandary and should be skirted.

The days we spent dragging and hauling were exhausting ones, especially for leg muscles that hadn't been trained for the work of huskies. Yet there was beauty in the inexorable process going on around us. In the shelter of the channels and off in the forest, the warm sun spread the feeling of an early-summer day. But once out on the edges of the vast frozen fields of the lake, the wind across the ice gave a late-winter chill. And all about the wind and water were doing their work; the water making its way up the honeycomb, eating out small columns of space; and the wind setting the ice to grinding slowly, imperceptibly at first. But even with only a slight breeze, the delicate chinking and cracking sounded from all parts of the lake. The afternoon of the third day dragging, we pulled into an island for a late lunch. The wind had picked up and the sound of ice floes battering each other increased. We hiked to the end of the island and there, about a half mile beyond, were the whitecaps of open waves. We had lunch; then a siesta to let the midday wind die down. When we woke an hour or so later, the ice line had blown within a hundred yards of the island and shortly we crossed our last sea of bobbing black diamonds out to clear passage.

6. Flatwater

Of all the sections in a canoeing guidebook, the one on basic strokes is probably the most useless. Not because the information peddled therein is wrong; just blatantly obvious. Why, a cigar-store Indian could get himself around a lake without all that business about a straight back, slight bend at the elbow, and so forth. What we plan to do here is keep the comments on physical mechanics down to a minimum and instead concentrate on the basic principles behind them. If you know *why* a canoe behaves the way it obviously does, the more complex methods of maneuvering on a river will come easier. But first, for the complete novice, the basic mechanics:

GOING NOWHERE. The forward paddler sits in the bow seat. The rear paddler sits in the stern seat. Ideally the bow and stern ought to ride evenly (keep an even "trim" in the water); but in lake country, steering may be a bit easier with the bow a touch higher. Shifting your gear around amidships may help, especially if you have only one pack to distribute the way you want. But with a full load, the respective weights of bow and stern paddlers do more to determine trim than any minor shifting of gear.

Fanatics of the guidebook trade claim you should always kneel, which is nonsense; most of the time you can sit. Kneeling keeps your center of gravity lower in the boat, hence for heavy seas it minimizes the chance of an upset. It also unites you more closely with the boat, hence in whitewater it permits more control of the hull (through the levering action of knees and hips) as well as more precise control of paddling strokes. In these situations kneeling is helpful, but if your joints are as sensitive as ours, you'll sit on the quiet, flat stretches.

Matter of fact, as you gain experience and develop good bracing strokes, you may find yourself sitting through rougher and rougher water. Rug for one almost never kneels because he insists he can reach out farther from a high seat and would rather have his paddle in the best position than he would his hindquarters. He extends both feet or sometimes tucks one under

the seat; in either case, both thighs are braced against the sides of the canoe, so that they grip the gunwales when the boat rides the heavy water. Jim prefers a compromise position, one knee down and the other leg extended forward. The knee down keeps his weight low and the leg extended acts as a brace to prevent being thrown forward by a sudden jolt. Whatever your position in whitewater (and the novice should begin by kneeling), learn to ride the canoe much like you would a horse: with a swivel of the hips and firm pressure by the knees.

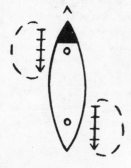

GOING FORWARD. Pretty much the way you'd imagine, even if you've only seen canoes in Hollywood movies. Hollywood doesn't always get the details right, so note the following points: Make your stroke parallel to the keel (not the hull) for maximum forward momentum. Reach forward when you put the blade in the water: the power of the stroke comes when the shaft is perpendicular to the water, not at the end when the blade sweeps up parallel to the surface. When you swing the paddle forward to begin the next stroke, keep the flat of the blade (as well as the entire shaft) parallel to the water. This is called feathering. Finally, grip the end of the paddle over the top; it is not held like a broom handle.

GOING BACKWARD. The same stroke as going forward, only do it backward.

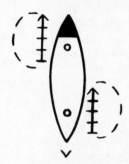

Some people argue that a stronger stroke can be achieved by shifting the top grip so that your palm instead of your knuckles is facing you. Probably true, but in whitewater, one stroke blends with the next, and it is inconvenient to switch grips.

Those are the simple, physical mechanics of getting around, except for steering. But steering is where the general principles come in, so we turn to them for a moment.

GENERAL PRINCIPLES. Stern-wheelers, as Huck could tell you, go in straight lines; side-wheelers don't. Canoes are side-wheelers.

Canoeists long ago hit on the same solution that the steamboats worked out. If you put two paddle wheels side by side at the middle of a boat and turn them in synchrony, you will run a true course. Likewise with paddles. The problem is that while paddle wheels come in identical pairs, paddlers don't. Canoe partners rarely match one another in either power or finesse; often they don't even paddle in stride. Nor do they ordinarily squeeze side by side in the middle of their craft.

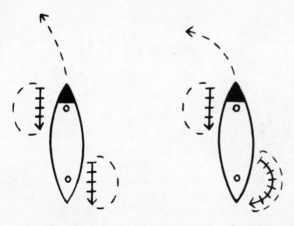

To gain turning leverage, each man instead positions himself as close as possible to his end of the boat. They gain leverage all right but lose symmetry since the bow seat has to be placed back to allow for leg room. This small allowance for human anatomy, a few inches only, is fatal to directional stability. Even a weak sternman will outlever and oversteer a strong bowman. Paddling on the right, he will cause the canoe to veer off in an arc to the left. If he extends his paddle out farther from the gunwale in a *sweep* stroke, he will accentuate the turn. The left-paddling bowman counteracts the off-course deviation, but only partially. If the stern paddles normally, of course, and the bow sweeps on the opposite side, the opposing lateral forces may balance out, but the sweep is an awkward and exhausting stroke and you'll find few bowmen volunteering to keep at it.

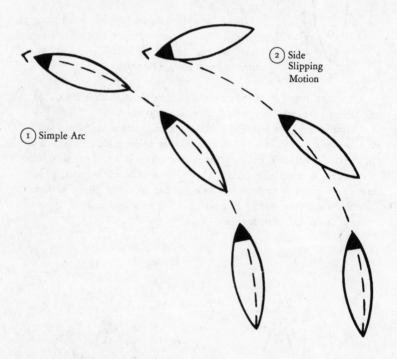

Directionally Unstable. Write these words in Technicolor. The canoe, you see, is more perverse than we have admitted. Instead of tracing out a simple arc, the canoe sideslips off course as well. The bow cuts out one curve while the stern, instead of following like a good troop, heads off in a wider orbit. The net product of all these crisscrossing vectors is that the whole boat skids toward the outside of the turn, and as it does, the turn becomes sharper and sharper. The canoe, if you will, runs not in circles, but in an ever-tightening spiral. For that reason, the sternman is in the best position to steer a flatwater course. By using his paddle to lever his end back to the inside of the turn, he corrects a complex deviation in a single motion.

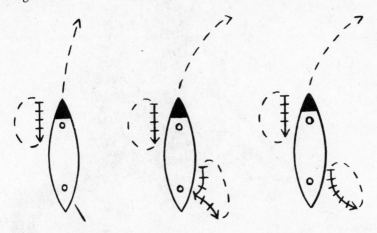

The most elementary stroke the sternman uses to turn the boat toward the side he's paddling on—whether to correct for the inevitable sideslipping or to avoid an obstruction—is the *stern rudder*. This maneuver simply entails sticking the paddle out from the boat at about a thirty-degree angle from the keel line. The force of water against the blade will turn the canoe just as any rudder would. A rudder on the right turns the boat to the right. This stroke is altogether passive, however, and is useless if the canoe does not have any forward speed. A much faster and more powerful version is the *pry*. Start with the rudder in close to the boat (the blade face parallel with the canoe) and push it in an outward sweep away from the boat. The disadvantage of this stroke for straight flat running is that it creates so much drag that it cuts dishearteningly into speed. That's why the experts incorporate the steering component of their effort into their forward stroke in one smooth motion called the *J*. Instead of turning the power face of the blade toward the boat as for the pry, turn it outward. As you complete the J, the thumb on the top of your paddle will point downward and your wrists will be cocked forward. With the pry, the thumb points up, and both wrists are cocked backward. The J is more efficient but also more awkward and harder on the muscles (the triceps). Mastery requires practice but pays off in speed and subtlety.

To sum up: On flatwater, the sternman controls the course. To steer the boat away from the side he's paddling on, he uses a sweep. To steer toward the side he's paddling on, he uses a stern rudder, a pry, or a J. There

are plenty of other strokes to learn (not to mention the ones you're better off not learning, such as the bow rudder). But these are enough to get you out on a lake for a day's outing. With two people in the boat, trade positions so both paddlers get experience steering. Switch paddling sides periodically to become proficient on both sides of the canoe, but whatever you do, don't switch every other stroke to correct incompetent steering. Large drunken zigzags, the frustration of every novice, are best overcome by practice in paddling a canoe alone. Kneel at the center thwart or sit backward on the bow seat for roughly proper trim. Now paddle toward a fixed point across a lake while stroking on only one side of the boat. To avoid the great circle route to your destination, you will need a J or pry after nearly every stroke.

For long journeys, two people paddling in synchrony with long easy strokes works best. For sprinting speeds, use short quick strokes (still in synchrony). The bow paddler sets the pace and the stern paddler if accomplished, will keep the straight course with a barely perceptible flick of the blade. And, if he is considerate, he will never let on to his partner just how much correcting he has to do.

7. Wind

Wind is to flatwater what current is to a river. Lakes lack the advantage of a downhill slope, but they put their open spaces to work. Give a big lake a stiff breeze and it will produce swells as large as the waves in a river's high-water rapids. The difference is that on lakes the wind pushes the waves along while the water remains stationary; on the river the downhill slope gets the water moving while the waves remain stationary. (The river also throws in rocks, which makes matters even worse.) All of which goes to say, the basics of canoeing may be enough to get you around ponds, but it is only a start for big water. Right now we want to turn to the problem of wind.

And here we're not concerned with moderate breezes. We assume that anyone versed in the simple steering strokes will manage well enough in one- or two-foot swells; they are business as usual. But on big lakes, a quick change of weather can transform even a glassy calm into five- or six-foot swells. For times like these you need an overall strategy for handling the lake. The nature of that strategy is determined by two factors: your direction of travel and the direction of the wind.

We'll take the situation which, so it would seem, occurs more often than any other: you are headed across a lake dead into the wind. The breeze is moderate at first, and you head straight into it, thinking to give the wind as narrow a profile as possible to work on. As the breeze increases, however, try swinging the boat just a point off the wind. What happens? If you point the bow a bit to the right, the wind is going to try and swing the boat even farther in that direction. And with the sternman paddling on the left, his stroke is also going to push the boat to the right. This double push to the right forces the sternman to spend most of his time J-stroking or prying to keep on course. But if the paddlers switch sides, then the sternman's stroke turns the boat to the left, which offsets the wind's pull to the right. Now there's no need to rudder (which you had to do paddling straight into the wind) and all energy can be put into paddling forward. If the wind gets much stronger in fact, both paddlers may have to stroke on one side of the boat to keep a straight course.

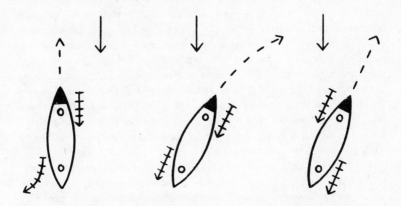

The second reason for angling a point off the wind has to do not with the breeze itself but with the waves. As they grow, the bow is more likely to cut through them rather than ride over. By "quartering" (the term for this angling), the bow instead offers a broader profile to the wave and rises with it. But by solving one problem, quartering creates another. As the bow begins to climb up the next slope, the stern is still coming down the last one, and the two waves encourage the canoe to go broadside in the trough (that is, to broach). Thus the bowman and sternman must develop a rhythm to maintain control of the canoe: Keep up enough speed so the canoe's momentum helps to prevent broaching—yet not enough speed to plunge the bow in the wave. The sternman, in addition, must work especially hard as he descends into the trough to keep the quartering angle from becoming too broad. In such situations, the bow generally maintains the momentum with strong short strokes, while the stern concentrates on keeping the proper angle. Paddling in synchrony is neither possible nor desirable here.

With the canoe bucking up and down these waves, mastery of the whitewater strokes known as the high and low braces proves useful. We'll go into those in a later chapter (see pages 179–83); for now it's enough to know that both strokes enable a person to lean (or brace) on his paddle so that the canoe gains stability in turbulent water.

Suppose that the wind is heading across the lake, and you need to paddle at right angles to it. That would mean taking the waves broadside, which with large swells could result in a capsize. The remedy, once again, is to head at an angle into the waves at about forty-five degrees. You are quartering, this time at a broader angle. The lateral component of your direction will carry you across; the upwind component will prevent you from being blown down the lake.

The law of averages would indicate that the wind will be blowing in your direction of travel some time or other—though with us it's generally been other. When fortune smiles, rig a poncho sail and take the afternoon off. A nine-by-twelve fire tarp serves even better as the makeshift sail, rigged up as ingenuity dictates. With a gusty, unpredictable breeze you may want nothing elaborate: the bowman simply steps on the bottom corners of the tarp and stands up, arms apart holding the sail. Guy ropes of five or six feet on the upper corners allow the sail to billow. Either way, however, your arms will soon tire; one remedy is to drape them over a paddle placed across the shoulders like an oxen yoke. This is much less tiring, but after a while it tends to put your arms to sleep.

A long lake and a steady wind make more elaborate preparations worth-while. Two poles cut to serve as masts at each end of the tarp eliminates arm fatigue, and an even broader sail (plus increased stability) is gained by joining two canoes catamaran style. Lash the boats firmly with two poles across the forward and rear thwarts. To prevent waves from piling up and splashing aboard in the close space between boats, keep the two bows slightly closer together (say four feet) than the sterns, which ought to have six feet distance between them. Each bowman then holds a mast end of the sail. The sternmen relax with their rudders and the canoes slice through the waves with refreshing speed.

Running with the wind on a long lake can start off deceptively easy, because you are beginning your trip on the lee, sheltered end of the water. By the time you near the end of the lake the wind has had the whole expanse to build up the waves. What starts as a pleasant sail thus can end with some very tricky boating. When the swells become too large or the wind too strong, stow the sail. If you're hooked up catamaran style, stay that way for the sake of stability. (Paddlers may wish to use the catamaran even when heading into the wind, just for this reason.) Even with the sail down, the wind will zip the boat smartly along; as you paddle, the stern end will rise on a big wave working to catch up. Soon the canoe is being carried along by the crest of the wave; you paddle quickly now, riding the wave with almost as much exhilaration as a surfer.

Almost—that's the problem. The canoe is much heavier than a surf-board and can't keep up with the waves. No matter how hard you paddle, you'll soon find yourself sliding back into the trough of the wave behind it. And here is where your danger lies: the stern may swamp as the next wave cuts it, just as the bow was threatened in a head wind. One precaution is to trim the stern a bit lighter—the opposite of normal practice. A second measure is to guard against the broaching likely to occur in the trough. As with a head wind, the bow maintains the momentum of the canoe, while the stern keeps the boat's angle from getting too broad.

Running with the wind in really big waves calls for a sea anchor to keep a canoe from broaching. With long lakes and a stiff breeze, anticipate the need for one before you get into big stuff. Set it up by tying about fifteen or twenty feet of nylon cord to the wire handle of your biggest cooking pot (or use any pail). If your stern painter is attached on the stem near the waterline, just attach the anchor rope there too. If the painter is attached high on the boat, you'll have to loop another cord around the stern seat and under the boat, and attach the end of the anchor line at the keel to this "bridle." The pail stays with its line under the seat until the waves get rough; then it's thrown overboard. Paddle forward vigorously, as before. The anchor immediately fills with water and acts as a drag on the canoe, keeping the boat from going broadside to the waves. The anchor line must be attached low on the boat (near the keel or waterline) because the last thing you want is the anchor also pulling the boat down.

With these techniques, you can run amazing big seas, but it hardly makes sense to go courting disaster. Always have gear tied in (see our system, page 111). Wherever possible, seek the shelter leeward of islands and bays; keep close to shore. Especially in head winds, a detour to avoid wind may in the end save time and energy. Finally, it is good to know that, as a rule, calmer seas are found early in the morning and later in the afternoon. The day we broke free of the ice on Ashuanipi, we took a siesta on an island for a couple of hours, then ate an early dinner and took to the calmer water at five for four good hours of paddling.

In a real gale, of course, you may have to wait several days while the waters rage. This can be frustrating, especially when you're itching to get to your headwaters. But remember, there's one more difference between the waves of a lake and the haystacks of a river: winds, sooner or later, blow themselves out; a river slope does not. Rest assured, it will be waiting for you.

8. Navigation

Canoe navigation, when executed from the perspective of the armchair, is a simple matter of maneuvering your finger through bays, around islands, and across open water. At first glance, actual navigation might not seem much more difficult: a look at the map as you start across the lake and then back go the charts to your pack until after the next portage. That's good enough for medium-size ponds. But with big lakes, one elementary, scientific fact cannot be ignored: people can see only in straight lines, not around corners. A simple enough statement, but give us a minute to demonstrate some of its ramifications.

To do that, we want you to do a bit of imagining. On the next page, you'll find a map of one section of big-lake country: we've labeled it Lake Penobsca. As you can see, Penobsca is an open lake: lots of water and three or four islands. Off to the east, a land mass is marked; to the south, a couple of peninsulas. Suppose you were plunked down at the spot indicated by the canoe on the map. Take a moment to imagine the view you would have as you looked around.

After doing that, consider another situation—the one shown in our map of Beaver Lake. Here you note there is less open water and large land masses to the northeast and southwest. The map also indicates a couple of islands, but they are nowhere near the size of those on Penobsca. Misty Bay extends off to the southwest. Supposing your canoe was placed at the spot indicated, take another moment to imagine that view.

Finally, we're going to put your imagination to one last test. Suppose, if you can, you are a backcountry fur trapper, and four wild, unruly men from Hudson Bay paddle up and accuse you of poaching. Your denials are in vain and the men blindfold you, tow your canoe to an unknown lake, and depart in their own boats, leaving you adrift and bound to your center thwart. Somehow you work your blindfold off and discover, as luck would have it, that the only articles left in the boat are your maps of Penobsca and Beaver lakes, each with the little canoe on them. You study them and try

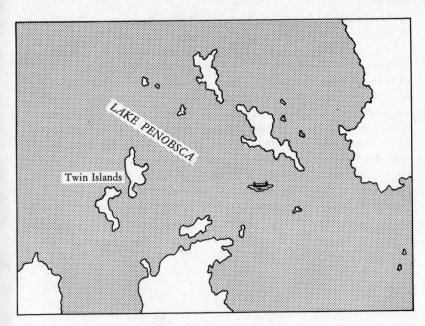

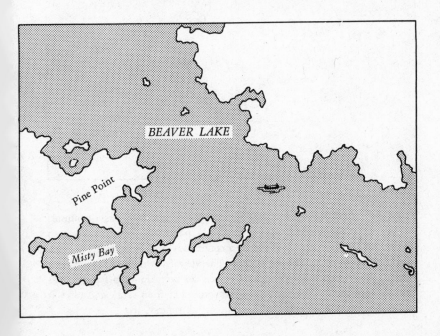

to discover whether you are at the point marked on Penobsca or the one on Beaver Lake. How successful are you at your task?

If you think we are about to tell you that after reading our section on navigation you'll be able to solve the problem, think again. Not even an experienced woodsman would be able to arrive at an answer. That's because *the views you would get looking at the countryside from the marked positions on either lake are identical.* If you don't believe us, look at our third map. It has the lines of the first chart superimposed on the second. Keep in mind our principle of seeing in straight lines: from either canoe, the only areas visible are the unshaded portions of the third map. The land to the west *might* be the Twin Islands on Penobsca, but it also might be the end of Pine Point on the north side of Misty Bay. Of course, in leaving you bound to the center thwart, we've exaggerated your difficulties.

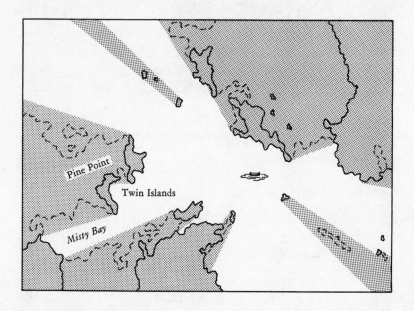

If you had a paddle you could go find out whether that land was a peninsula or only Twin Islands. But that's precisely the point we want to make: map reading in big-lake country is usually a continuous affair, not merely a casual check of the topos from time to time. The view from only one point on a lake is always a partial and incomplete one. So keep the map·for the day's journey in a transparent plastic case (to protect it from rain) and place it so as to be easily visible to your navigator at all times.

Continual vigilance and common sense go a long way in big-lake navigation. Yet "common sense" is a deceptive term: part of it, certainly, is straightforward logic and clearheaded thinking. But most of it is simply the unreasoned lessons derived from experiences "common" to everyday life. We're going on the assumption that big-lake navigating may not be part of your everyday life, and so will try to give you a set of experiences on which to build: namely, our own.

You see, it wasn't long after we broke through the last ice that we had our own navigating problems. Ashuanipi Lake stretches out to a length of fifty or sixty miles and is maybe twenty or twenty-five miles broad. Much of it consists of crooked bays, large islands, and above all, narrow and unlikely passes. The particular one we were headed for was at a place called Grosse Ile, which is French for "Large Island." Beyond Grosse Ile lay Ashuanipi's Northwest Bay: our key to the Moisie watershed. The route through that pass was complicated enough to provide several object lessons in canoe navigating, as you can see by a quick look at the map on page 98. You'll want to take more than a perfunctory look. We're going to use the chart to outline some navigational techniques you may find useful for your own big-lake mazes. After you familiarize yourself with the features of the chart (you may want to plot your own tentative route through the area before reading further), we'll take up our points one by one, using sections of the map to illustrate them.

POINT ONE: *Compass bearings and distance canoeing.* Our first task was to find the entrance to Ashuanipi Pass, the opening leading around the south side of Grosse Ile. We came across the lake from south of Ile Hélène, which is visible on the smaller-scale map. When you canoe across a space of open water four or five miles wide, it is difficult to distinguish any features on the far shore—especially where the flat topography and stunted evergreen lend a uniformity to the shoreline. In order to discover the precise direction we wanted to travel, we used the map to take a compass bearing. This process is a simple one if you have a decent compass and know how to make the few adjustments for translating findings on the map into actual directions in the field. The handiest compasses come equipped with a transparent plastic base, liquid-filled housing, and calibration in degrees. Cost ranges from five to ten dollars and up.

To begin your operation, ignore the terrain and concentrate on the map. You know your location—in this case, just south of Ile Hélène, on the small-scale map. Place the transparent base on the map with the direction-of-travel arrow running in a line from where you are toward the point you wish to go: Ashuanipi Pass. (Don't bother to orient the map so it actually faces

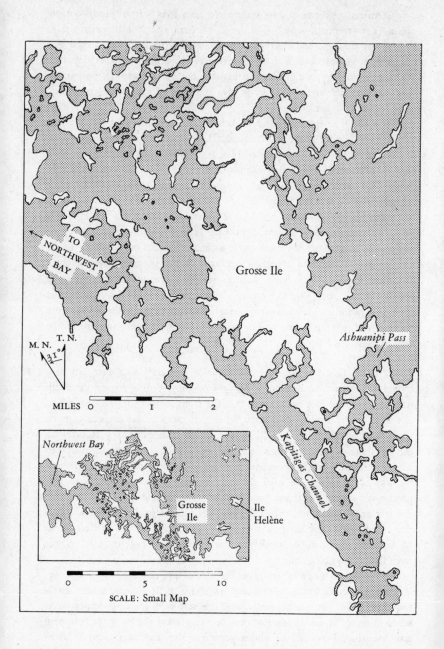

Grosse Ile

Ashuanipi Pass

Kahitigas Channel

TO NORTHWEST BAY

M. N. T. N.
37½°

MILES 0   1   2

Northwest Bay

Grosse Ile

Ile Helène

0   5   10

SCALE: Small Map

north. No need to do that.) When the direction-of-travel arrow is properly pointed, turn the compass housing ring until the "N" (and the arrow that rotates with the housing) points in the direction of true north as indicated on the map legend. (Ignore the *magnetic* needle of the compass for the moment.) Next check the reading in degrees at the direction-of-travel arrow. If you're using our map to practice, you should get a bearing of about 255°.

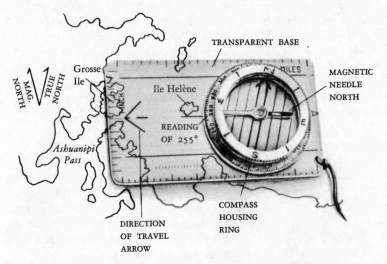

What remains is to translate your reading on the map into actual directions. That would be simple if the magnetic needle pointed to true north; but as most people know, it points toward the magnetic north pole. (Technically speaking, the needle is said to run parallel with the magnetic field, not "point" to the pole.) How much difference there is between the direction of magnetic and true north depends on where you are. Any good topographical map will note the variance in degrees of declination. As you can see from our chart, magnetic north is 31° to the west of true north: That meant we had to add 31° to our bearing, making our direction of travel 286°. (Had we been in an area where magnetic north was to the east, we would have had to subtract, not add. When translating directions *from the map to the field,* western declinations are *added* and eastern ones *subtracted.*) To sum up our method:

    1. Line the direction-of-travel arrow properly on the map.

    2. Point north on the compass housing the same direction as true north on the map.

    3. Add (or subtract) the declination to the bearing reading.

4. Rotate the entire compass until the magnetic needle points toward N (360°). Then canoe along the bearing marked as the direction of travel.

Whatever you do, don't neglect to adjust your compass for declination. An error of one degree doesn't amount to much over a short distance: only 88 feet for one mile. But if we had ignored the 31° on Ashuanipi, we would have wound up two miles south of our goal after only four miles of paddling. Even more important, never mix yourself up on whether to add or subtract the angle of declination: 31° subtracted instead of added means you're 62° off course! There are innumerable ways—all satisfactory—to remember when to add and when to subtract. Jim made up a ditty, "From map to field, the proper yield is East is Least (subtract) and West is Best (add)," which somehow helps him. Rug just keeps in mind the actual location of the magnetic pole in the Arctic Archipelago and deduces fresh each time the direction of the declination.

POINT TWO: *Dead-end bays that look like passes and passes that look like dead-end bays.* This is one of the many deceptions based on the central

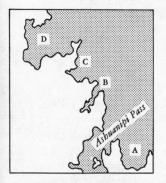

premise that the canoeist can only see in straight lines. In the inset you can see that the general area around Ashuanipi Pass presents four other bays. On the map, they are all easily recognizable as dead ends. But if you approached the area not completely sure of your course, some of them might give you pause. Not A and C: you can see to the end of them easily enough. But D could lure you around its corner before you discovered the blind alley. From the map, B looks too small to deceive anyone. But if you compare the size of its entrance with the narrowest neck of Ashuanipi Pass, the difference is not great. And the false bay would appear to be heading in the right direction. Note also (again using the straight-line test) that Ashuanipi Pass itself would look very much like another bay from offshore. No large stretches of water are visible beyond the end of it. Your best defense against wasting time bay hunting is to keep the map handy to compare features of the bays you enter and do an accurate job of compassing in the first place.

POINT THREE: *The pitfalls of mazes.* Originally Rug had planned to take the northern route around Grosse Ile. Fortunately we looked up an Indian familiar with the country who warned us away from the route. Looking at the next inset, you can see part of the reason why. The labyrinth around the top of the island is enough to challenge even a sharp map reader. The narrow passages, numerous islands, peninsulas, and blind-alley bays would make it imperative that you check your progress constantly. Once confused, it might take several hours of careful cruising to sniff out the trail again. What the map does not show about this particular maze is that much of the land is marshy. The bogs made it difficult to tell where the land stopped and the water began.

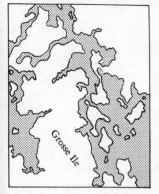

POINT FOUR: *Sense of scale and relative position.* One of the trickiest skills to pick up is the ability to translate correctly the scale of a map into real-life terms, especially when using the 1:250,000 scale. Does that little nick shown on your chart actually translate into a normal-sized bay, or is it really just a small indentation along the shore? And that little dot of an island—does it refer to the small expanse of bare rock off the left of your bow, or that larger island with the trees a little farther away? The best defense against this sort of confusion is a check of the landscape before you get into any really difficult sections. Compare a small bay or an island you can positively identify and note its size on the map.

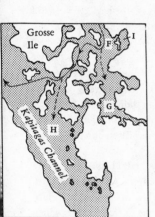

Even more difficult than scale of size is sense of position. It is easy enough to see on the map that the proper route through Ashuanipi Pass meant circling around to the right, past the southern point of Grosse Ile. But when moving at the snail's pace of a canoeist, distances and directions can easily be confused, especially when islands and peninsulas block the larger view of the terrain. Suppose, for instance, that you follow the east shore of the island at the top of the inset. When you near F, you know you want to stay to the right. But the sharp turn you need to get into the proper bay may appear on the water to look like you are making too much of a U turn. The tempting alternative is to conclude that you want to stay clear of the bay on the left (I) and head to the "right," down what appears to be the main passage—the inviting dead end at G. The combination of map and compass always handy makes it possible to map out your strategy. At the bottom of Grosse Ile, the map would tell you to keep to the right shore, rounding the bend in order to avoid straying the wrong way down Kapitagas Channel (H). When your compass showed you had turned enough of the corner and were heading roughly northwest again up the channel, the regular shoreline on the left would make it easier to cut to that side and avoid the confusing bays on the right.

POINT FIVE: *The open-water trap.* Even vigilant navigators have their lapses. We have to admit to that proposition or else lose the right to call ourselves vigilant. The sad fact of the matter is that Rug, who was the current man on duty with the maps, let down his guard for a few crucial moments as we paddled northwest along the left shore of Kapitagas. If you look at the inset,

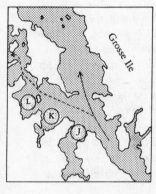

you'll see that the turn we ought to have made was to the left as indicated by the dotted line. Rug had studied the map, and noticed that of the three bays (J, K, and L) we wanted only the last one. If you look even a little closer than Rug did, you'll notice two more things. First, the bay at L is one of those passes that looks more like a dead-end bay. The configuration of the land, especially when viewed at a distance of more than a mile (as we did), blocks any view of the outlet at its end. Secondly, the peninsula between bays K and L is not very prominent. If you didn't look too closely, it would be possible to conclude that K and L were actually only one big bay. Rug didn't look too closely.

Turning north, you can see the reason why. The straight line of vision in that direction points attractively toward more open water—several miles of it. It looked like the natural route to follow, and Rug had his eye on it. "Third bay to the left," he said to himself, and counted the large expanse which looked like a dead end as only the second. The map was lying just behind his bow seat, but Joe was in the midst of a story about the time he and his dad rescued a lobsterman whose boat had foundered off the Maine coast in a gale nor'easter. Joe is a tolerably good storyteller—and certainly more interesting than two or three bays on a map. So away we went, right up the deceptive open-water trap to the north.

POINT SIX: *Triangulation.* The process of getting lost can be a long one, depending on how good a lobsterman story you have and how slow you are to finally admit you don't know your whereabouts. When Rug finally got back to the maps, he was not at first uneasy about our plight. He figured things would clear up around the next bend, and waited for a "better perspective" to be had a little farther up the channel. We kept paddling until finally we found ourselves in a bay with numerous islands about, something the charts definitely did not indicate.

Had we known our mistake right from the beginning, it would have been easy enough to determine where we were. But all Rug could ascertain in his confusion was that we had been paddling in a general northerly direction for some time. As the inset below indicates, there were several spots that corresponded with our possible whereabouts. One might have been the narrows at M; but Peach had an idea we had passed some islands back about the time Joe was pulling the lobsterman through ten-foot swells in the Atlantic. Then there was the possibility we had wandered up into the area of N—or maybe around to the left at O? Then again, could we have been foolish enough to get all the way up to P?

At this stage of the game, things can begin to get confusing. Long after the trip was over, Rug tried to explain the feeling to a disbelieving acquaintance. "Once you lose your position," he said, "nothing seems fixed, and every farfetched notion of where or how you took the wrong turn becomes possible —indeed you don't dare discount it because it may contain the solution to the whole damn mystery. Who knows? Maybe you *did* pass by a little iron deposit and screw up the compass. How else could you have overshot the passage you had your eyes open for the whole time? The more wild schemes and explanations you dream up, the less plausible the more straightforward interpretations begin to sound."

One way out of the problem would have been a morning's worth of snooping around for a check of the placement and configuration of the islands. Fortunately, we had a quicker method. Off to the north was one of the few

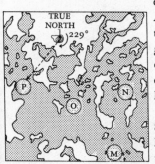

elevated hills which broke the flat horizon of Ashuanipi. A quick look at the contour lines on the topo showed there was only one hill in that general region. If we could take a compass bearing on the hill and then draw a line on our map according to that bearing, we would know we were located somewhere along the line.

Sighting toward the hill, Rug got a bearing of 80°, which meant that if he drew an imaginary line from where he was through the hilltop, it would run at an angle of 80° from magnetic north. Conversely, if a man were standing on top of the hill sighting down the same imaginary line toward Rug, he would be looking 180° in the opposite direction, 180 plus 80 being a bearing of 260°. So now Rug knew that if he drew a line on the map starting from the hill and running in the direction of 260° magnetic north, it would somewhere cross his position. To correct his field bearing (which was magnetic north) to true north on the map, he subtracted the declination of 31°, getting 229°.* He then penciled in a line at that angle from the hill as we've shown in our diagram. Once done, it was clear enough where we were. We still didn't know exactly, but it gave us enough of a direction to prove we were at P, and not N, M, or O. And we could take it from there.

If we had been able to see another hill, or if we could have sighted any two landmarks we were sure of, we could have drawn lines from both of them. Where the two lines crossed would be exactly where our canoes lay. This process is known as triangulation. Although our calculations may sound a bit complicated at first, if you practice by taking your compass and following the procedure step by step, you'll see most of it is straightforward, common-sense thinking. Just keep your mind off the stories about Maine lobstermen, that's all.

* This is just the opposite of what you do to translate a true-north map bearing to a magnetic-north field bearing, as in our example under Point One. If you add declination to translate from map to field, subtract it to translate from field to map.

III. HEADWATERS

9. Portaging

It's one thing for a traveler to trace his own route through strange country. It's another to track down someone else's trail when no one has thought to mark it on any map.

Our original plans were to try the former method: bushwhack our own portage trail out of Northwest Bay into the Moisie watershed. But Rug, who had more experience than the rest of us at trying to mire through the northern muskeg, kept worrying and looking at our maps. "I know, I know," he would say. "By all rights, we should be able to hike to the little stream, and from there paddle or wade or at least drag our way to Lac Gagné. But if Labrador is anything like Hudson Bay country, we can't count on that. In a wet season, the whole distance between Northwest Bay and Gagné will hike like oatmeal; and in a dry season, the stream may be nothing more than a tangle of spruce." Both prospects had worried us enough to insure that before we left Sept-Iles we looked up the nearest thing we could find to a local authority on lake crossings and portage routes.

That was Eugene, a Montagnais trapper of indeterminate age who had retired to the shanty town the national government set aside as an Indian reservation. Eugene assured us there was indeed a portage trail west from Ashuanipi, though it hadn't been used for twenty years—not since the railroad was put in. According to Joe (who blamed his deficiencies as a translator on the remnants of Montagnais which laced Eugene's French), the old trapper remembered just three things about the crossing: The trail was short, only a quarter mile; its blazes would by now be very old; and it met the lake "right here"—at which point Eugene squinted at our map and swept two gnarled fingers up and down the entire arm at the top of Northwest Bay.

Now we are actually paddling the area beneath the sweep of those gnarled fingers, and we begin to have doubts. Especially Jim.

"You did the same thing as those guys who went looking for the Franklin Expedition," he says to Joe. "They always asked the Eskimos if they hadn't heard of any survivors of the wreck, and the Eskimos said sure. They had good manners and all, so they said sure, they'd heard of some whites living in the next village. If you ask *me,* Eugene's just sent us packing to the next village on account of your asking polite questions."

"No," Joe replies, "I don't think my French is that subtle."

"Well, *something's* fishy. Three times we've paddled this stretch and what do we have to show? If Eugene was on the up and up, how come he led you on so long in that pidgin French and then at the end piped up in perfect English, 'Take it easy, and have a good time'?"

One thing is sure: we don't have to worry about looking sharp to pick out a solitary blaze mark from the canoe. Along shore we see literally hundreds of them. Unfortunately, they are not the ax bites of thoughtful Indians but the mindless gouging of the winter's ice. The four of us check dozens of likely-looking signs only to find each one leading to a trailless bog. Finally Joe suggests a different tack. "There's no chance of our smelling out the trail from the lake," he says. "We haven't got the noses for it. What we've got to do is *think* it out. Put ourselves in the place of that first Indian and imagine where he'd lay out the trail and then go find it. For my money, what we want is to head for this 'Lac Petit-Portage.' Start a beeline in that direction and search the territory on either side for a path. That should flush Eugene's trail."

The idea sounds good in theory, but we spend the better part of an afternoon crisscrossing an area that amounts to little more than a square mile. We find five small ponds, several stands of higher ground, and many broad swashes of wetlands where the swamp water sits a little deeper than the boot top. But no trail. Eugene's reputation is up to his hip waders in mud and Joe's good name is suffering by association. As we head back for the canoes, sloshing along single file with our heads down, Peach lets out a growl from the rear. "Dammit, Joe, you're not returning the way we came. You've got us off on some caribou path." Joe stops in his tracks too defeated to manage a retort; but then his eyes fall on the next tree. No blaze mark, but alongside is a narrow, weather-bleached platform with long broken runners. He turns very slowly but can't quite damp his triumph. "Now, Peach," he says. "I guess I wandered a bit, but you wouldn't have wanted to miss seeing this old Indian sled, would you?"

On the next tree and every so often after that, we manage to identify waist-high niches. Tracing out that line of blazes, we follow a remarkably dry and open route back to a tiny cove not fifty yards from where our boats are moored. There at trail's end, Peach spots that hand-carved paddle left behind by some passing Montagnais. Jim for his part notes with mixed satisfaction that not even the Indians had relied on their blazes to mark the landing—not judging by the Coke bottle hung upside down on a stick at the shoreline. Not tö be outdone by Peach's archaeological finds, he decides to carry out the bottle in the hope of eventually having it dated, sort of like carbon 14, by the Coca-Cola Company.

Noble Torture

With the sun fast approaching the horizon, it's time for us to turn our attention to the noble torture of canoe portaging. Noble, we say, because portaging tells something of *Homo sapiens'* remarkable ability to envision and seek out something beyond the compass of his horizon. Torture, we admit, because all this still means hauling a lot of cumbersome gear through the woods.

Now a little torture, if it's high-minded and self-inflicted, is fine tonic for the flagging spirit. But too many canoeists indulge needlessly. They drag gear between lakes in ways calculated to double their time. They carry around falls with studied inefficiency. And in the end, they drain themselves of the grand vision which provides the motive power in the first place. Most people, we're convinced, simply don't realize how much effort and time they could save by working out an effective portaging system. Think of it in terms of our current example. Eugene's "quarter mile" actually turned out to be a mile and a half. Counting one trip for scouting and two for lugging gear, we faced a seven-and-a-half-mile hike to transport 600 pounds of gear between neighboring lakes. Nothing monumental by fur-trade standards, but a logistical problem deserving careful planning. Multiply that one example by the thirty or so portages on our trip and you begin to see the amount of time to be saved by judicious carrying techniques.

LOADING AND UNLOADING. The first rule of efficient portaging is to carry your camping gear—all of it—inside the packs and duffels. At the beginning of a trip, your pack will seem absolutely incapable of holding all its equipment. The temptation is to leave something, perhaps the cook set, to sit in the bottom of the canoe. There's plenty of room for it there, you figure, and why not just carry it in one hand on the portages? Steel yourself, dig through the duffels an eighteenth time, and find a place to stuff it. Otherwise those dangling pots will catch every passing bush, swing you off balance hopscotching feeder streams, and leave you handless and helpless clambering up steep banks. Besides, you'll find you have plenty of legitimate canoeing gear to carry—life preserver, paddle, camera, and maybe a stray fishing rod.

The rest of your canoe's paraphernalia should be stowed. Leave the spare paddles lashed along the gunwales. (For whitewater, tie them with a slip knot so they can be instantly freed with a tug on the line.) The bailer remains

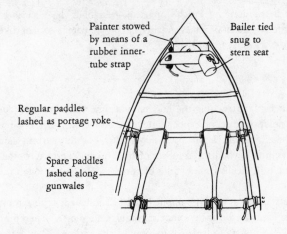

Painter stowed by means of a rubber inner-tube strap

Bailer tied snug to stern seat

Regular paddles lashed as portage yoke

Spare paddles lashed along gunwales

fastened to the stern seat, pulled snug so it doesn't dangle. Secure the painters either by looping them around the thwarts or by coiling them under the decks. Jim has glued straps of rubber inner tubing at the inside of his bow and stern to hold the ropes out of the way.

Unloading several sixty-pound packs at a precarious wilderness mooring requires a modicum of dexterity. If the beaching area leaves room for only one canoe, the whole portage is slowed down as each boat waits for the previous one to unload. If possible, then, haul the entire loaded boat out of the water first. This advice will horrify the Boy Scouts as roughneck and ir-reverent, but the new tough canoe materials will easily survive the ordeal. Two people just pull the boat far enough up on land for each to grab a gun-wale and then continue to slide the boat, hand over hand, far enough along to reach the packs. If the mooring is a deep one, the two can lift the bow end a bit higher to allow the buoyancy of the water to absorb most of the heavy load in the stern. If the shoreline is shallow, keep the boat more parallel to the bottom to distribute its weight more evenly and minimize scraping.

When it's impossible to beach or partly ground the canoe (such as along a steep rocky shoreline, or next to a dock), you'll have to unload with the canoe still floating free in the water. One person should steady the boat from the dock while the other does the unloading. Keep a balanced position while freeing the cumbersome pack frames, either on your knees or, when stand-ing is necessary, with both feet spread wide toward the gunwales.* Work the pack frame up to a perpendicular position, and then after readjusting your balance, swing the pack to shore, keeping your center of gravity low and

* When walking in a canoe, feet should be kept near the center keel line, since a person's weight is alternately placed on one foot and then the other. When standing in place, the wide stance gives better balance.

near the middle of the boat. A heavy and unwieldy pack can make this move tricky, as our diagrams show. In A, you'll notice we've mapped out canoe, dock, and pack frame ready to go ashore, leaving it to your imagination to draw yourself into the picture. How would you make the transfer? One way would be to place your grip low, at the black dot. That would keep your weight centered in the boat as you swing the top of the pack to the dock. But don't forget, while you're holding the pack that way, it becomes part of your center of gravity. Now the tip's resting on the dock, and the only way to get it all the way ashore is to push it up, as the dotted arrow in B indicates. But as Sir Isaac Newton observed, for every action there is an equal and opposite reaction (the solid arrow). Hence you may find your boat and pack in the unfortunate position at C. We leave you to connect yourself to that black dot as you see fit.

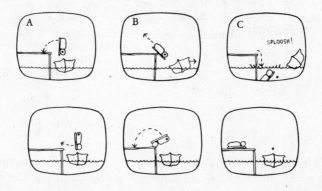

On the other hand, if you kneel or stand in a low crouch and grab the pack at the top, as in our second set of diagrams, you can pivot the bottom of the frame over the dock. In that position, the frame is not simply an extension of your center of gravity, but has a pivot point on shore. The boat is more easily kept from drifting away, and even if it moves with the final push, the pack remains safe and you free to regain your balance.

TYING IN. Wherever you moor, a notorious time waster is the tying, untying, and retying of packs to the boat. For some reason, this bit of rope handling is a source of frustration, short tempers, and banged knuckles all out of proportion to the time it takes. The explanation may be that the retying is not only the last chore but also the final straw for the overworked portager. Some canoeists just skip tying gear over the easy stretches, and to these people we are indebted for an abundance of colorful lore about scattering and retrieving camp goods along river bottoms. Our feeling is that nothing is as unpredictable or as diabolical as a capsize; you usually dump when you least expect and can least afford to. Call it superstition or good sense, we don't care, but we lash in all our gear all the time. This philosophy has given us lots of experience in devising a tie-down system (see our diagram) that combines easy threading, absolute security, and quick release.

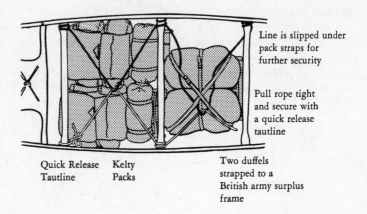

Line is slipped under pack straps for further security

Pull rope tight and secure with a quick release tautline

Quick Release Tautline   Kelty Packs

Two duffels strapped to a British army surplus frame

Carrying

In most cases, the sensible and easy way to portage a canoe is to flip the boat up onto your shoulders and carry it single-handed. Those who have never tried this maneuver will perhaps shudder at the idea, but if done correctly, it's not the burden it might appear to be. On short, vertical portages where boulder hopping and rock scrambling with a canoe would be dangerous, the best solution is someone at each end of the canoe carrying the boat right side up. In the case of a cascade requiring only a short lift-over, just leave all the gear in the boat and have four·folks haul the whole outfit intact. Avoid two men carrying the boat inverted on their shoulders. The bowman's head is too close to the front of the canoe for him to see where he's going. Unless the two men walk in step, an unpleasant rhythm sets the thwarts to shaking and jarring the shoulders. And in bushwhacking through a thicket, it's impossible to turn the boat with two people stumbling, jockeying, and swearing at the same time. With one person swearing, it's only *next* to impossible—which in some situations has to serve.

Single-carrying a canoe can be torture, but it's not primarily the heavy load that's to blame. Seventy-five-pound packs carry much more easily than seventy-five-pound canoes, for the simple reason that their frame distributes the weight more comfortably. A canoeing yoke doesn't do the job as well, but it's better than carrying the boat without. Differences in human anatomy make it impossible to specify one yoke system which beats all others, so experiment on your outings to find the one which works best for you. Some canoe manufacturers sell yokes to go with their canoes. You may want to buy one, but the following homemade versions have satisfied us.

Peach depends on the blades of his paddles to cushion the load on his shoulders. The key to this yoke is making sure the paddles keep the canoe well balanced. The boat's trim should be even (that is, parallel to the ground), with the rear end a touch lower, so you can see where you're going without constantly having to lift the bow up. The placement of the yoke, the spare paddles, or even the smallest extra weight in the bow or stern can upset the balance. On one portage we tried to cram a homemade fishing net into the stern of Peach's boat, but it dragged the back end down too far.

You can see Peach's yoke system in the sketch on page 110. He carried the boat bow first with the T-grips of the paddles pointing in that direction. But you may find the balance on your own canoe works better with a different arrangement of paddles.

Jim has tried the paddle yoke on several occasions, but found that two shoulder bones of unknown origin protruded right where the flat of the blade lay. So he prefers to use one of the cheap horseshoe-collar life preservers as a yoke. The only adjustment he makes is to tie the top chest straps behind his neck instead of in their usual position. This raises the preserver in the front and sets the horseshoe farther away from the neck, which makes it a more effective pad for the center thwart of the canoe. Some people find this modification unsatisfactory on longer portages because the preserver works its way back too far and the bottom chest strap in front rides up and begins to choke at the neck. Experiment a little, and practice holding your breath.

DOUBLE CARRY

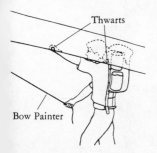

Thwarts

Bow Painter

As you can see, much of the discomfort takes place when the yoke fails to cradle the weight of the canoe comfortably, or when the canoe slips from its original position on longer carries. One means of correcting these deficiencies is the double carry: toting your pack and canoe at the same time. This may seem like sheer insanity, but Jim and

Lift canoe by gunwales
so it rests on your
thighs

Shift hands to
proper grip
on center thwart

Swing canoe to your
shoulders

Ready to go

Peach use it wherever possible. If you carry the canoe without your pack, all the canoe's weight remains on the shoulder and back muscles, but by carrying your pack at the same time, the center thwart of the canoe rests on the pack's shoulder pads (between your shoulders and the frame itself). This transfers much of the canoe's weight (via the hip belt) to the hip and leg muscles, which are better able to bear it. Furthermore, with the thwart securely resting in between the shoulders and the pack frame, it cannot slip off, and the hands are needed less often to hold the canoe in place. The double carry does have its limits. The added weight of the pack along with the already heavy canoe shows up especially when hiking an uphill slope, and it also cuts down on a man's balance and dexterity—so beware portages with bad footing. But on fairly flat stretches with well-marked trails or through open country, the double carry saves the labor and time of an extra trip.

The hours spent lugging your boat around the woods will inspire you to devise additional torture-saving devices. Some of them may even work. Whitewater helmets serve as good headrests; or use your hat, with a shirt stuffed inside for padding. Either allows you to lean the canoe forward from time to time, putting the weight on neck muscles for a change of pace. This is more naturally done on downhill slopes, when the canoe has a tendency to tilt forward anyway. Of course, not all brainstorms pan out. Jim suggested Joe wear his knee pads like epaulets on the shoulders. It was a dismal idea.

After getting the yoke in place, it remains to hoist the canoe to your shoulders. First, drain any water from the bottom of the boat. (Being doused with a quart of dirty splash water is a discouraging way to begin a carry.) Then stand at the center thwart, grab the near gunwale with a hand on either side of the thwart, and lift the canoe so it rests across your thighs. Next shift your grip from the gunwale to the center thwart, in preparation for hefting the boat to its position on your shoulders. Make sure you have the grip right. There are two proper ways of grasping the thwarts: with one, you end with the boat on your shoulders and you facing the bow; with the other, you end facing the stern. Either grip will have your thumbs to the inside of the thwart, facing each other. Your wrists (not your knuckle joints) point toward the direction you will end facing. Remember that: we've seen novices gallantly wing the boat in place and find themselves ready to walk right back into the water with the canoe. On a narrow trail where the clearing is not wide enough to pivot the boat, this lack of foresight can be embarrassing.

Now for the hoist itself. The key is to put your whole body into the effort and not try to brazen out the lift using only your arm muscles. At the same time that your arms are swinging the boat up, your thighs are giving it a boost, your back is arching up from its bent-over position, and your hips and pelvis straighten up. All this should be with a quick rocking motion. When it's done with vigor, the canoe will swing up to your shoulders easily. Most beginners are too cautious in their movements, so they wind up losing the force of the rocking motion which makes the whole process easy. If you *are* new to portaging, practice your vigor with two friends at either end of the canoe spotting your moves. Then if the vigor ends in overexuberance, the boat is saved an unexpected bounce from five feet up.

At the end of a portage, simply reverse the loading process. After a long carry, your arm muscles may well be too tired to lift the boat off by themselves—so once again, the whole body is used to hunch the boat into the air. The key at this point is to be sufficiently ready to catch the canoe back on your thighs before it crashes to the ground. Jim likes to help cushion the downward movement by having his lower arm cradle the outside of the canoe as it comes down. He has rather long arms, however, and you may find this move inconvenient.

There are alternate (though less elegant) ways of raising and lowering the boat. One is to invert the canoe and have a friend lift the bow above his head while the point of the stern remains on the ground. You can then get under the canoe, set the center thwart on your shoulders and tilt the stern end up to its balanced position. This is especially convenient when double-carrying with a pack, since it takes practice to hoist the canoe into place with the high pack frame in the way of the boat's arc.

Hiking with a canoe differs little from hiking with a pack. Keep a steady, rhythmic stride. The boat is kept in place by extending either one or both hands forward along the edges of the gunwales. When double-carrying, the pack frame helps steady the boat, so that often only one arm is used to keep things in balance, or sometimes none at all. It is also possible to control the angle of the boat by keeping a rein on the bow painter. Either of these methods cuts down on arm fatigue. The differences from normal hiking become noticeable when bushwhacking. Here above all is where patience is needed. In the middle of boggy places, keep your temper and go slowly. In stream and rock hopping, choose your path cautiously; but you'll be surprised how much balance is maintained with a canoe on your back. Tightrope walkers, after all, use long bamboo poles to provide overall stability; just think of your canoe as a seventy-five-pound balance pole.

No matter how well you master the art of portaging, there are just too many carries which feel unconscionably long. Brief rests can be taken without getting out from under the canoe: just let the stern tilt back to the ground while cradling the point of the bow in the Y of two tree branches. As you march along, try keeping yourself in good spirits by humming some forceful and inspirational tune. (To yourself, of course: doing so out loud wastes energy.) Jim's favorite for the long hauls is "Battle Hymn of the Republic," although when the final clearing comes in sight, he breaks into the climactic "Great Gate of Kiev" from Moussorgsky's *Pictures at an Exhibition*. If your route lies through civilized areas, you will also derive encouragement from the neophytes who are struggling along the trail, dangling pots and pans, and staring at you in amazement for even *thinking* of trying to carry a pack plus canoe single-handed. When you feel really merciless, you can do what Jim's friend Les Bechdel did when he and Jim were guiding a group of campers one summer on a portage around Raquette Falls. Les had marched ahead at a furious pace, with pack and canoe, and soon passed four guys from another camp who were all stumbling along with one boat. "I couldn't resist," Les later told Jim. "After passing them at a trot and rock-hopping a couple of small streams, I gave a little jump and clicked both heels in mid-air before going around the bend."

We should warn you though, Les was in perfect shape and National Slalom Kayak Champion at the time. If your leg muscles are more like ours, you'll try his maneuver only at the risk of ending your pirouette with two broken ankles and a passel of horselaughs from the guys four-manning their canoe past you.

Trail Finding and Bushwhack Portages

On a bona fide wilderness trip, of course, no spectators are likely to be on hand to laugh at your gaffes or gape at your proficiency. Chances are, you won't even have anything remotely resembling a trail. In that case, any portage of respectable length (that is, one that leads out of sight) usually deserves scouting. Don't become overconfident just because there is an old trail which is well marked at the beginning; it can very quickly run into a maze of wandering animal paths, lead to an open meadow with no sign of where it picks on the other side, head into a blowdown, or simply disappear in the next thicket. On the other hand, trappers who prefer to keep their trails hidden may leave the first two hundred yards or so uncared for, and only farther inland will you find the path well maintained. At the first indication that you've lost the path, retrace your steps to the last definite blaze or other landmark, leave one man there, and let the others fan out, working their way forward until they regain the trace. Once you've lost the trail completely, you have to start just as you would for bushwhacking— with compass, map and horse sense. If you're looking for the next lake across the watershed, for example, it may be a good idea to head for the point on the horizon where the trees dip lowest, but not if the topo shows it to be the Dismal Swamp. Animal trails will often take the shortest (or at least most convenient) route between two bodies of water. If you run across one, it's worth following up. Remember too, if your Indian trail is an old one, that blazes notched twenty years ago will look only like gnarled and swollen knots; but once discovered, they serve almost as well as when they were first cut.

When carrying around rapids, uncertainty about your destination is replaced by the quandary of choosing which side of the river to portage. As always, you will glean as much information as you can from the maps. In general, the best bet is to prefer the inside curves of the river bend. The water is slower and often allows you to take out farther downstream, the riverbank is less likely to have been cut away, and in some places the river will make a sharp enough U turn to warrant a shortcut across the inside of the curve. But look closely at the map and at the terrain as you approach it for any sizable tributaries, deep ravines, high cliffs, or other obstacles to avoid. The odds say that a blind man would pick the better side 50 percent of the time, right? And an educated decision by experienced scouts should only improve those odds. Yet, by some anomaly of river running, most of the time when you are struggling down a riverbank under sixty pounds of patched-up duffels on a gerrymandered frame, you will look across the rapids and notice that on the other side the way is less steep, the footing less rocky, and the grass a little greener. We call this misperception the Bovine Distortion.

Mostly your chosen path will lie along the shoreline of the river, but there will be places where you will be forced to cut away from the bank—such as at sufficiently large waterfalls. Once again we recommend scouting ahead without packs. On your return trip, try to follow the exact route you will take with the canoes. Study a few of the unmistakable landmarks along the way and use these to break a long portage into a number of clearly remembered segments. On crucial turnoffs and cutbacks, it's also helpful to mark the route with bright objects that can be spotted at a distance. Orange life jackets, red kerchiefs, and yellow hats are all good candidates to stick in trees and hang on bushes. Cutting a fresh blaze would work as well but even in Labrador a woodsman with a conscience would no more leave this scar behind than he would an empty can of Schlitz.

As you memorize the portage route on your return to the canoes, look back to where you've been. A route coming can look quite different from a route going. We are thinking especially of Y junctions. The novice who doesn't notice a trail branching in from the left will be surprised and puzzled to find his trail divide in two on the return. The same lesson applies in trail-less country. Let's say you're returning from point A in the sketch by descending a knoll and hitting a well-used animal path which takes you back to your canoes. Getting to the boats may be easy, but unless you note the turnoff point,

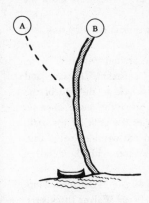

the return trip with gear may find you following the well-defined animal trail too far, toward B.

If you didn't lug the packs over on the scouting trip, you may want to take them first (instead of the canoes), just because it will be easier to familiarize yourself with the route. When the boats are carried, it's helpful for the hiker with the pack to lead his canoe partner. Although a canoe does not block the view of the immediate path, it's easy on bushwhacks to get confused without a friend ahead to keep the larger perspective. If your gear is compact enough so that only one man needs to make a return trip, take the canoe first. That way, while the one partner is returning for the last load, the other can be getting the packs tied in so everything is ready to go when the final pack arrives. With the double-carry system, many portages can be made hauling the gear across with only one trip, saving even more time.

Saving time. That's the reason we figured Rug was so determined to carry his pack on our scouting trip over the watershed portage. And it was—partly. By the time we found the old blaze in Northwest Bay, Peach's watch said close to five, and we knew we'd have to move quick to set up a decent camp on the far side of the carry. But the rest of us weren't so optimistic about the chances of following twenty-year-old blazes. So we left our packs with the canoes, pointing out to Rug it wouldn't speed things any for him to lug his solo, we're all in this together, and so on. But no, he's obstinate.

"We get to the other side," he says, "and that'll be another fifty or sixty pounds on the right side of the watershed."

He keeps saying this to himself as we meander around, backtrack, pick up the trail, lose it, pick it up again, head across some white moss meadows, and finally straight into the middle of a good thicket. Jim stands guard at the last blaze while the others fan out, and thinks to himself Rug would have done better to leave the pack. But then there's a yell from Joe.

"Hi, there! I think I've got us our last clearing."

We all break for the sound of his voice, Jim being less than cautious about noting the blaze in case Joe's wrong. Not far through the brush is another meadow, and in the middle of it, what seems a small pond.

"Here's your intermittent stream marked on the topo," says Joe. "We're into the new watershed."

Rug is the last one to come up, lumbering along with his pack. He gazes suspiciously at the water.

"You sure this is the intermittent stream?" he asks.

"It looks that way to me, Jawn. My compass says we've been going the right direction—and the trail was heading this way."

"It looks to me more like a pond than a stream. You sure this is a stream?"

"Sure. There's the outlet over there. It disappears around that bend."

"I want to see current before I call anything a stream," he says, and without another word trudges off, pack still on his back, to the end of the pond. We see him stoop over, thrust a hand down, study the reeds. Then he comes back, says not a word to us, and slowly juggles the pack off his back. Deep inside he gropes around and pulls out a brown and wrinkled paper bag. Then he turns around to face us, full square and solemn, with the pond or intermittent stream or whatever behind.

"Gentlemen," he says. "The headwaters of the Moisie." And then flourishes off that paper bag to reveal a tiny bottle of Hiram Walker blackberry brandy.

So we take a pull, all around, and acknowledge Rug his reason for persevering with the pack.

The brandy amounts to only a swallow, but goes down with a warmth we can use, the sun having gotten below the trees, and most of our gear a mile and a half back at Northwest Bay. We make a quick decision to camp partway across the portage in one of the fine white meadows, and head at a trot for the canoes. Peach leaves a preserver and kerchief here and there, especially since things are getting dusky. We pick a cluster of pines in the middle of one of the smaller clearings for our spot that night. Then Peach and Joe and Jim hurry on in the dimness while Rug sets his pack aside and commences work on a fire to take the chill off the evening air.

10. Fire

We'd like to give you some practical information on building fires. Note we said *practical.* One of the most romantic and swashbuckling parts of any guidebook is the section which details the many ways you can start fires without matches. The bow and drill, the flint and steel, the magnifying glass are the methods most commonly described, but those are only starters for anyone with a little imagination. Here, for example, is one of the more inventive guidebook authors at work:

> The magnifying properties of water can be capitalized upon for fire making by, for example,
>
> a) holding the crystals from two watches or pocket compasses of about the same size back to back,
>
> b) filling the space between with water,
>
> c) directing this makeshift enlarging lens so as to converge the rays of the sun in a point sharp enough to start tinder glowing.

The same intrepid bushman also suggests making a lens by "shaving, and then smoothing with the warm hand, a piece of clear ice." He concludes (in his best straight-faced Sage of the Woods Deadpan) with the hopeful remark that "it is possible with ingenuity to devise other such improvisations." This makes wonderful reading, but forget about actually *using* these techniques. Two hours of holding leaky watch crystals together and you should be sufficiently tired of having water run down your sleeve while waiting for the sun to come out.

We are not saying that all methods of starting fires without matches are unworkable or useless. But if you've never tried them, don't assume they will work in a tight spot. For the time being, then, we're going to skip the frills and concentrate on the basics of fire building.

BRING PLENTY OF GOOD MATCHES. This means wooden, self-lighting kitchen matches. Paper matches absorb dampness all too easily, and safety matches are worthless if the striking surface on the box is wet or lost. Pack the matches in waterproof cases that each of you will keep tied to your belt loop and in your pocket at all times. Test the waterproof case *before* you leave on your trip; some leak. In addition, scatter packets of reserve supplies (waterproofed, in plastic bags) throughout your packs and duffels. For a twenty-five-day trip, five hundred of them scattered in twenty packets should ensure that no matter what gets dunked in the river, most of your lights will stay dry. After you have taken the trouble to get all these matches together, you may be surprised to learn that our next rule is:

DON'T USE MOST OF ALL THOSE GOOD MATCHES YOU BROUGHT. A twenty-five-day trip with two hot meals a day requires fifty fires, and in theory you shouldn't need much more than fifty matches to do the job. The rest are packed as backup supplies in case you lose some or most of your gear. Most beginners use more matches than they need because they think their fire is ready to go before it actually is. If the materials for a fire have been properly assembled, you need only one match to get things started; if they have not, any number of lights will not serve the purpose. You should not consider yourself a good fire builder unless you can consistently light one-match fires under most circumstances. In desperate straits and a downpour besides, the use of a candle virtually guarantees a fire on the first strike, but other times it is an unnecessary waste of wax. In either case, you need wood that will burn.

GOOD AND BAD WOOD. Good wood is dry wood. Even slight dampness, such as the moisture in any living tree, is enough to prevent wood from being good fuel. The first requirement, then, is to make sure a tree is dead. Obviously, a dead tree is devoid of leaves or needles. But in some stands of heavy forest, the bottom part of the tree, kept in perpetual shade, will have no greenery, while the topmost part at the height of the canopy is still healthy. Don't fell one of these. Instead, shake your prospect to see if any leaves or needles at the top sway at your touch.

In the winter, deciduous trees have lost their leaves. In that case, take a branch and break it. If it snaps cleanly with a good crack, it's dead. If you have to twist it back and forth to break the fibrous connection, or if it breaks only halfway through, then it is still green. (In medicine, a bone which is broken only partway through is called a "green stick" fracture.) You may also run across trees felled by a storm whose leaves are dead but still have not dropped from the tree. As a rule, this means the tree was alive too recently to count as seasoned wood. In some sheltered spots, the leaves or needles will remain after the wood is sufficiently dry. Then the foliage should fall easily when the tree is vigorously shaken; and the wood will again snap sharply when broken.

Even dead trees do not always make good burning. If they have been lying on the damp ground, they are likely to be too wet or rotten. You can identify this "punkwood" either by sawing a cross section of it or taking a chunk out with your ax. If the innards have the appearance of the grain beginning to crumble, or seem soft and flaky to the bite of the ax, then you'd best look for other material. Dead birch is especially likely to rot this way, because the bark remains on the dead tree and seals in the accumulated moisture. Thus your best bet is a small (five to seven inches in diameter) standing dead tree, or else fallen logs whose branches have kept the trunk away from the ground.

We should note that these guidelines for gathering wood apply to wilderness sections of the country only. Many parks and forest preserves have prohibited the use of standing deadwood as firewood, often because inexperienced campers don't know enough to discriminate between dead and living trees—and increasingly, because high-use camping areas have become alarmingly defoliated. When camping in such spots, we recommend taking one of the compact camp stoves presently on the market. If wood fires are permitted (and they are not in some cases) you may want to use the stove anyway and then after dinner collect whatever scrounge wood is around to make the flickering campfire that is so much a part of a night in the woods.

KINDLING. The crucial part of building a fire is gathering enough momentum in the heat produced by the initial flame from the match. The beginner's usual mistake is to underestimate both the quality and the quantity of wood needed to produce a blaze big enough to ignite the larger splits of a cooking fire. Here above all is where the wood must be dry. One of the best sources of kindling is the small dead branches on the lower parts of evergreen trunks. These are especially good if found in a thicket of pine where the dense needles overhead serve to shelter the wood from light and moderate rains. In northern latitudes, beware the branches adorned with moss. Even the wispy variety, which often looks dry, is generally moist enough to dampen the kindling. Collect a *large* handful of these tiny twigs, along with the next level of kindling, which is the dead branches ranging in sizes up to the thickness of your thumb. A good standing dead tree can furnish material for your entire fire.

If no small branches are readily available for kindling, large logs may be split with an ax. Novices should be warned, however, that kindling splits must be small. As a rule of thumb, when we figure our kindling is split small enough, we split it about two more times. One particularly choice source of kindling is the charred pine stumps found in burned-over forests. When the "stumps" (often more than five or six feet high) are split open, the fat-saturated innards can be used with excellent results.

Another prime fire starter is birch bark, as even the neophyte knows. Get in the habit of pocketing a strip or two whenever you have the opportunity, since not every campsite has a stand of birch nearby. Don't peel it directly off living trees—this is bad conservation, and you'll find enough bark which trees have shed. Birch works especially well because it will light even when wet, and burns with considerable heat. The bark naturally forms in many thin layers, and you can peel them apart according to the kind of results wanted. For something that will catch quickly, separate your sheets as thinly as possible; in thicker layers, the bark won't catch as easily, but once ignited will burn longer and give the additional time to get the bigger wood going.

We should also say a word about paper: don't use it. Not because it is a bad habit to get into—which it is—but simply because it does not work well. Fires are started in either wet weather or dry weather. If it's dry out, there is no need for paper because sufficient kindling of all kinds is available. On a wet day, dry tinder is admittedly harder to find, but paper absorbs moisture very quickly from the air. Dew and humidity, let alone rain, is sufficient detriment. Those paper bags we advised as one way of packing your meals are an actual hindrance to starting a blaze: they light with difficulty, burn slowly, and give off little heat. Paper seems like such a good idea because it's often used on indoor fires, where wood is dry, the paper has not been exposed to moisture in the air, and likely enough you have a gas jet to help things along. The conditions are just not comparable.

FIREPLACES. Try to keep your fire on noncombustible material like rock or dirt. Beware especially the moss in northern Canadian wilderness areas. Circumstances forced us one late night to set our fire on that kind of ground without hauling up any rocks from the river's edge to form a protective shield. We doused it well before bed, and then again after breakfast. But when Peach applied the acid test before leaving—thrusting his hand into the dead embers—they seemed warmer than they had a warrant. Peach dug about with a stick. Sure enough, the sphagnum layer went down a good ways before hitting dirt, and the fire from the night before had begun smoldering its way deeper. We excavated with that stick and continued dousing down to a depth of a foot before putting the fire dead out. If you've never camped in this kind of terrain, we can't stress too much how important it is to double-check on this point. Underground fires can smolder for months, or even longer, then break out when the opportunity is right. In

Alaska, such burnings sometimes continue all winter under the cover of snow. And the general government policy on forest fires is, you start 'em, you pay for 'em. "Mmmph," said Peach as we finally left our campsite. "How many appendixes you think we'd have to take out to pay for the entire province of Labrador?"

LAYING THE FIRE. No doubt you've seen the innumerable diagrams showing the different kinds of fires: log cabin, tepee, all-night stoker, trench fire. Each has its place, but don't spend time constructing an elaborate edifice before you light your fire. If something goes wrong, you'll pull apart your skyscraper in a matter of seconds, and unless you're lucky, it will collapse and put out what little flame you had going. *Do* spend whatever time you need getting the raw materials *ready and at hand,* but build the fire as you go, putting on sticks as the flames increase.

Suppose you've gotten all your supplies ready, from tinder to the quarter splits of a six- or seven-inch log. With all your material within arm's reach, kneel down and take your clump of tinder. Lay down a sheet of birch bark if you wish, but on a dry day that's not needed. Make sure your tinder is crushed together close enough. A common error is to lay down twigs as if laying down larger branches on an already established fire. The first flames spread by your match will be small ones; and if the tinder is not packed tightly enough, you won't be able to amass the collective heat and flame to ignite the bigger materials. With a stiff wind blowing, it may be easier just to take the tinder, crush it down to about the size of a football, hold it in one hand, and cup the lighted match under it with the other, your body serving as a windbreak until the flame catches. Then set the fire down and begin laying on the larger material, starting with the sticks only slightly larger than the tinder and working up to the one- or two-inch logs. Anything much larger you'll probably want to split with the ax.

Under most conditions, these preparations should suffice to get a fire safely on its way, and you can then begin to think about what sort of shape you want to give it, be it tepee, log cabin, or bonfire.

11. Small-Stream Work

Some rivers begin their journeys as the outlets of large lakes; consequently they are good-sized streams to begin with. But many others spring from humbler origins: even the Mississippi at its head is small enough to step across. Thus your initial encounter with a river is likely to be through the challenges and intimate pleasures of small-stream work.

If your headwaters are only moderately small, time along these stretches will be a singular pleasure. The banks remain close enough on either side to provide a comfortable, easygoing atmosphere. In the early season, when the mosses and pine pollen and fiddleheads are coming to life, the closeness of the forest and the dampness of the earth allows the scent of the land to hover along the stream. The way to take these passages is comfortably; poking along and getting out often to ease the boat around rocks and, as gently as possible, over the shallows.

Here is where the high-top sneakers are indispensable. Put them on—over the wet-suit booties when the water is cold enough to merit them. (With borderline weather, be prepared for sniping from your friends. Rug was the only one of us timorous enough to bring booties, and Peach made the most of it with some stage-whispered harrumphing about the need to bite the bullet.) In most summer weather, sneakers alone will do, plus a pair of cutoff shorts or a bathing suit. Regular pants legs roll up, but they also roll down, and you'll usually wade deeper than you anticipate.

As the boat passes from boulder-garden wading into deeper pools, be ready to hop back in. The bowman hefts himself over one gunwale back into his seat as the boat goes off into deep water; then swings one of his legs over to the other gunwale, and lets both of them extend lazily out over the sides, draining his sneakers of water. The sternman hops aboard the same way the Lone Ranger used to come flying at Silver from behind, with a two-handed vault (mind the high tip of that stern, please) up onto the end of the boat. He can comfortably remain in the extreme sternward position draining (a hell of a long wait if he is Jim and wears size fifteens); or if deep water promises, then he may ease himself forward into the seat and continue paddling, legs akimbo.

As the aroma of a lazy day goes to your head, you may want to avoid wading, and try to get by instead with a modicum of scraping. Aluminum boats will tolerate much of this; fiber-glass and ABS boats deserve a shade more watchfulness. Wooden paddle blades should not be subjected to the constant hard wear of pushing and levering; a copper bang plate or strip of fiber glass will protect the edges. Fiber-glass blades stand much greater wear, but even their corners round off after repeated scraping. Remember that the paddle can be used not only to push the canoe forward but as a prop to lean on. By transferring your weight to the shaft, you lighten the canoe and permit it to pass over shallows where it would balk with a full load.

Headwater work is not always lazy, however. The forest banks may crowd so close that fallen trees bar the way. Late in the season, the water level may sink so low that travel becomes a matter of constant dragging instead of leisurely gliding. At the Moisie headwaters, our stream meandered and became so shallow that it made more sense to drag the boats across the shortcuts of the stream bends, gear and all. This is possible, of course, only when the country is moderately open and the ground cover makes sliding the canoes a workable solution.

We've been forced to travel creeks where the distance between banks narrows to only six feet, and it helps to have a Sven saw handy for occasional stubborn logs. For the most part though, it's easier to raise the branches and pull the canoes under, or press them down and haul over. Either way, if the current is moving with conviction, be extremely careful in approaching such fallen trees. If your canoe swings broadside and bumps against the trunk, the undertow will flip you, sharp as a mule kick. Worse, the current will pull you down into the tree. If it is just a bare log, no harm is done, but if branches hang down into the water, a swimmer can be trapped in the cobweb. From there the margin of safety until your friends can pull you out depends on how long you can hold your breath. Take our advice and give low-riding sweepers plenty of range.

Beaver dams are a common sight along headwaters. They are easily enough crossed in many cases without even getting feet wet. If the impetus of your paddling won't scrape you through the lowest breach of the subsidiary dam, the bowman hops out onto the damwork. This buoys up the bow, making it easy to haul the boat up till the middle thwart straddles the dam. The sternman then climbs amidships and out onto the dam; the boat is shifted so it now tips downstream over the dam fulcrum; and the bowman crawls forward, leaving the high end easily moved off its mooring by the sternman.

In areas where canoe travel is through swamps and stream current is negligible, you may encounter leeches. These blood-sucking parasites attach themselves painlessly, so it is a good idea to remove sneakers and check for them after wading in stagnant water for several hours. The ones we've run across (none on the Moisie) have varied in size from tiny quarter-inch black worms to repulsive six-inch monsters. Keep calm if you find one attached. They are easily removed by covering them with salt (which dehydrates them). Some people recommend applying the end of a still-glowing match head or cigarette ash. If you yank them off straightway, they're more likely to leave some of their sucking parts embedded, which can lead to infection.

None of us has ever tangled with mud bogs or quicksand, but if you should encounter them on your portages, don't panic. (This is easier said than done—we would probably panic shamelessly.) The density of mud or quicksand is greater than that of water; since you can float on water, you can float on quicksand. The minute you find yourself sinking in, throw yourself flat on your back, regardless of how disagreeable it may seem to wallow in ooze. Once flat and free of any pack, swim, slide, or roll your legs back to the solid ground. If you're traveling over suspicious ground in the first place, use your paddle to test it as you advance.

Getting to your river may entail traveling up another stream to the watershed boundary, and in that case you will need to know a few rudiments of working the currents. If the upstream work is of the dragging and hauling variety, the technique of grunt and muscle remains essentially the same. But with a larger current to work against, you must know how to use the areas of least resistance.

That brings us to one of the most basic concepts of whitewater: the eddy. If all rivers traveled downhill in ideally rounded sluices, there wouldn't be any eddies, nor, for that matter, much of a current differential at all. A concrete sluiceway creates some friction, and so the water near the shallow sides of the channel travels more slowly than the deeper, fast-moving current in the center. But even so, it would be difficult to make headway up such a river. On the other hand, notice what happens if we drop a large boulder into the middle of an otherwise uniformly moving current. The water piles up on the upstream side of the rock and flows around to join the current on either side. Just below the rock, the current has been interrupted, and so resistance to an upstream boat would be less. More than that: since the rock prevents the current from filling the space below with water, it must be filled by the water rushing past on either side. If the water rushes fast enough, it will have gotten a ways downstream before it can stop itself enough to fill the empty space, and in fact will have to flow back upstream to do so. In other words, not only does the rock create a calm eddy below it, but the stronger the current downstream, the more of an upstream current in the eddy!

An understanding of this principle makes it easier to see that a surprising amount of progress will be made paddling upstream in the eddies rather than in the main current. As you begin paddling any whitewater, be on the alert for them—not only because of the help they lend in upstream work, but also because the prime skill of "reading" rapids depends on your being able to recognize the varying speeds and directions of whitewater. To the novice, any set of white foam looks like a seething mass of downstream action; to the expert, it is a series of main currents, cross currents, boils, souse holes, and eddies—water working in many different ways. Picking out the eddies is the first step to learning the ways of the river.

The most obvious eddies are the sort we've already described: big boulders stuck in the middle of the river. But notice the less obvious ones. Deeper rocks that sit just below the river's surface turn currents around too. The riverbank, where the current is generally slower, sometimes dips into enough of a bay to set up a leisurely eddy. When a stream rounds a bend, inertia takes most of the water to the outside of the curve and leaves the inside current slower and shallower. The more you look, the more you will notice the river's second thoughts.

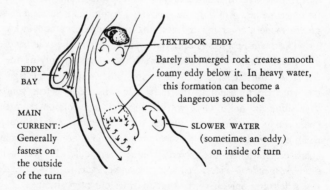

EDDY
BAY

TEXTBOOK EDDY

Barely submerged rock creates smooth foamy eddy below it. In heavy water, this formation can become a dangerous souse hole

MAIN
CURRENT:
Generally
fastest on
the outside
of the turn

SLOWER WATER
(sometimes an eddy)
on inside of turn

The usefulness of eddies and slow spots to the upstream paddler is obvious. They are the steppingstones of progress. Crossing and climbing the currents between them, you will instinctively reach down with your paddle for a firm hold on the stream bottom. If you are serious about covering ground instead of just playing with the currents, you better go the way of Mike Fink and cut yourself a pole.

The best poles are hardwood, smooth-skinned, and about twelve feet long. We have used maple saplings that are about one and a half inches in diameter at the base. Serious polers get the finished product from the lumberyard complete with a bulb at the top and a metal shoe at the bottom, but we have always eliminated the middleman. If you do the same, make sure your sapling is not taken in a preserve where cutting green wood is forbidden. More important, observe good conservation practices, such as cutting one of two twins that are blocking one another's sunlight. We have puzzled some over obtaining a proper shoe, but whenever we've tried poling we have never had a tuna can the right size. After a while, our working end gets frazzled and that's when we trim it back to good wood.

Before we go any further we should warn you: poling sounds a lot simpler on paper than it is on the water. Getting a balanced stance right, slipping the pole up for another push, switching sides—all these maneuvers come only with a lot of practice. We suggest a shallow, placid stream to start with, plus weather and wardrobe suitable for swimming—voluntary or involuntary.

The sternman, to use his pole, stands with his feet wide-based, one a little ahead of the other. When the canoe is angling into the current, the pole should be placed off the upstream gunwale so that the boat cannot drift down on it and create a catapult. If you change your tack to the current, switch poling sides at the same time. Either lift the bottom end of the pole over the canoe or just switch your hands so that the top end becomes the new working end. The latter technique is faster, but with home-grown models, reversing the pole makes it top-heavy and awkward.

Upstream progress is achieved by climbing up the pole hand over hand. The proper angle of boat to current is maintained by prying the stern into the right position. The most important thing is to pick the right tempo. If you are used to paddling upstream, you will likely defeat yourself poling by rushing too much. Once you have secured the pole on the creek bottom, you need not go hell-bent for leather to keep up momentum as you do paddling. It is better to relax for a moment and concentrate on refining your boat's orientation to the current. Unlike the paddle, the pole will hold the canoe suspended—*unless* you lose the angle. And in that case, sheer speed won't help but only drive the canoe farther out of position.

When the angle is perfect and you have taken a breath, work your way up the pole, accelerating the canoe as you go. When you get almost to the top, slip it up and out of the current, again hand over hand. Resetting the pole takes much longer than recovering a paddle stroke and can be nerve-racking for the experienced paddler. Keep cool and don't waste motion (and time) trying to hurry. Synchronize the setting of your pole to the two or three seconds when the current has stopped forward motion but has not yet pushed it back. This is the time when it is easiest to get a hold on the bottom without slipping over the rocks. Once the pole is set, you are back at the beginning of the rhythm and ready to re-establish the exact angle.

If the current is so swift that you haven't time to reset your pole before sliding downstream, it is too fast for poling. You will then need to find more eddies to hop or head for the bank where you can haul the boat hand over hand along the overhanging bushes. Or turn the boat around and run the stream as it was meant to be.

12. Riffles

Back on still waters, you trained your canoe to travel in straight lines. Once you cross into the flow of headwaters, straight lines are hard to find. The river (if you can yet dignify it with the name) meanders, hesitates, twists back on itself uncertainly. Even where it picks a surer course, thousands of boulders tumble it, shunt it, strain it into greater chaos and confusion. Straight lines are broken into countless ripples; plane geometry encounters relativity and disintegrates whirling. So it is time to let the canoe cavort after the fashion of her own lines, to outdo the river with her own play— to pivot and wiggle, to sashay, and now and then to sing down corduroy riffles. Deep down, that's the career the canoe was born to, and you can well forgive Rug his bottle of blackberry brandy.

Any paddler of small streams who attempts a literal straight line will of course be turned back haughtily. To run any twisting stream requires movements more nimble and precise than any lake demands. On flatwater, you remember, the sternman steers because canoeing is asymmetrical. But the genius of the canoe is that the craft itself is symmetrical; it works equally well backward and forward, starboard and port. In whitewater, the bowman as well as the sternman must help take the boat along the curves of the river. When that happens, the canoe recovers its natural symmetry.

It makes sense, then, that while forward and backward strokes have their place in running rapids, the lateral strokes which enable bow and stern

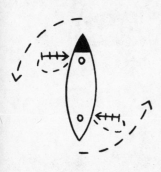

to power their ends sideways are equally important. To illustrate the laterals, let's put Rug and Peach in their canoe. Rug, as always, is bowman and paddling left; Peach is stern and on the right. Suppose they want to pivot counterclockwise (turning sharply on that almost worn-out proverbial dime). Both men perform the same stroke, the *draw*, on opposite sides of the boat. They place their paddle blades vertically in the water parallel with the keel line and straight out from the shoulder. The power side of the blade is toward the boat

(so the thumb at the T-grip faces sternward).* The key is to lean out as far as possible, farther than is comfortable at first. This will encourage you to put your whole weight over the paddle and will enable you to use the long muscles of your back in the pull of the stroke. As you bear down and pull in, the paddle will return to the gunwale, but more important, the boat will slide over to the paddle. With three or four of these strong strokes, Peach and Rug can have the boat pivoted full circle.

Properly done, the draw stroke is a firm, steadying stroke. As we'll see later, the farther out the lean, the more the paddle's motion stabilizes the whole canoe. As the canoeist reaches out, the canoe may roll a little, but should never pitch violently or bank down very far (unless it's intentional— see page 179). Actually, the tippiest part of the sequence is during recovery, when the paddle is brought closest to the gunwale: don't draw it all the way back to touch the canoe. If it strikes the stream bottom or catches a rock in that position, the paddle can wedge against the boat and lever you over-board.

Now suppose Rug and Peach want to pivot in the other direction (clockwise), as indeed they will half the time. Peach can effectively move the stern left by prying along his right gunwale. The technique is the same

---

* When we talk about the "power" face of the blade anywhere in this book, we mean the side facing the stern during a forward stroke. That is called the power face even when it is not the side pushing the water (which it is in the draw, but is not in the stern pry and some other strokes).

as for flatwater steering, except that in white-water it requires greater vigor and decisiveness. The paddle is held at an acute angle to the water-line; the grip hand is pulled in and across the chest, and the lower hand serves as an oarlock holding the shaft against the gunwale for lever-ing power. When done in a fast, pumping motion, the pry is a stronger stroke than the draw, especially when the return for the next pry is made by simply feathering the blade through the water instead of lifting it out altogether. Since the paddle is angled backward into the water, the working half (the blade) can be effectively submerged without the tip extending deep enough to hit stream bottoms. If the paddle does strike a rock, it will slide past or over it without upsetting the larger equilibrium. With experience, you'll find your-self not always clipping the paddle shaft to the gunwale in textbook fashion, but instead pushing out with your lower hand while leaving the upper hand fixed. This variation converts the pry into a longer, smoother stroke, though one that is slower to recover from. The standard pry is more useful for fish-tailing the stern between offset boulders; pushing off with the shaft feels steadier in big waves.

While Peach is prying, Rug has a choice of two radically different strokes —both of them flawed beauties. One possibility is the bow pry. It will obviously serve to move the canoe away from the paddle side just as the stern pry does, though the mechanical advantage and hence the power is reduced by the bowman's position farther from the end of the boat. Unlike the sternman, however, the bowman has to hold his paddle vertically and his stroke is limited to a shorter range of motion: a quick chop-chop, black-belt

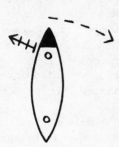

style of lever/feather/lever/feather. Just be careful not to catch a rock off balance or it becomes lever/feather/over and out. Even more serious, the pad-dle slices through the water in an awkward posi-tion that does nothing to steady the canoe. Should a wave or rock catch the canoe off guard, the stern-man prying will instinctively lay his paddle flat in the water and prop himself on it in a low brace (see page 181). The bowman prying has neither the long extension of the draw (which allows him to lean on the power face of his blade) nor the backward angle of the stern pry (which allows a low brace lean on the non-power face). So he counts on his partner's good instincts or else winds up drinking water.

Why doesn't the left-paddling bowman simply switch sides and draw to turn right? For one thing, a bowman who precipitously changes hands will create a river craft with two side wheels on the same side of the boat. Asymmetry is one thing, but this is a lopsided disaster. In the second place, it takes a certain finite time, about one quarter of a paddle beat, to accomplish the changeover. Only a short time, you say, but would you ever try to fly an airplane without one wing, even for a short time? The old truism still holds: never switch in a crisis midstream.

The bow pry does have an alternative. Somebody a long time ago (we've seen photos from the last century) learned how to do a draw stroke on the opposite side of the canoe without changing hands. Paddling on the left side, you begin this "crossdraw" holding the paddle straight out over the water in the feathered position. Next, twist your whole trunk around 90 degrees until your shoulders face the right gunwale; at the same time, your arms swing the paddle across the boat parallel to the water so the blade just clears the bow deck. The paddle should now be *parallel to* and a little above the right gunwale, and the blade face (not the shaft) perpendicular to the plane of the water. Finally you are ready to extend the paddle out and into the water, at just about the same angle as the sternman's pry (pointing ahead instead of backward, of course). Straighten your left arm and keep the right bent,

the stroke being executed by punching out with a hard right jab. Feathering the blade through the water on the return stroke is impossibly awkward; lift the paddle out of the water and start again for a series of quick jams.

We describe this stroke in such agonizing detail because it is the one most beginners get wrong. The common error is to try and put in the crossdraw the same way the draw is done—the paddle held vertically, grip hand high in the air. Hold the grip hand low and back at belt level; then the blade angles forward properly. Fortunately the stroke takes less time to perform than to describe, but even so, the paddle must still be switched from on side to off side and back again when completed. Furthermore, like the bow pry, the crossdraw leaves the bowman in a less than ideal position for bracing. All this means the stroke occasionally invites miscalculations. The hand may be quicker than the eye, but the river's eyes are faster than yours or ours.

Choosing between the bow pry and the crossdraw is largely a matter of previous training, current fashion, and personal style. For wilderness cruising with heavy boats we generally prefer the crossdraw. It is a stroke which is at

first difficult to conceive, but the bow pry is the one more difficult to perfect. And a misplaced or unlucky pry can snap a paddle, while even the best-placed stroke wears the shaft as the paddle strains against the gunwale. Fiberglass and aluminum paddles, however, obviate these complaints enough to turn the choice back to individual idiosyncrasies. Some canoe teams as they anticipate certain maneuvers work out a system for both men to switch sides during a quieter interlude so that the bowman can work from his strong draw side. This method works well for a single paddler and for two people racing a familiar course; less so for free-lance rambling on a strange river.

So much for pinwheeling and the basic whitewater strokes. Two people doing complementary draws and pries can spin a canoe, but small-stream canoeing is at the third remove from such simple maneuvering, requiring a whole choreography of infinitely varying paddle sequences. Let's take things slowly. We started with a simple pinwheel around one point. Now we want to show you how the complexity of maneuvering increases, layer by layer, as you work away from the pinwheel and into the various curves in a stream course.

At first remove: Obviously, one person's stroke does not commit his partner to its equivalent. For this reason, it's important to understand that a canoe reacts differently to one person drawing than it does to two. Not only is the applied force cut in half but the canoe turns along a different axis.

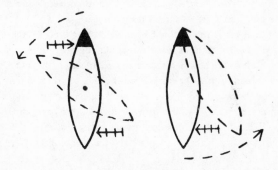

Suppose Peach is busy drawing while Rug takes a breather. Instead of spinning around its center point, the boat's fulcrum shifts to a point very near where the bow meets the waterline. Try it in your own canoe or push a pencil around your kitchen sink to convince yourself. Thus if only one man is working to turn the boat, he can with some extra effort set the canoe at the same angle to the current, but his absolute position in that current will be quite different than if his partner helps.

Let's have Rug and Peach launch their canoe into a straight stretch on a fast little stream that is conveniently flowing toward the top of our page. The only obstacle in sight is a solitary boulder directly downstream. Once again Rug is napping and Peach, too proud to ask for help, decides to clear it himself. Look what happens. Whichever way he decides to go, right or left, the stern stroke will place the canoe at a suitable angle for paddling clear but unfortunately will also position the canoe farther downstream and closer to the rock as well as on the opposite side from which it now has to go.

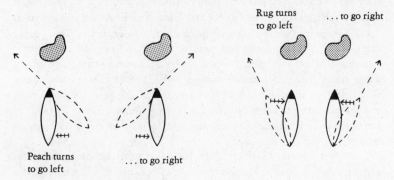

Rug turns
to go left

. . . to go right

Peach turns
to go left

. . . to go right

Better to let Rug in the bow initiate the turn; he will draw the bow upstream away from the rock and will pull the whole canoe to the side of the rock he's heading for. Then Peach is in the best position to kick the stern around and set the canoe back on its downstream course.

This maneuver is the simplest imaginable, but even so, the timing and coordination of strokes leads to a staggering number of small variations. Going by the book, the bowman crossdraws, then both men paddle, and finally the sternman draws. But if the initial turn is critical, both men may be needed to power the boat around; therefore the sequence may run: bow crossdraw/stern pry, forward/forward, forward/draw. Other times the rhythm may reverse itself: forward/pry, forward/forward, draw/draw. Or the tempo may quicken: crossdraw/pry, forward/draw. And the mapping of dance steps goes on and on.

How does a pair of canoeists agree on what variation is best? The answer of course is that the river calls the tune. Now and then it may present only a single obstruction and allow you to improvise, but in a genuine boulder garden the score is far more specific. So we must hike our calculations a step and view the situation. . . .

At second remove: Here we've got Peach and Rug approaching the same boulder as before, only this time it's among friends. At position A, Peach and Rug already have to anticipate the proper angle for finding the break in that first string of beads. The only chute is to the right of our original boulder,

and at B, Rug is crossdrawing mightily to reach it. But once there, another boulder threatens, so at C, both men will be drawing and prying to arrive at D. Once past that gap, they must decide which course to take around the big boulder. And so it goes.

At third remove: Canoes, as we have said, aren't inspired and don't move by straight lines. All combinations of strokes take on meaning and direction only in relation to the roving current you are riding. River currents have curiosity and you will find them searching from bank to bank, pausing (for air?) behind ledges, going back to take a second look at a passing rock. And since curiosity implies exuberance, they will tug you along too. Let's put that last nest of boulders in realistic perspective, somewhere on the Moisie where the river's needle suddenly veers west around a bend (page 140).

Points to note: The chute through the first line of rocks is aligned perfectly with the main current of the stream; our canoe has no business being at position A and Rug has no business napping. The trickiest spot, however, is at D. As you can see, the current leading to the outside of the stream is threatening to smash the canoe on the next rock amidships. More than that though, the current itself is differential, being faster to the outside of the turn and at the stern of our canoe. Thus the river is working not only to run the canoe amok but also to swing it broadside both to the rock below and to the general direction of flow. The solution is not difficult so long as the canoeists, especially Peach in the stern, anticipate the action of the water.

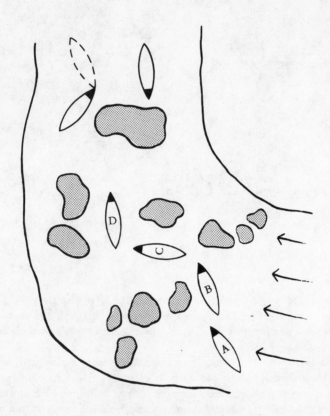

The danger lies with overturning. Peach in fact hardly needs to pry at all to get from C to D. The river will do his work, and, if it is feeling frisky, Peach had better be prepared to *draw* his end over right, to the inside of the bank! Rug has responsibilities too. A draw on the bow's left to keep the boat parallel to the current may become necessary if Peach's timing is slow. More important, Rug should choose to head left of the big rock downstream. This is the river's own inclination and to fight it needlessly is a violation of first principles.

This is not to say that the expert canoeist simply trundles along in the mainstream: his philosophy of motion is rather to use all the river's currents to his own purposes, to work elaborations on the river's own baroque. Imagine that the current here is at riptide, the turn below our last set of rocks is sharp, and the view below obscured by overhanging evergreen. The prudent voyageur is not about to take chances in the river's deepest channel—he wants to work his way to shore for a look-see. To do so, he will cut to the inside bank, where the current slows to an amble. With the bow pointing to shore, the faster midstream current spins the canoe about-face so that it beaches bow upstream.

An even more convenient landing field may be the eddy directly below the last rock. A swift current will throw thirty feet or more of quiet water behind a barrier, plenty of room to spot a canoe.

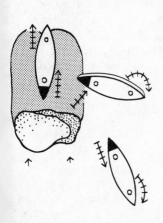

This maneuver, the *eddy turn,* is a basic component of successful river running and a work of grace if you allow the river to amplify your strokes. Approach the eddy at an angle of about thirty degrees—the wider the angle, the easier the turn—and aim to cut into the eddy only inches downstream from the master rock. As the nose of the canoe crosses the eddy line, the bowman reaches out to draw or crossdraw; the paddle is placed in the calm spot just below the rock. Lean out strongly on this draw—it serves to steady the canoe, which can be expected to flutter a bit if the current differential is large and the water turbulent. The primary intent and function of the stroke of course is to turn the boat, which it does admirably. Give credit where it's due, though: bow in slow water, stern in fast—the river does the rest. On an authoritative draw, the bowman feels like he is swinging on a maypole. If smartly placed, a single stroke will do; the recovery phase will be a forward stroke prodding the canoe right up to butt the rock. The sternman meanwhile feels like he is on the snap end of crack-the-whip. His job is to help the river swing his end around, and keep the bow pushed up snug to the eddy.

The main mistake novices make in an eddy turn is a failure to keep the turn tight. By the time the boat has swung its U turn, they are too far downstream to catch the eddy. The following points should be of help. *Bowman:* Put your draw or crossdraw in *only* when the bow's nose is in the calm eddy water. A draw in the main current is counterproductive, since it allows the fast current to sweep you downstream. Secondly, be ready to switch back to a forward stroke once your boat has completed its turn, especially if you've pivoted on a crossdraw. With the boat tending to slip downstream, the stern will want your help in keeping snug to the eddy. Once the pivot's done, the crossdraw is of no use. *Sternman:* Once the nose is in the eddy, a quick pry or draw helps the river to make the turn; but don't forget that you will need a series of forward strokes to keep the boat heading upstream. With the bow-man using the draw to turn, the stern draw or sweep is the natural com-bination; with a bow crossdraw, the stern pries—and has to work harder be-cause the pry itself tends to push the boat downstream. At the end of the stroke, quickly slice your blade forward in the water and begin a regular forward stroke. The vigor of your moves is what counts: lean hard into the forward stroke, use the knees and hips to lever the end of the boat around during the pry.

With practice, the whole sequence becomes fast, intuitive, fluid. Bowman hangs in the eddy, sternman pries and shifts with a hip, canoe and river careen on their curves. Then the quiet satisfaction of arrival, the ease of watching the canoe bobble and bump in its shelter. Time perhaps for a nature break, and the chance to crane around to inspect the river that is waiting below.

IV. THE UPPER STRETCHES

13. Scouting

Youngsters each have their own way of growing up. For some, the transition through adolescence into adulthood is placid, uneventful, imperceptible. Others tear into this middle period more uproariously before slowing down to settle the primary direction of their lives. Of the remainder, there are a few delinquents who turn savage as if overnight. Their development contains no subtlety; and the mayhem they wreak warns all bystanders of the violent turbulence within. The Moisie, we love her, but she has a delinquent heart.

And she has grown in her first forty miles: through some little lakes and one large one, enlarged by feeder streams and invisible seeping springs, swollen now by the ice melting on the upper lakes. We know we've missed the river's crest (water's down six feet on some bushes) but judging by the roots it has another six to drop. The rapids we're on begin innocently enough. The slope is gentle and dotted with roundheads, only here and there pockmarked by a few jagged boulders. But around the first bend, the river's murmur takes on an edge of excitement. Rug stands for a longer view and then sits abruptly in deference to an approaching rock. Without need of spoken command, his boat starts to prefer the left boundary of upcoming boulders; soon it is out of the midriver channel and cruising within hailing distance of the east bank. Joe's boat follows as if on a string. The middle now is chopped up into standing waves of respectable stature but the roundheads are stout and keep the tall waves busy with conversation. This would make a sporting run in unloaded boats and somewhere close to a farmhouse stove, but here our wilderness trucks are glad to take safe convoy in the moderate swells along the river's edge.

The inside of the next turn hugs a large, sharp bluff comprised of crumbling red rock. Rug's eyes are on the river as the lead canoe points around the bend, but a blind man could do as well. Once past that baffle of soft rock, the river speaks in thunderclaps. Again without a word, Rug backpaddles, and two strokes behind, Peach pries the stern into the bank. The second canoe catches the vine of an alder ten feet upriver. From our vantage, we can see that the brush-cut surface of the bluff wraps around to form a small plateau through which the river cuts deeply.

And now, for the first time, we begin to understand the import of the Mayor's unsolicited and unwanted advice. It appears that at low water, a passable rock shelf exists between cliff wall and river current. For us, in late June during the winter's runoff, rushing water and solid ground meet at perpendicular angles. We had expected rapids here from the step-up in gradient on the topos, but how in Lord's name had we overlooked the three contour lines that squeeze together at the river? Rug turns to Peach and says, "Looks like we get a chance to scout these chutes from a hundred and fifty feet up."

In the most literal sense, scouting is part of all whitewater runs; every rapids has to be read before it can be paddled or detoured. But everybody knows the scout is the fellow who cruises ahead of the wagons to spy out dangers and mark the route. On a long wilderness river, plenty of stretches are going to require a thorough job, the kind that means leaving the canoes and legging it along the shore. It's usually not difficult to decide whether a piece of water deserves a close look from the bank. If the rapids look borderline, you obviously scout. If you can hear but can't see around a blind corner, you scout. If the rapids are negotiable but you're not sure what's beyond the turn, get out and scout. If you catch butterflies from the view ahead, take the time and scout. Even if a drop like Niagara makes the need for portage obvious, you'll be better off scouting your route than charging through unbroken country without a trail or clear destination.

A reliable scout (and a scout is either reliable or worse than worthless) is careful to check the whole length of the rapids being surveyed. Elementary on paper, but this principle needs all the moral force of the Ten Commandments to push a hiker through muskeg and briars when he is tired and more interested in canoeing than in trailblazing. Rim Canyon (for so we named that stretch on the Moisie) discouraged a close look by surrounding its bluff cliffs with draws, ravines, tangles of evergreen, and everywhere sharp boulders more appropriate to a moonscape. But Rug knew enough to persevere from the time he had scouted Long Rapids on the Missinaibi River, a three-mile stretch much like Rim Canyon. There, he had almost overlooked a twenty-foot falls at the midpoint. Near misses like this can happen when the terrain is a jumble of vertical pitches, but make sure they remain *near* misses —there may be no return from total oversight.

Just as important as catching a glimpse of the full length of the river is the chance to study any questionable water from several vantage points upstream and downstream. When the topography is stubborn and refuses the opportunity, certain allowances have to be made quite consciously for your limited perspective. If you are only able to view a rapids from above, say from the top of a cliff, its features will be drastically flattened. Consequently, it becomes quite impossible to evaluate the height of standing waves. Wet experience has convinced us that if you can even see a wave from fifty feet up, it is probably a monster, the variety that eats uncovered canoes for lunch. Distance can lead to misperceptions that may be equally dangerous. Rug learned this lesson back at Long Rapids (that water hole was an admirable primer). The only view he got of that middle falls was from the rim of the wall opposite where he intended to route his party. The falls looked ferocious enough—no trouble with that call; and the far side seemed to offer a broad expanse of gravel that would serve nearly as well as blacktop to portage canoes and gear. After Rug and the others committed themselves to following the shoreline instead of going overland, they found that the gravel viewed from afar had enlarged itself to rocks six feet high. Just remember, large obstacles shrink over long distances; Sanforize your judgments when you can't get close.

The most helpful perspectives, if you can beat your way to them, are from directly upstream and downstream. The easiest and clearest view is from below looking up. The back sides of the rocks are exposed and the eddies stand in plain sight. With your mind's eye tracing a path of least resistance and maybe a finger in the dirt translating for your partner's benefit, reading rapids from downstream is as enjoyable a leisure as skimming the morning paper. Find what you like best and memorize it; but before you return to your canoe for the run, hike the shoreline and study the river from upstream.

At first glance on the return trip, it won't look like the same river. Most rapids appear more violent from above and all appear more confusing. Where once you saw bare rock, now you see water congealing into dark mounds, then slewing off in white foam; the eddies disappear altogether behind these fluid hillocks while the white flotsam runs together in swirls that obscure what from below looked like the self-evident single best course. With more study you will discern the correlation between up and down, Yin and Yang, but even so it helps to pick out the two or three most unmistakable landmarks, features of the river or shoreline that you can key on when you finally get to see the rapids from the final and most critical perspective—that is, when the rocks are moving past and the current is standing still.

The essence of reading white water, of course, is learning the language. As with any form of communication, mastery requires exposure and practice, but familiarity with the alphabet and basic vocabulary is easily learned. Let's begin, then, syllable by syllable, with one rock in a straight current. Any rock at or close to water level will create a hummock as the current slides over it, as well as a following wave downstream. The size of the wave depends (in part) on the velocity of the flow. A still current produces no wake at all, which is why canvas canoe bottoms are threatened more by shallow lakes than by swiftly moving streams: the canoeist looks for and reads *water,* not

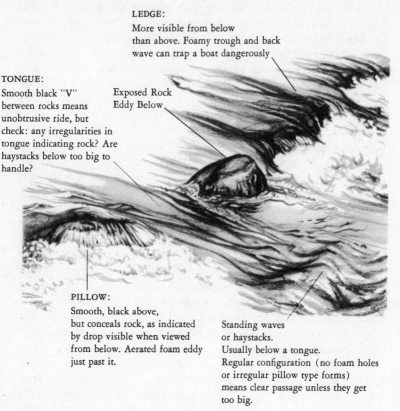

LEDGE:
More visible from below
than above. Foamy trough and back
wave can trap a boat dangerously

TONGUE:
Smooth black "V"
between rocks means
unobtrusive ride, but
check: any irregularities in
tongue indicating rock? Are
haystacks below too big to
handle?

Exposed Rock
Eddy Below

PILLOW:
Smooth, black above,
but conceals rock, as indicated
by drop visible when viewed
from below. Aerated foam eddy
just past it.

Standing waves
or haystacks.
Usually below a tongue.
Regular configuration (no foam holes
or irregular pillow type forms)
means clear passage unless they get
too big.

rocks. At one end of the scale are the water hummocks overlying small stones; at the other, are huge *souse holes,* caused by a fast, full river cascading over large boulders. Between these extremes the waves come in all sizes. The seasoned eye can estimate the depth of the rock by the way the current spits below it, and can thus tell whether a canoe stern will clear or grunch.

The shape of the underlying rock also contributes to the shape of its wave. With round rocks in moderate current, the water passes over them in a smooth hump, not a wave. Whatever turbulence is engendered follows *downstream* of the rock—how far downstream depending on how fast the current and how deep the rock. The deeper the rock, the more downstream the waves; as the boulder becomes bigger and obstructs closer to the water's surface, water pillows over smoothly and drops more steeply below. The key

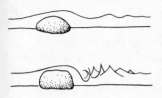

on these round rocks is to realize that you will hang up not in the waves below, but on the deceptive smooth pillow above. Jagged rocks produce less regular wave configurations, and fortunately for the canoeist, they are a tiny (though vocal) minority. The problem is that their sharp edges can slice water and therefore minimize commotion. They are harder to spot, easier to clip, and do more damage to the victimized boat. This is why rapids under bridges where the builders have dropped granite debris are more treacherous than they look. Even worse are those stretches of river where industrial man has planted poles or spikes for logging or other purposes. They can spear a boat dead, yet send up hardly a ripple to betray their existence.

Rocks in fast rivers rarely live alone, and neighbors will deflect, redraw, and otherwise disturb the wave pattern of any rock. Two rocks a canoe width apart will join forces, squeeze the flow between them, and then pile it up below into a standing wave larger than either would merit alone. The smooth V of the tongue between rocks usually marks a clear path through the chute, so long as that standing wave is manageable. On the other hand, one rock may hide in the quiet water of another's eddy and become nearly invisible. A hard-running bowman should be on the lookout to steer clear of them; even more emphatically, that bowman had better watch before attempting to swing into any eddy. A rock two inches below the surface that inspires only a diffident little wave can bump the keel of a spinning boat sharply, and send it spinning in new directions.

Ledges behave differently than rocks, differently even than a long row of flat rocks. Instead of jumping up at the river, rivers jump down from

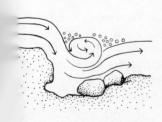

them. The resulting wave pattern is not only different, but also more dangerous. Water tumbling over any vertical pitch, even one as short as a foot or two, wears a hole in the water and rock below and then curls back upstream to set up a rolling circular motion. The down-moving half of the circle creates a hydraulic jump, a watery reef that traps whatever—or whoever—is unlucky enough to enter Davy Jones's lagoon. The logical way out is to swim down deep underwater and catch the main undertow out, but this act of faith might be difficult to bring yourself to the first time. Ledges and small falls are also justifiably notorious for great quantities of white foam. This froth is dense enough to swamp a canoe but not dense enough to float one. Nor will it float any ejected occupants. The best policy for open boats is to avoid dropping over ledges big enough to create rollers and back waves.

Even this, the simplest of all solutions, requires care because ledges have a deceit of their own to work. One of our favorite spots is a ledge on the upper Hudson we call the Hook. In medium water, the entire river turns and rips through a rocky chute on the left side. The whole right and middle is a ledge with perhaps three feet of drop. At this water level, hardly any current flows over it, so it is quite harmless. But it looks like any other ledge—that is, from upstream *it is invisible.* The approaching canoeist's line of vision passes straight overhead; all he sees is smooth water. The only indication of a ledge on a strange river may be the roar of the cascading current or the presence of rough water along a parallel line. Think about it; if you can see whitewater on one half of the river and not the other, what looks flat has to be dropping so fast that it falls completely out of sight. Anyway, Rug especially enjoys the Hook for baiting novice paddlers. The only beginner so far who didn't have to step out red-faced and drag his boat over dry ledge was Peach; not because he reasoned the problem out, but because he wanted to shoot the big stuff.

So the rule holds: canoeists read water, not rocks or ledges or other obstacles. The paddler thus has to know that not all waves are formed by water striking solid surfaces. *Standing waves,* or *"haystacks,"* represent the dissipation of energy that occurs when current coming off a steep slope arrives at deeper water traveling at a slower pace. Thus neat orderly rows of tall waves that gradually decrease in amplitude offer a real joyride, until they swamp you. The smallest variation in the contour of one of these waves, however, should warn you of a lurking rock. Whether or not it is high enough to knock keels you will learn in time, from what can be truly hard experience.

Once you have read a particular rapids, you are left with the decision of whether to run it. First consideration naturally goes to the sheer difficulty of the whitewater. The river's gradient, as we told you earlier, offers a useful, though imperfect guide. Equally important is the complexity, not so much of the whole rapids but of the specific course you would run. The sequence of events within a rapids may be decisive. For example, large standing waves near the top of a run might discourage you from an attempt, though you would be willing to chance swamping at the end of the same set. Volume of water is another factor. Even a fractional rise in water level will increase velocity, exaggerate existing current differentials, create new ones, raise tall standing waves from the dead, and make giants of their low-water survivors.

All this diminishes lead time for decisions and demands greater precision in handling a boat. A heavy rain can increase even a moderate-sized river's level of difficulty by an order of magnitude; spring flood, as any good mayor can tell you, will transform a river beyond recognition.

One of the most useful ways to classify whitewater is by the international rating system sanctioned in this country by the American Whitewater Affiliation. Rapids are graded from I (very easy) to VI (risk to life) according to the scale we've reprinted in the accompanying table. While it

A Summary of River Difficulty Classification

I   EASY   Sand banks, bends without difficulty, occasional small rapids with waves regular and low. Correct course easy to find, with only minor obstacles like pebble banks, riffles at bridge piers. River speed less than hard backpaddling speed.

II   MEDIUM   Fairly frequent but unobstructed rapids, usually with regular waves, easy eddies, and easy bends. Course generally easy to recognize.

III   DIFFICULT   Maneuvering in rapids necessary. Small falls, large regular waves covering boat, numerous rapids. Passages clear though narrow, requiring expertise in maneuver. Scouting usually needed.

IV   VERY DIFFICULT   Long extended stretches of rapids, high irregular waves with boulders directly in current. Boiling eddies, broken water, abrupt bends. Scouting mandatory first time. Powerful and precise maneuvering required.

V   EXTRAORDINARILY DIFFICULT   Extremely difficult, long, and very violent rapids, following each other almost without interruption. River bed extremely obstructed. Big drops, violent current, very steep gradient. Scouting necessary but difficult; extensive experience necessary.

VI   LIMIT OF NAVIGABILITY   Grade V carried to the extreme. Nearly impossible and very dangerous. Only for teams of experts, at favorable levels and after close study with all precautions.

tells nothing of the river's individuality to say that Racehorse Rapids below the Hook is grade II–III in medium water and grade III at higher levels, it does give the next paddler down a rough idea of what he can expect.

Factors other than the quality of water itself, none of them trivial, will bear upon wilderness scouting decisions. Your experience, obviously. If you are out with expert friends, they may be willing to offer commentary and guidance; but you should always be making your own assessments too, since your ultimate aim is to become yourself a qualified judge. The size of the pool below a rapids can be crucial. Sane whitewater men don't risk even moderate runs that conclude with waterfalls, a power-plant turbine, or other dangerous formations. Cold water should deter any long risky runs unless all paddlers are protected by wet suits. Time of day may tip the balance if a rescue would carry into dark or too many muscles have already stretched beyond the call of duty. Finally, there is the question of accessibility or lack of it. A capsize in an isolated wilderness area can cause more anguish and certainly more lost time than losing a boat altogether on an afternoon outing. On the other hand, canoeists don't run wilderness rivers for the sake of perfect comfort and absolute security. Our own compromise once we get fifty miles or so away from a friendly hand is to apply the nine-of-ten test. Don't ask yourself if you could run a particular rapids; ask if you would be able to run it nine times out of ten without mishap. Someone will ask about the tenth time, but it seems to us that if you could run the thing ten times over, you probably aren't scouting it in the first place.

Some rapids will look all right for seven or eight times only. If the problem is swamper waves, you may gain sufficient advantage (with open boats) by portaging your gear and running the canoe through empty. If the problem is really huge waves, one man can sometimes bring a boat down single. Other times it may be possible to line the canoe from shore or to improvise some combination of all these techniques.

If capsizing is a real or even remote possibility, give some thought to organizing a rescue. The first boat, after a successful run, should turn and wait for the others as a mobile emergency unit. Before that first passage, it is sometimes worth stationing one or two people below with safety lines. Secure the fixed end to a sizable dowager of a tree or rock but tie no other knots or monkey fists; they catch more rocks and crevices than boats and swimmers.

We intend to cover the details of rescue work later; for now, we mention it only as one of the possibilities. That is the essence of scouting after all: assessing a set of possibles. As for Rim Canyon, we made our way to the rude animal trail that followed the top of the cliff, nerved ourselves to the edge of the precipice, and studied hard. Between the waves we eyed from a hundred and fifty feet up and the brushy animal path, the possibles narrowed fast toward the latter.

14. Lining

If your rivers run anything like ours, you'll wind up scouting a fair share of teasers, the almost runnables. Maybe it's a twisting staircase that looks worth trying except for a vertical falls at the end. Or a fast turn on a smaller stream that threatens to pull any entering boat straight into a low-hanging tree. Another time, it's the problem of crossing a powerful current where the slightest sideslip will rip you into midriver and heavy water. The variations are endless. A narrows filled with rollicking big waves but no room to pull over and bail. A boulder garden requiring sixteen-foot pivots by a seventeen-foot boat. An overhanging ledge diabolically placed to knock off a passing head.

Any of these situations and plenty more are good reasons for lining. The strategy is simple: you secure one rope each to the bow and stern of the canoe, send the loaded boat back into the river, and by remote control maneuver the whole outfit downriver (or upriver as the case may be).* The theory works because a rope snubbed at the right moment carries an absolute authority that a paddle can purchase only in the best of times.

In the abstract, lining a canoe through whitewater is elegant and appealing. Out on the riverbank, it's mosquitoes, black flies, and bulldogs† fighting over poaching rights, ropes tangling in your hands, and the damn alder bushes trying to decide whether to keep barking at your shins or to pitch you into the river and have done with it. Nobody who has given lining a fair try would ever go back to it except that the only alternatives are portaging or risking your necks in some rapids you don't belong in. For our part, when it comes down to those choices, we pull over and dig out the tracking lines.

---

* Some canoeists prefer to secure their lines looped *around* the bow and stern of the canoe; and we've noticed the technique mentioned in nineteenth-century accounts. We've always just used our long painters, which have worked fine for us, and so can't comment on the advantages or disadvantages of the other technique.

† North Country horseflies.

Experts will differ on the best rope to use. Manila is heavy, gets heavier when it soaks up water, and rots. Nylon and the other synthetics are extremely strong for weight, but at least a quarter-inch braid is necessary to offer a firm grip. Three-eighths-inch rope hefts even better and has less tendency to snarl. Nylon stretches, a property you'll hardly notice in short lengths, but a loaded canoe at the end of fifty feet of it behaves like a monkey on a rubber band. Dacron and polypropylene are not so elastic but because they are stiffer they don't fold into neat coils like nylon. They also bite deeper into the wallet. Polyethylene floats, which helps in rescue work, but it is impossibly slippery for this and many other uses. Our choice was nylon.

We don't feel we can maintain even a semblance of control over a canoe on a rope longer than fifty feet. Call that the maximum length for each painter. If you can manage with twenty-five feet, so much the better; boat control will be tighter and there is no sense coping with an extra twenty-five feet of trouble, bow and stern. But in crabby terrain and in high-water conditions (when the foliage extends right over the river) you may find the longer lengths handy. Of course, it's all right to remain flexible and keep a couple of extra twenty-five-foot coils in the pack to tie on when necessary. The best knot for joining the two lines is the sheet bend, though you might want to overdo with a double sheet bend when trusting your entire outfit to it. The fisherman's knot, used by climbers on their big ropes, also works well.

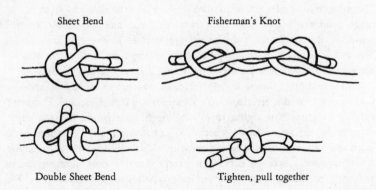

Sheet Bend

Fisherman's Knot

Double Sheet Bend

Tighten, pull together

The American storybook is full of lone trappers one-manning their fur-laden boats up mountain streams with bow line in one hand, stern line in the other. Adventurers these days are unlikely to come across well-groomed towpaths that would make this technique feasible. In the most congenial country, we found that two people, one on each line, could walk the boat along at a comfortable snail's pace—a drunken snail, mind you. In rougher topography, we found it faster to bring one canoe through at a time—two people on the ropes, a third and perhaps the fourth splashing or thrashing to an outcrop downstream to await a toss of the line. The first two would then work their way down and repeat the piggyback routine.

Successful execution naturally depends on successful tosses. If there is a secret, it lies with the proper coiling of the ropes. The rope can never be allowed to fall haphazardly or it will snag in the underbrush, catch under rocks, and if that doesn't roil you enough, twist by itself into knots of frustration. Never coil the rope around your bent elbow, as you would to stuff it in your pack or hang it on a nail; it will contort even more miserably. Instead, lay the coils one by one into the flat of your left hand (if you are

right-handed), and grasp them with your thumb. The free end of the rope remains nearest the wrist. In this manner you can guide the canoe via the painter with your free right hand while the line plays out smoothly and effortlessly from the left as if it were wound on a drum with a brake. To toss the line to the next man, slide the coil into your right hand so that the free end faces out. Or, if there is plenty of open space and good footing, you can divide the loops between both hands and throw two-handed. With practice, though, you'll learn to throw as far with one.

There are a number of ways to set the canoe out into the current. A shove, a kick, or a poke with a stick will do. Controlling the movements of the boat once it's out in the river is scarcely more complicated. To bring the canoe upstream, downstream, or toward the bank, simply tug the lines in the appropriate direction. Moving the canoe away from the near shore is done by the same physical principles that make tacking a sailboat possible. The bow line is pulled in while the stern line is held slack until the boat is set at an angle of twenty to forty degrees to the current (the slower the current, the broader the angle). By holding the canoe in this fixed position and not allowing downstream drift, the current striking the keel line will push the canoe nearly straight out.

The important point is that the key relationships are between the canoe and the current it is riding, not the configuration of the shoreline. The canoe, if it is placed into a jet that is ripping away from the bank, is going to zoom out with it regardless of the setting angle. After all, your boat is going to be canoeing whitewater even if you are not. Therefore everything you know about running rapids is useful in lining them. Stopper waves, for example, will hold up a lined boat as surely as one that's paddled. (More surely. Lining a boat deprives it of three hundred pounds of momentum.) Similarly, the uphill slope of any large haystack will slow up the drifting boat and tempt it to broach. And once the canoe swings broadside, it can crunch rocks, dip into curlers, hang in eddies, and in dozens of ways confound the man who wants desperately to push with rope that is good only for pulling. Desperation quickly turns to despair if the sternman panics and pulls too sharply on the rear line when the canoe is caught in big water. The stern will burrow into the downslope of the wave behind it; if the sternman doesn't catch on and continues his tug of war with the river, that wave will climb the upstream gunwale and sink the whole barge.

Conservative judgment has its place, but not in the middle of a pot-boiler. Scouting is the time, as much for lining as for paddling, to anticipate the action of the water and its cross currents. Before you commit your canoe to a stretch of wild water you dare not run yourself, plan the whole sequence of maneuvers that will be necessary to negotiate it. You may work out surprising stunts: we have lined through boulder gardens by hopping boulder to boulder ourselves in midriver, have lined through chutes from the top of small cliffs, and have shuttled one another out to exposed ledge rock in the middle of a thirty-foot falls so that we could portage down the slanting rock to the pool below. In none of these spots nor in the more conventional lining does safety or success lie with halfhearted measures or with hugging the boat in trouble directly back to shore.

If a veteran river rat can be teased by the almost runnables, his temptation is tenfold when it comes to that other class of water—the almost linables. On the Moisie we knew that, and did our best to allow for it. Especially after the shock of Rim Canyon, especially on blind turns where the river drops out of sight.

Rug and Peach are giving one such turn the scout, with Jim and Joe waiting upstream with the flies. Fifteen minutes later, Rug and Peach return.

"Well," says Rug. "You're not going to like this one."

"We portage," says Joe. "I was afraid of that."

"Maybe. But Peach and I would like to try lining it. You two can choose for yourselves after watching our luck. It's a nice rapids all the way down, except this big rooster at the end would swamp us. Packs alone should survive, *if* the curl on the wave doesn't sink us."

"The bowman will just have to be quick about pulling the boat through it, that's all," says Jim.

Peach laughs.

"There's a catch," says Rug. "The bowman won't be able to see the canoe."

"What's that supposed to mean?"

"The rooster is right at the corner of the river where a big rock juts out. It's maybe eight feet high, about the size of a house trailer. But we got a scheme to get around it. We station one man up from the rock, one guy on it, and the other guys downstream. The upstream guy—we figure that'll be Joe—starts with both lines; he works the boat down, then throws the bow rope to Peach on the rock. We lower the boat some more until Peach has enough line to toss it to me and Jim. It'll take at least two of us to hold the boat if she fills up. When the boat hits the big wave, Peach shouts to us to pull the bow through. Meanwhile Joe will throw the stern rope to Peach."

"It's your boat, Peach," says Jim.

"Well," says Peach. "Just don't miss my toss, is all."

So we take our places. It turns out Jim is tall enough to see the boat poke its nose into the rooster tail and he pulls on cue. Since he is pulling from shore the boat cuts into the uphill slope at a steep angle. At that instant, Peach's stern rope catches on the edge of the table rock. Instead of pivoting freely the canoe starts to hog into the trough. A little water curls over the gunwale but just as things look serious the stern rope slips over the corner and the canoe breasts over the wave triumphant. We score against the river—by millimeters.

Rug and Jim go into conference.

"That was a little close," Rug says. "What do you think about your boat?"

"You mean *Joe's* boat. I don't know. The rock gave us some trouble, but we ought to be able to learn from that mistake and do better on the second run." He shrugs his shoulders, "Let's leave it up to Joe. If Admiral Cautious is game, so am I."

At that moment, without prompting of any kind, Joe calls down, "Let's start the second one through." Jim and Rug are amazed, wonder if they're the ones turning into Nellies. Joe does not bother to mention—indeed has no way of knowing—that his upstream position above the table rock prevented him from seeing the first canoe's spectacular broach in the wave.

Jim, Nellie or not, takes the extra precaution of tying the free end of the bow line to a rock. Peach shouts, "Pull!" and simultaneously receives the stern toss from Joe. This time he takes care it doesn't catch on the table. Without that brake, the canoe pivots in the wave with full force, so fast that it tears the rope out of Peach's hand, all except one loop of the coil, which spins down into a clove hitch that locks his wrist in a death grip. Running across the width of the big rock, Peach is barely able to extricate himself in time. This struggle, a contest between one wave and another, water against adrenaline, pulls the canoe up short as if in astonishment. Failing to climb the wave on first wind, it broadsides and swamps in one gulp.

Satisfied at last, the Moisie grabs the boat bodily and flings it downstream—through the rooster, not over it. Forty-five feet of nylon stretch and stretch but slowly our silver whale swings a giant arc toward shore.

Rug, breathless, turns to Jim. "For Christ's sake, get your camera out. What a sight!"

"I know," says Jim. He goes nowhere.

"*Well?*"

"The camera's in the boat."

15. For the Record

The camera was out there all right, bucking the waves with the rest of the gear. Until we hauled in our fifty-foot tether, Jim naturally had his apprehensions—but they were not major ones. A two-hundred-dollar investment in camera equipment is well worth protecting in advance, and he had. Photography gear needs to be as absolutely waterproof as a sleeping bag—more so, since cameras dry out with even less grace than down bags. At the same time, a camera is no good packed inside three layers of plastic. All the best pictures are unexpected ones, and the object in nature photography is to stalk the moose, not the camera.

Our solution was simple, cheap, and effective: we bought an army surplus ammunition box. The size suitable for holding a camera and extra film goes for only a couple of dollars; it opens and closes quickly, and withstands the knocks and abrasions of an expedition better than the plastic stowage bags now available in some outdoor shops. The key area to watch is the rubber gasket seal. Load your ammo box with rocks and sink it in the nearest bathtub for a couple hours to check for seepage. (Jim's brother Pete neglected this test once, and his SLR camera drowned in a subsequent capsize.) Even with a watertight seal, you may find that on cold mornings a film of moisture has condensed on the inside of the camera lens. This is not the fault of the ammo box, and can be remedied by taking the camera out into the sun, where the condensation will evaporate in about ten minutes' time. During the day's paddle, the box fits easily under either the bow or stern seat, ready for quick access. Always tie it with good nylon cord to the seat.

It's funny, though: here we were hauling in our boat, when we'd ought to be concentrating only on that nylon rope—and Rug thinks of taking pictures. It's the kind of thing that dispells the notion that you're so far away from the civilized world that you've forgotten the routine of one day after another—plain history, if you will. You'd think being on a big river like that would force you to focus on the present moment alone: the rooster tail, the falls around Rim Canyon, whatever. That's true enough; but then there's the camera. Deep down, there's no getting around the fact that the camera's an intrusion. Joe had the clearness of perception to understand better than any of us. He never could see why we took so much time getting a piece of paper with a picture of the canoe in the water instead of drinking in the sight right *then and there.* He's right, of course, but we have the last word. Here and now has become then and there. The camera is tacit recognition that even the river can't hold us in its presence (or should we say presents?) forever. However much we savor, the time will come when we won't be able to, save secondhand. So the camera is there, diluting the present with a little bit of past and future.

Everyone has to make his own compromise on this issue. Some will be purists and leave Kodak behind. But even they should take along a small five-by-eight spiral notebook and pen or pencil. Whatever you do, keep a journal and keep it religiously. Time and distance blur memories of an encounter with a river, no matter how powerful. Go back to the journals and your concrete notations will spark a train of recollections you never believed you possessed. It doesn't matter how you write; just put down what comes. Hearne was remarkably matter-of-fact about his travels on the Barren Grounds, and Mackenzie often satisfied himself with notations about the number of Indians met and the progress in miles per day. Stefansson had the analytical mind of the sociologist; his insights could be penetrating not only when he studied Eskimo cultures as an anthropologist but also when he turned his mind to others on his own expeditions. Canoeists we've known have also kept naturalists' journals, pressing leaves and ferns between covers; one erstwhile philosopher friend sandwiched his records between reflections on the works of the Indian savant Krishnamurti.

In short, different folks write different journals—even on the same trip. One enjoyable (and revealing) diversion is to compare notes after a trip is over. Our lining incident, for instance. The account you've already read was based on Rug's recollections. Joe's diary tells a different story:

Day 14—A really tough day. Beginning to think this river is just one set after another of unrunnable rapids—actually ledges, each set dropping sufficient elevation to cause us to either line or portage the boats. On this day, in fact, this journal was submerged. We were lining the boats through a rather difficult bit of water. Dave's boat, with all four of us working the lines, made it through, but did ship a little water. I agreed to have mine follow, though I was very uneasy about it. In fact, at the last minute, I hustled to the boat and, holding up operations, took my sleeping bag out of the canoe. Well, sure enough, she swamped. . . . This really got me down, since all my stuff, just dried out yesterday, was soaked. *Completely*. I was very upset with John for being so time-conscious in the previous rapids; for with time, I would have taken out my whole pack—perhaps all the stuff. But he seemed to be tired of delays, and prodded me to hurry and get my bag out of the boat. . . .

Joe, it seems, saw more of that broach than Rug remembered. Jim corroborates the point in one of his journals (he kept two, a short one for logistics, another for personal recollections). "Joe is dubious, wants to take his pack out," goes the entry for June 29, "but Rug chides him into removing just his sleeping bag." As for the swamp itself, Jim remembers that "the boat descends well through the chute and appears home free when Peach makes the mistake of trying to pull it in too quick."

Peach, on the other hand, if he realizes his mistake, makes little of it. His entry for the day reads *in toto:*

29 June—Day 14
Hot & sunny, worked 9 a.m.—8 p.m., 6 portages,
3–4 miles progress, exhausted, discouraged. Swamped
Joe's canoe lining.

Most expeditioners are willing to put up with the encumbrance of a camera as well as a journal. If it is one of the new "pocket" cameras which take the 110 film, there is hardly an encumbrance worth mentioning. According to an inside source we have at Kodak's research labs, the best value in their 110 line is either the bottom or top models. (The cheap one works well; we haven't any experience with the others.) The grain of the finished snapshots is not quite as fine as that of the regular Instamatic, but some people prefer the texture of 110 prints as well as their rectangular format—

we do. We haven't seen the 110 slides, but some photography magazines have rated them even better in brilliance and resolution than the regular Instamatics.

Cheaper cameras have their limitations, however; especially for white-water shots. Their slow shutters make it difficult to freeze action, and their generally wide-angle lenses make dramatic pictures difficult when the river is wide and the photographer forced to take his shots from shore. A single-lens reflex camera with a telephoto attachment is the solution. One particular 35-mm. camera which might be mentioned is the Nikon Nikonos II. Whitewater buffs claim it is waterproof even in an upset. It retails for a sizable sum, and indeed does advertise itself as waterproof. We've never tried one, though, so must remain noncommittal and envious.

Still shots can capture drama; if composed well, they can even hint at the vast kinetic energy at work when two paddlers come face to face with one big souse hole. But frozen motion, however graphic, is frozen, and the essence of any whitewater is *motion*. It seems to us that anyone who wants to bring home palpable evidence of the river at work has to deal in motion pictures.

Those who have hesitated about getting into movies because of their high cost should think again. The outlay for equipment is little more than you might spend for a moderately good still camera and slide projector. And the cost of three minutes of film (fifty feet) plus developing comes to just about the same price that you would pay for twenty 110 snapshot prints. A basic point-and-shoot camera is available for as little as thirty dollars, but you should purchase one equipped with an automatic exposure which allows panning from a shady scene to a lighted one without stopping to adjust f-stops. If you can afford the even more expensive cameras ($100–$200) their features will pay dividends. Among the more important aids:

Through-the-lens viewing: lets you see exactly what you're shooting, which is not otherwise possible in close-up shots. *Existing-light cameras:* the faster lens combined with ASA 160 film allows shots at dusk and marginally decent pictures around a campfire at night (the campfire has to be roaring). The 160 film should not be used for shooting sunny scenes on the river. The bright sky combined with the sparkle and reflection of the water will lead to overexposure at worst, and a grainy picture at best. (This occurred even when Jim stopped down his lens with a neutral density filter). *Zoom lens:* this is perhaps the most useful accessory to have. Most amateurs like it because its focal length can be varied from a wide angle ("short" lens) to telephoto ("long" lens) while the camera is shooting—giving the dramatic "zoom" effect. In general, the larger the zoom ratio, the more versatile (and expensive) the lens. 5:1 is adequate and even 3:1 will serve. The zoom's advantage for wilderness trips is not the zoom itself; simply that you will find yourself in tight situations where it is not easy to move forward or backward in order to frame your picture the way you want it. The zoom lens gives greater flexibility in composing. Furthermore, the telephoto position allows a more detailed and dramatic view of a canoe running a chute in midriver.

The key to taking full advantage of movies is to understand the essential difference between stills and motion pictures. Good snapshots make horrible movies, so you should avoid the natural temptation to use the movie camera to take what are, in effect, a series of snapshots. The moose you see briefly on shore before it heads off to the woods will do better captured through the telephoto of a still camera. The snap freezes details and your viewers can study it. On movies, you'll have four seconds in which to hurriedly tell your audience what it was that disappeared among the alders. Of course, it's a different story if you have someone enterprising enough to rise with the sun and spend time waiting along an animal trail to catch caribou browsing. The principle applies as well to people as to animals. A shot of Rug eating a plate of spaghetti followed by a shot of the next morning's rapids followed by a shot of Joe at breakfast the day after is snapshots on film—and it's horrible.

The plain fact of the matter is, good movies take more time because they are shot as series of sequences which comprise a scene, not as snaps which stand by themselves. If you are serious about coming home with a good film, you can economize on time spent with the camera by deciding what you want to capture in advance. For scenes of eating, take your shots all at one breakfast or dinner, and not spread over five or six different campsites. For portaging, take one carry and shoot it from start to finish: people scouting, unloading boats, carrying packs and canoes, resting at the end, loading up. On whitewater shots, concentrate on those where you have ample time to set up the best shooting angles. Then most of the time you're free to enjoy meals in peace, to run rooster tails without worrying how you'll look dumping headfirst, and to employ your finest French on the alder-tangle portages.

Of all the shots taken on a wilderness trip, the ones most likely to be disappointing are the whitewater sequences. Out in the woods, a drop may have seemed particularly ferocious; on the screen it appears routine. Conversely, you may be surprised to find that some shots appear hair-raising when in fact they were easily run. The surprise is a result of the natural assumption that a camera records what is *actually* happening (as opposed, for instance, to the impressionistic canvas of a painter). But the camera is recording the scene from one perspective—and unless you're carrying and shooting as you paddle, it's not likely yours. Furthermore, different photographic lenses see in different ways, even though their vantage point may be the same. Your job as filmmaker is to use the camera to give any viewer the same feelings which you experienced from your own perspective in the boat. To do that well, we provide some basic principles to keep in mind when dealing with two elementary facets of whitewater boating: speed and motion.

PERSPECTIVE AND SPEED. Any canoeist who has drifted to the lip of a drop and then plunged into its swift, shifting currents knows how much speed has to do with the exhilaration (and terror) of running whitewater. A moment's reflection, however, shows that actual speed is not what contributes to the feeling so much as the psychological pressure of accomplishing a complex set of maneuvers within a limited amount of time. The camera sees only the outward moves—which (if you are good) may be precise and rather deliberate; it misses the sensation of speed produced by the inner turmoil. To reproduce those feelings, you can use the camera to emphasize the speed in a number of ways, especially with a zoom-telephoto lens. A long lens (the telephoto end of the zoom) *emphasizes motion perpendicular to the camera and compresses motion parallel to the camera.* To see what we mean, sight across some rapids from the riverbank, your camera on the wide-angle setting. Then zoom out to telephoto and notice how much faster the water seems to be moving along. If you're shooting a boat coming through a drop from the side, your natural inclination might be to get as close as possible and shoot on wide angle. If you move farther back and get the same picture area on telephoto, the feeling of speed is increased. When you shoot from up or downstream, however, the boat seems to be covering less ground. This perspective is not effective in portraying speed, but is excellent for recording a boulder garden where maneuvering is the prime consideration. The long lens compresses space as well as motion; consequently, shooting upstream through the boulders makes distances between them seem tighter than they actually are.

Telephoto shots enhance movies, but only if the camera is braced properly. Jim has found that in general, any focal length longer than 30 mm. suffers from hand-held shooting. The jiggling is not always apparent when sighting through the lens because the human eye compensates for such motion; but the result is sadly apparent in the final print. Our remedy is to take along a small camera clamp, one of the several models available in the larger outdoor stores. It fits in our ammo box, and can be used in three ways: as a tripod whose tiny legs can be unscrewed and stored in the barrel; as a clamp to be attached to a pack frame or some steadying object; or with a wood-screw attachment for trees.

The cameraman without a zoom has fewer options open to him. One is the editing job done once the footage has been processed. Fast pacing of shots helps to quicken the tempo of a movie, and filming from a variety of different angles makes this possible. Take some close-ups, concentrating on facial expressions and intersperse them with the medium shots of the whole boat going through a drop. A low camera angle, looking up as the boat comes over the drop, increases the drama of a run. And if you trust your sternman's maneuvering abilities, you can get interesting shots taken looking forward out of the bow. Once Jim even strapped his cheap camera to a paddle and stuck it like a boom behind the stern seat. This left both men free to paddle as the boat went over several drops.

PERSPECTIVE AND MOTION. Closely allied with the subjective feeling of speed is that of motion. Speed, of course, is one kind of motion; but even more basic is the simple fact that running a river immerses you in several different relative systems of movement. The main current takes you downstream, the side current from another chute shifts the direction, the eddies move upstream—and throughout this your canoe travels across constantly changing vectors. One way to capture this feeling is to take away the viewers' stable frame of reference, just as the river has taken away yours. Compose shots to eliminate the far shoreline, so that only water and the canoe are visible. This is done more easily from higher-angle vantage points. (Direct overhead shots, taken from an overhanging rock, tree, or bridge, give an even more extreme view, although they tend to minimize the height of the waves or the drop in a chute.)

The zoom shot is helpful here also. Photography manuals note that novices usually overwork the zoom—and that's true. But in the case of a shot where moving water is the only frame of reference, the zoom is less obtrusive as a technique. With everything in the picture already shifting, the zoom to telephoto will be less noticeable, yet at the same time the changing focal length contributes to that feeling of motion.

Cameras lacking a zoom can produce some striking effects with motion. Relative movements can be captured best if shots are taken neither from the stable reference point (the shore) nor from the moving system (the canoe) but from a third perspective, another moving canoe. Have one boat run a big chute in the center of the river while the camera boat tags along parallel in safer waters. The feeling of movement is twice as impressive when one canoe passes another and the camera pans to follow it. On these shots, always use the widest-angle lens available in order to minimize the jiggle of the hand-held camera.

Working with film takes time and effort, and like we said, it's not for everybody. But as you live with the river more and more, and concentrate on filming its motion and essence rather than on photographing your trip as history, even a camera can become a lens through which your present is enlarged.

16. A River Camp

After we hauled the boat from the river, Joe wrung out his clothes while Jim checked the food duffel to see if there were any leaks. There were, the main one being a large pack of biscuits stowed in a plastic bag without a "twist 'em." Joe thought we should salvage them by adding sugar and cinnamon to make bread pudding, and so we talked over the merits of throwing good sugar after bad biscuits and finally went ahead with Joe's recipe. We all ate a little, said it was pretty good considering, and chucked it in the garbage bag. In the middle of lunch, we had a sun shower; then the weather settled into a drizzle for our afternoon paddle. About four or five, the rain seemed to pick up enthusiasm, and so we decided to stop for the night.

Pitching camp on a rainy day is a more deliberate, rationally thought out affair than on a sunny day, so we might as well take the time now to outline the process. With good weather, things kind of unwind naturally and it's a toss-up whether you take a swim or set up the tents or take a walk around to explore. Rain helps to focus on the essentials: keeping dry, keeping warm, getting fed.

All the same, you're not going to hear much from us about traditional campcraft. For one thing, setting up camp seems to us mostly a self-taught, self-evident exercise. For another, lightweight, sophisticated equipment combined with an ecological conscience makes modern campcraft less complicated than the old spruce-bough-mattress, hand-lashed-table variety. So we won't insult you with the obvious principles of camping but will content ourselves with an embellishment of details.

Here's what we mean: The first step in setting up camp is picking one, and it inspires lists of desirable (and often contradictory) woodland attributes. A location should be flat, for comfortable bedding, but not so flat that water fails to drain well in case of a storm. It should be sheltered enough to provide protection in a gale, but breezy enough to keep the bugs at bay. It should be close to water, but not close to the wrong sort of water (swamps and lowland grounds). If you heed all the advice tendered on ideal campsites, chances are you'll find yourself pitched on the doormat of the nearest Hilton. The truth is, any rational person knows what a good campsite looks like, and he generally winds up settling for less than the textbook case.

While these basic principles are obvious, it may be worth noting that good campsites are often not readily apparent from the perspective of the canoe. Vegetation can change once away from the riverbank; alders, for example, often give way to more open country only twenty yards inland. Climbing a steep bluff may reveal a magnificent plateau campsite at the top. Common-sense reading of topos can also help. In Labrador, we found consistently good sites along eskers (ridges created by the deposits of subglacial streams) and learned to look for them on the maps. Topos can also warn you of poor camping. If you are heading for a steep gorge, you may want to look for a flat spot earlier than usual.

Actually, remarkably little level space is necessary for a comfortable night if you try out the ground you plan to sleep on before pitching your tent. Pay particular attention to the upper two thirds of your body. Below the thighs, your legs can generally work a *modus vivendi* with roots, declivities, and minor craters. In genuine wilderness, small-bush undergrowth makes surprisingly good tent space. The bushes are soft enough to provide a cushion-like mattress for the evening, yet hardy enough to spring back to their usual demeanor the next morning. Staking down the tent becomes more difficult, but Rug has replaced his corner pegs with long shish-kebab skewers. In well-traveled areas, however, make a habit of sleeping on bare ground. Otherwise you will be helping to create it.

If you can't afford the luxury of a good full sized tent, purchase an 8-by-10 or 9-by-12 tarp and make yourself a canoe shelter. The idea is an old one—used by the Canadian fur traders for hundreds of years. Their *maître canots* had some advantages your canoe won't: overall length could be a roomy 36 feet and beam was as wide as 70 inches. When the boats were tipped over and a tarp extended out from the high gunwale, it made a fine canopy of a shelter. Their high ends combined with the wide beam gave greater head clearance than modern canoe designs, but you can prop up the gunwale with forked sticks at both ends of your boat. The tarp slants off the gunwale like a lean-to, one end parallel and next to the keel (fastened with cords run around the hull and anchored underneath at bow and stern seats), the other end fastened to trees, bushes, or rocks. Short sticks propped at the low ends of the tarp increase clearance for the feet.

Canoe shelters have their disadvantages, the main one being they are not bug-proof. They are also not as easily pitched in sites tight on space and a chore to haul to the top of high bluffs. Yet we've gotten good service from them on many trips. The duffels are stored at the low end of the tarp, and act

as guards to prevent your feet from sliding down too far; a pair of Keltys fit nicely under the bow and stern eaves. If the ground slants, pitch the canoe along the high end; then the majority of water in a downpour drains downhill off the far end of the tarp. One final note of caution: the aerodynamic characteristics of the canoe shelter are not exactly ideal. On stormy nights pitch the canoe bottom into the wind and seek the shelter of forest instead of an open sand beach. It's hell to have to go hopping around in skivvies at 2 A.M. retying a ripped-out grommet.

So much for keeping dry at night. When you arrive on shore in the middle of a rain, you'll be equally interested in keeping warm. No point in starting a fire without some sort of a rain shelter in place, so first look for a good spot for the fire tarp. Pitch it high enough to keep the heat from melting the plastic and to give you standing room around the fire; low enough for adequate protection in a driving rain. That amounts to roughly six feet on the high end, about four on the low (and windward) end. There are many ways to set up guy lines, but we've found the easiest and most adjustable method is to carry two lengths of nylon cord about thirty or forty feet long. String each between two trees, roughly parallel to each other and somewhat wider than the 9-by-12 tarp. Have enough rope so each line loops around one of its trees and can be adjusted by a tautline hitch. The tarp is fastened anywhere along the lines by the stick/loop method shown in our sketch. Adjust overall tension with the tautlines; move the tarp along the ropes as you wish by sliding the stick/loops. The variations are many and you can shift the tarp as the wind shifts.

Don't switch canoe and fire shelters, or assume one tarp can do double duty. After a few days' use, the fire tarp reeks of smoke and sports a layer of char. Even Dirty Rug's liberal olfactory tolerances would be offended.

In a soaking rain, starting a fire is often a group effort. Three or four days of steady drizzle will wet even the sheltered thicket tinder. You can try looking under large dead logs and other out-of-the-way places, but it may be easiest to rely on shavings from the splits of logs big enough to have a dry inner core. Preparation becomes a matter of meticulous care: at this particular campsite, Rug was quartering the splits, then splitting the quarters and slicing tinderlike splits off of those. Jim had taken a couple of the bigger splits under the fire tarp and was whittling shaving after shaving with his hunting knife. As each splinter flipped off, Joe quickly gathered it up before it could absorb moisture from the ground. He cradled his collection in his fist, the warmth of his hand (which he carefully kept dry) serving as further protection against the damp of the air. When the shavings had expanded to fill two generous fists, he passed them on to Peach, who had been clearing a fireplace and sorting Rug's larger kindlings into piles. Peach laid his birch bark, placed upon it a small handful of the thinnest shavings, and lit the match.

As the flames spread upward, he carefully fed them, shaving by shaving, so as not to disturb the delicate balance. The small cluster began to catch.

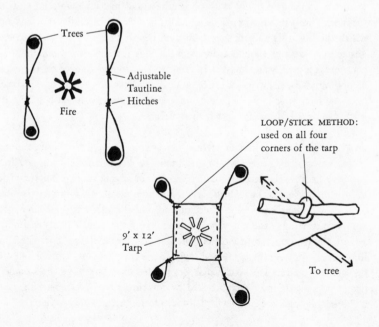

Peach stuck three or four of the larger, thumb-sized splits into the dirt so their tips touched each other in a small tepee over the tiny fire. He didn't lay them on the shavings (which wouldn't stand the weight), and the top of the tepee remained about three inches above the flames. Peach continued to add Joe's shavings, but all the while the heat was drying out the thumb-sized sticks, so that as the fire grew and reached them they burned more easily. Then came the quarter splits, again balanced to dry as a high tepee. Slowly the fire gained its own momentum, and we could turn to the chore of getting dinner.

A lot has been written about the art of wilderness cooking, from Ruth Mendenhall's *Backpack Cookery* to Bradford Angier's romances of lining a hole with moosehide and cooking leek leaves and water with hot stones. We commend all this to you, but on a rainy night you are likely to be less inventive. Fortunately the world of dehydration and freeze-drying has made the basics of cooking just as obvious as those of setting up camp. We leave the gourmet points to the gourmet and offer here only a few pointers about the various methods of food preparation.

BOILING. Raising the temperature of water to 212° F. takes more energy than novices sometimes suspect, especially when what's involved is five or six quarts for spaghetti. The higher the grill, the more heat is lost; that's why we often prefer to dispense with one entirely and just build the fire around the pot. This gets the job done quickly, but watch carefully the logs on which the pot rests and replace them with new ones before the old become unstable. Also keep enough space between logs for adequate ventilation. If you do use a grill, water may often seem to be hanging forever on the edge of boiling; a fistful of quick-catching small tinder will push it over. Lastly, once you have your broth bubbling, don't overdo, since too much boiling will leach spaghetti and macaroni of their nutrients.

FRYING. This is the common method of cooking freeze-dried burgers, pork chops, and steaks. The secret is to spend most of the preparation time soaking and very little in the actual cooking. Sear the meat quickly and only enough to brown and get hot enough to serve (a minute a side, say)—otherwise the meat turns tough. Some people recommend parboiling but we've found that too much cooking is bad any way it's done. Frying the regular foods is simply a matter of getting the proportions of heat and grease right (slow fire and little grease for eggs, high fire and little grease for pancakes, hot fire and all the grease you can lay your hands on for hashbrowns). One after-dinner luxury is popcorn, most easily cooked by covering a well-greased frying pan with the big cook-set pot (which usually forms a tight seal). Get the oil quite hot *before* you add the corn—kernels are less likely to burn that way. Shake over a hot fire, using the frying-pan handle.

BAKING. Our methods are primitive, but they seem to work. Joe came praising fancy reflector ovens and was argued out of his own en route, not by Jim's vehement theories but simply by the oven's slow results. We had success with basic bannock (1 c. flour, 1 tsp. baking powder, ¼ tsp. salt) toasted on sticks or else fried in a skillet. Joe became master of cornbread in the well-buttered frying pan, sticking the pan half over the coals at the slowest end of the fire and rotating periodically. (Make very sure the fire's slow.) Jim was most at home with the double-frying-pan Dutch oven: batter in the small pan, the larger one laid upside down to cover it. He put this on hot coals and heaped more on top. In evergreen forests, where hardwood for good coals is lacking, you may have to build a fire on top and use coals only on the bottom. A fire underneath the pan would burn the cake, but on top most of the heat rises, with enough radiating downward to bake the center.

You'll be surprised how well you can eat with such primitive techniques. The taste of prepackaged dehydrated meals can be improved dramatically by only a few thoughtful additions, the main one being margarine. Extra margarine in the noodles, extra margarine in the stew, rafts of margarine on the cornbread, truckloads in the powdered mashed potatoes. Vienna sausages to pep up the macaroni and cheese; hard-cased sausage to spice the spaghetti. Bring along extra seasonings: garlic and onion salt; cinnamon for an occasional sweet roll instead of biscuit (add some sugar to the batter too).

If the climax of the evening's meal is the production of a baked dessert such as sweet rolls, the inevitable denouement is the dishes. Careful washing with soap and thorough rinsing can be accomplished without hot water, but with especially greasy meals it's easy enough to heat a frying pan of hot water. Leftover garbage goes into the plastic bag reserved for food remains. We kept all our garbage (tin cans burned and stomped flat, aluminum foil rescued from the fire) in an old army surplus duffel carried expressly for the purpose. The hiker's maxim holds equally well for the canoeist: if you pack it in, pack it out. Soapy dishwater is never returned to the river, but tossed in the latrine. At the evening meal we generally rinsed the whole outfit in near-boiling water, just to keep persistent grease from accumulating.

All these details of setting up camp have their ritualistic overtones—especially when performed in the rain. Rug splitting the quarters for Jim, Jim slicing the shavings for Joe, Joe cupping the tinder for Peach. The four of us shuffling like solemn rabbis around the fire, each periodically giving way so the next man could stand in the sheltered corner of the fire tarp without the smoke. Then there were the set pieces at the end of the evening: Peach heating his little bucket of hot water for a steaming washcloth on the face; Rug getting the honey from Jim for a small dollop in his tea; Joe off for a few minutes alone with the river. All these rituals of the river camp are repeated and shared one with another. Like all rituals, they work to bring us together.

Down at the river that night, Jim finds Joe in the misty drizzle. "This will sound silly," says Joe, "but it just strikes me how the river never stops for the night."

"You know, I was wondering," says Jim. "Suppose you floated a stick out there tonight—let the current take it. Which do you think would get to the bottom of the river first, us or the stick?"

"Us," says Joe. "You're forgetting the eddies."

"But the river runs all night. And the eddies move, even slowly."

"We would still win," says Joe with an air of placid confidence.

To this day, Jim does not know why he did it, but when he returned to his pack for a toothbrush, he also fished out a small role of bright yellow utility tape. He broke a small stick off a dead evergreen limb and returned to Joe and the river. Wrapped the tape two, three times in a band around the stick; showed it to Joe (who was looking anyway); then threw it as far as he could out into the river.

"Empirical verification," he says.

"We'll beat it, easy," says Joe, playing along.

Then the two of them went off to bed and left the stick to its own designs.

V. THE RIVER CANYON

17. Whirlpool Pass

One of the undoubted privileges of a voyager on a Major Expedition is naming the prominent landmarks. Map makers may have already drawn boundaries and thus names, but these are of their own sort. You have the right to fashion your own after contact with the real thing. When you name something significant, write it down at the end of the day on your maps. Do it confidently, and don't worry whether you've apportioned titles accurately in terms of the maps. Your name has to conform with your actuality, and hang the rest.

For instance: the final length of our river threaded its way through canyons whose walls climbed fifteen hundred feet into the air. After getting there, we decided to name the area the High Moisie. Now, technically, those valley walls got higher and higher gradually; and the cliffs at the end of the canyon tapered off slowly too. But we can tell you the very rapids where you can look back and see the end of the High Moisie; and in retrospect, we can tell you the very spot that the river canyon begins—though the maps will prove beyond a shadow of a doubt we are wrong.

Name it anyway. Whirlpool Pass, entrance to the High Moisie, is a spot where the whole of the boiling river passes through a gate no wider than forty feet. That is not unusual in itself—we have passed other narrows that size. But with this one, all the river fits itself through without so much as a ripple of rapids. We name it, leave our mark on it so to speak, drawing boundaries to suit our fancies. But the river has its chance too, and recipro-cates by leaving its mark on us, redrawing the lines we had tried to set so firmly on the rest of the world. As we close with the gate, we know what is coming, this exchanging of names and essences. But we don't say anything—only wait.

The day is quite still. We can tell as we approach the bottleneck that the water, smooth on the surface, is doing strange things along the irregular bottom. For the first time jagged rock walls begin to climb steeply and close to the sides of the river. The calm is an oppressive one, portending more rain on the heels of the day's earlier squall, and the overcast gives an eerie quality to that dark pass. Instinctively we stop paddling, the current and the silence of the gate pulling us into its vortex. That's what it is in there—a silence; and not merely the translation of visual gloom by our imaginations. Those high walls cut off the noise of birds, wind, and such. But you can't help mixing up the two, the visual and the aural. Though we keep quiet, it seems like those fluorescent-orange dollar-ninety-eight raincoats on Rug and Peach are sounding off our presence to the river.

Rug makes a comment about all the water strained through the gate; puts his paddle in for a slow stroke—quiet, though—at the same time. On cue, that river mutters from its bottom with a whirlpool. And not the sort of whirlpool made by the usual bow stroke. It *slithers,* with a sucking noise which the high rock gate amplifies. Then another pool starts, as if shook off that last one; then two more around our boat. The current sways the canoe, gentle but firm, to a track we didn't plan, but aren't about to change in our unease. Not that we're in any danger, make no mistake. But maybe here, more than in any of the big roiling rumbles above and below, we can tell what power the river has. In the big haystacks, you are too busy thinking about insignificant short-run things, like ways to keep the boat upright. Here we are quiet and the river gets our full attention. It says, *Look, friend: it's me, the river. A grip like iron and this only a calm spot. Watch what you do, you and your dollar-ninety-eight specials.*

18. Heavy Water

Heavy water, according to nuclear chemists, is a rare variant of the ordinary stuff. Each molecule contains a couple of extra neutrons: atomic particles that give it unusual physical properties. A new boiling point, for example. What rivermen call heavy water is chemically and atomically identical to slack water, but physically it is utterly transformed by the river's gift of energy. In their plain terms, water is heavy when it boils cold.

The canoeist knows it by what it will do to his boat. Even on small streams, the river current can pull the unwary paddler into trees and dash him against rocks. In heavy water, the river has no need for wooden implements or stone tools; the water forms its own retaining walls and delivers its own hammerblows. Step up the power by notches and the water will dig holes, shape funnels, and finally disintegrate into a froth as treacherous as quicksand. Never mind (for now) the complicity of boulders, ledges, and sidewalls. The force and inventiveness of the currents themselves threaten any craft as small, flimsy, and lacking in horsepower as a canoe.

Even before the new canoeist ventures out into truly big water (and he had better well venture in the company of old hands) the river will teach him about the power of shifting currents. To see how, we need only return to that safe landing area in whitewater, the eddy—exactly where we left two paddlers (on page 141). Suppose these two want to leave the eddy and continue downstream in the main current. How do they do it? One way might be to paddle downstream and out the bottom of the eddy as at left. But this has its problems. You remember that our two paddlers turned into the eddy by sticking their bow in just downstream of the rock and letting the boat pivot around in a U turn. So now the bow is facing up-

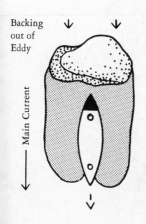

Backing
out of
Eddy

Main Current

stream and they have to turn it back around in order to continue on down the river. Another problem is that there may be a rock or chute downstream of their eddy, leaving no room to drift out the bottom. For these reasons, our two paddlers decide to do an eddy turn out of the eddy to their left side ("eddy out left"). They are neophytes, but at least know the basic principles. The bowman paddles up the eddy until his nose sticks out into the downstream current. Now the canoe is on the eddy-line boundary. The bow gets spun downstream, while the stern remains in the calm of the eddy. The boat pivots quickly and cleanly, and our paddlers are on their way.

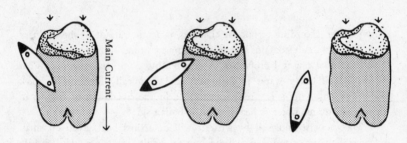

That's the theory anyway; but the neophytes have forgotten one thing. The fast downstream current will pivot the bow around, true, but it is acting primarily on the bottom of the hull, and will pull that part of the boat harder than the rest. A good hard current will thus also tend to roll the boat, pulling the upstream gunwale down toward the water. In a slow current, this undertow effect may go unnoticed, but in swift water, the results are roughly the same as having a rug yanked out from under you. The boat rolls quickly and cleanly into an upstream capsize.

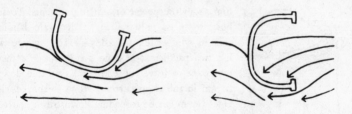

Now let's put Rug and Peach into the same eddy. Rug is still paddling left in the bow, Peach is sternman and on the right. As they eddy out left, they know the swift current will tend to pull down the upstream gunwale, so they *lean downstream* to counteract the effect. With experience and a few dumps, this leaning becomes automatic. Canoeists in covered canoes actually lean downstream enough to offer the flat bottom of the boat to the oncoming current, since this maneuver prevents the water from grabbing the upstream bilge and pulling it under. Without a cover, Rug and Peach bank their boat less dramatically. Raising the upstream gunwale helps keep the current from piling over the top, but the downstream gunwale also has to be kept above the waterline.

Skillful canoeists soon become good leaners, but leaning by itself cannot guarantee a secure eddy turn. After all, the canoe is not entering a smooth and even flow but a heaving, shifting current. The key, therefore, to crossing eddy lines (or negotiating any heavy water) lies not with the canoe but with the paddle. Coming out of that eddy, Rug not only needs to lean—he needs something to lean *on*. He gets it by reaching out in a hanging stroke called the *high brace*. This stroke is a modified draw. To do it, lean far out over the water and plant your paddle vertically in the current, but instead of

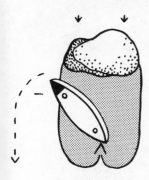

pulling it back to the boat, keep it anchored in the current at arm's length. Don't fix the angle of the blade in relation to the boat as you would for a draw; set it instead in relation to the current. The power face of the blade should be facing upstream, dead against the oncoming water; in order to do that, you'll have to cock your wrists way back. The position may feel awkward at first, but with the face of the blade being supported by the rush of the main current, you can lean downstream on the paddle with confidence—just as you're supposed to when turning out of an eddy.

The interplay between the man and the river is everything. The more violent the downstream flow, the harder Rug leans—and the more weight he can put on his paddle. The strong current will hold him up. The farther out he reaches, the more he widens the effective beam of his river craft—and the more stable the canoe becomes. These relationships account for why the intrinsically "tippy" canoe can survive in waters much too turbulent for tubby rowboats and behemoth Chris-Crafts. A well-placed paddle is the riverman's gyroscope, his canoe's self-leveling device. The faster the current strikes the canoe to twist it out of control, the more power that same current imparts to the paddle to keep the equilibrium. The paddler never matches his strength against the main force of the river; instead he taps its energy for his own use.

The most common mistake of the inexperienced canoeist is to paddle timidly. Leaning or "hanging" way out downstream on a high brace seems to

most beginners an improbable defiance of the law of gravity. So they fake it by dangling the paddle in the current without trusting the river enough to lean on it. Or worse, they become too jumpy to wait for the main current and try to brace in the calm water of the eddy. It doesn't work; a strong, steady brace requires a current to grab the paddle and run with it, which is why crossing eddy lines on a fast stream is the best preparation for canoeing the big waves and violent currents of really heavy water. If your brace is shaky or uncertain, practice doing eddy turns until you feel confident no matter how big the sheer between the main stream and eddy backspin.

With experience comes finesse. You will, for example, learn what happens when you vary the angle of your paddle to the current. Suppose you come out of your eddy in a high brace, the angle of the blade set just like a draw. The blade is set with its power side parallel to and facing the boat. But the blade angle is not set dead against the current. The result is that the bow pivots around in a relatively wide arc. Now suppose, in the same situation, that you rotate the blade angle (by cocking your wrists way back) so that the power side of the blade no longer faces the boat as in a draw stroke but instead faces the oncoming current. Since the angle of the blade now catches the full force of the downstream current, your brace will pivot the boat much more sharply, making for a tighter turn.

Wide Pivot   Tight Pivot

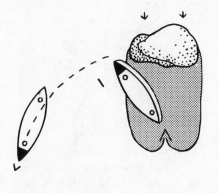
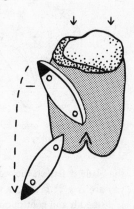

We have seen Rug and Peach turn left out of an eddy. Since paddling technique is asymmetric, we now have to consider the problem of turning into the current on the right ("eddy out right"). In this case, Rug's bow paddle is upstream of the boat and on the outside of the turn. What stroke is he to use? Well, why not lean for stability on another high brace, this time on the upstream side? Lots of reasons. For one, the high brace is a kind of draw, and serves to turn the canoe as well as steady it. Since Rug wants to turn the bow downstream, he will not draw (or brace) upstream. More importantly, the upstream brace is bad physics. As we have already seen, a boat turning out of an eddy tends to have its upstream gunwale pulled down by the main current. An upstream brace commits the paddler to lean in the same direction that the current is tipping his boat; if this current fails to flip him first, it gets a second chance when the experimenting bowman plants his paddle. The current will grab the blade and drive it downriver—this time right under the boat. Beware the upstream brace: it is theoretically unsound and in actual practice a sure capsize.

To turn right, therefore, Rug will lean downstream and use his cross-draw, depending on Peach to brace the canoe as it pivots around into the main current. Put yourself with Peach in the stern. As the bow hits the fast current and pivots downstream, your job is to hold the stern in the eddy. To make the U turn snappy, you have to pry or push your end upstream; to steady the canoe, you need a modified pry stroke, the *low brace*. The pry, you remember, is executed by trailing the paddle shaft behind the sternman at an acute angle to the water with the power side of the blade facing the canoe. To change it to a low brace, simply rotate the paddle 90 degrees so

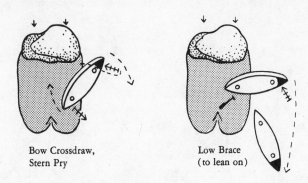

Bow Crossdraw,
Stern Pry

Low Brace
(to lean on)

the blade is flat on the water, a platform to lean on when you need it. Since you are free to flex your wrist at any angle between 0 and 90 degrees, there is a smooth and continuous gradation between the pry and the low brace, between maximum turning and maximum steadying effects. What's more, by increasing the climbing angle of the whole paddle in the water, you can gradually (or forcefully) convert the brace to a backwater stroke. These subtleties of emphasis are important, especially since the sternman can't lean for support on the strong downstream current the way the bowman can. He

has to sustain his brace by some sort of paddle motion—often by leaning through the wide arc of a reverse quarter sweep.

The low brace looks like a radically different stroke from the high brace, but the underlying dynamics are the same for both. The canoeist, bow or stern, shifts his center of gravity out over the water somewhere between his paddle blade and the canoe. As the currents roll and twist under the boat, the paddler's lean prevents a capsize to his off side, while the support of his paddle steadies him on the side of his lean. With practice, the high brace blends easily and gracefully into a draw stroke or the power phase of the forward stroke; the low brace blends into the pry or the recovery phase of the forward stroke. Eventually, strokes and braces mix with one another naturally, as the needs of propulsion and balance dictate. Out on the river away from explanations of paddle angles and leverage, it feels as if there is telepathy between the motions of the river and the little pools of lymph that occupy the inner ear. And the paddle is the medium.

The canoeist who has done a lot of paddling in heavy water may find it strange that we have taken so much time to discuss a fairly simple maneuver like turning out of an eddy. But a great many essentials of river running—leaning, crossing sharp current boundaries, high and low bracing, the blending of strokes—are all contained in this one simple maneuver. Having examined it in some detail, our next job is to apply these techniques in the chaotic water of the larger river.

And that calls first of all for scouting. *Never* enter heavy water until you look it over. One newly fallen tree can turn even a familiar rapids into a deathtrap. So make your way along the bank and assess carefully the course you plan to take. One of the most striking features of heavy water is simply the sheer size of the waves—and as anyone knows who's run the stuff, waves are twice as big when finally viewed from the canoe seat. (Part of the thrill of whitewater is bobbing in the current, enjoying the underview of the rough stuff shared in nature by only a few excited salmon.) Of course, the height of standing waves is not the only, or even the main, criterion of runnability. Wave length and formation are the keys. Waves spaced widely apart allow canoes to ride uphill and downhill without shipping water; but as wave length shortens, wave slopes become steeper, and your bow will be less likely to lift clear. Or maybe it does, but then hangs over the crest, plunges on the steep downslope, and buries in the next rise. Even more trouble than the regular waves are the roosters and curlers whose crests turn back on themselves. These can fill the canoe before the bow even hits the top of the wave. Above all, keep open boats away from the formations known in the trade as "souse holes" or "white eddies": seething pits of foamy turbulence where water has plunged over large boulders, sucked air along with it, and turned the whole area into a trap with hydraulic properties like those evidenced below ledges.

Wave features take on meaning when you match them against your boat. Some standing waves are long enough for fifteen-foot canoes to ride out, while a seventeen-footer will buck exuberantly and then sink shamelessly. (This is the exception that proves the rule about larger boats providing more buoyancy and surviving heavier water.) If you are out on a short trip, a decked canoe is the final solution. Otherwise, the wilderness canoeist has to take a hard look at the water and again at himself to decide what he's going to run and what to walk. One time, he may portage his gear and run empty; another, just shuffle his packs and run with his bow trimmed extra high. (If the stern rides too low though, his canoe can swamp from the rear or prove too much a river hog to maneuver.) Finally, he may keep the boat at its lightest and run solo, C-1. (For more on the C-1, see page 219.) There is no ideal approach; only an ever-shifting range of possibilities.

Back to the river. Rug's plan is to eddy out left (A) and follow the main current cutting across the river and to the left of the ledge in our diagram. The standing waves at B are smooth and regular; Rug and Peach take them at an angle of 20 to 30 degrees for the same reason they would quarter into big rollers in a head wind. By hitting the waves off center, the

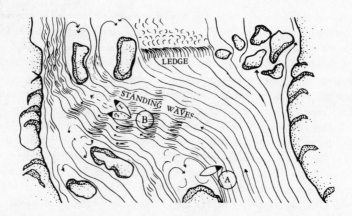

bow tends to lift instead of cut. Ever so gingerly, Peach rolls the boat to the rhythm of the waves; the canoe has to be kept level to the water, not to the ground beneath. As another tactic to avoid slicing deep into the waves, Rug and Peach keep the canoe at roughly the speed of the current. Since the canoe tends to slide downhill faster than current even without paddling forward,* they need to backpaddle, and if the river is very fast, to back-paddle with vigor. On the other hand, without the benefit of forward speed, our two paddlers have to rely on their braces. When not bracing or back-paddling or otherwise stroking, paddles are kept in a ready brace position. For the bowman, this usually means slicing the paddle vertically through the river a foot or two out from the boat, ready to convert to a high brace. For the sternman, it usually means trailing the paddle behind him in a low-brace lean.

In genuinely heavy water, the paddles should literally never leave the water. Draw strokes, for example, are not done one at a time, but in a single (and if need be, endless) continuous motion. The paddle swerves through the water in a figure-eight pattern that, when done properly, provides both a strong turning force and a good steadying effect through the whole motion. As a matter of fact, once you become proficient at this stroke, the *sculling draw,* you'll never go back to the inferior choppy version. The

Sculling Draw

sternman will also have occasion to use a continuous circular stroke, consisting of a regular forward motion (1) tailing off into a low brace (2) for balance, or a pry and reverse sweep (3) to turn the boat. At the end of either the brace or the sweep, the paddle slices forward through the water and around to the forward stroke again, using a draw–high brace (4) if balance is needed. You can begin to see, just from these two examples, how maneuvering in whitewater becomes a blending of strokes, one flowing imperceptibly into the next.

The heavy-water canoeist gets plenty of chances to use these combinations in big waves, especially because of the canoe's tendency to broach. With the bow angled into the upslope of one wave and the stern on the downslope of another, the canoe naturally tries to broadside in the trough. The tendency for broaching is further increased in "standing waves," which form at the bottom of rapids where the current is decelerating. Here the bow is in effect entering a slow current while the

Stern Circular Stroke

---

* For this observation we are indebted to John Urban, who suggests (in his *White Water Handbook for Canoe and Kayak*) that the hypothesis can be tested by floating a stick alongside the canoe and watching it drop behind. Alas, Jim never had his yellow tape ready when we could have used it.

stern remains in quicker water, so that the boat pivots. The remedy is a persistent and vigorous draw or pry to keep the canoe roughly parallel with the current.

If you look again at our river drawing, you will understand why Rug and Peach quarter the standing waves with their bow to the right of the line of current (1) instead of to the left (2). Not because that places the bow "downstream," but because it puts the whole boat in best position for turning into the chute below. Two long rocks, you can see, form two channels through which the main current divides. Which will Rug take? The outside (left) chute is the better alternative, for this reason: though the first channel is as wide as the second, only about one third of the current passes through it; inertia will carry the remainder to the outside. If Rug takes the smaller current, he may leave Peach's stern in serious jeopardy of being carried off by the majority sentiment, which would put the midships astraddle the middle rock. This possibility is especially worrisome if the canoe has by this time shipped some water. Not only does this extra weight make the canoe more prone to ship still more water, not only does it make balance more jittery by acting as shifting ballast; it also flows to the low end, the stern, to make Peach's work all the more difficult.

Since the more powerful current goes to the outside channel, you might wonder why Peach's stern wouldn't be even more likely to crash against the outside wall. The answer is that the current crashes against it first and bounces off again to provide a useful and much-valued pillow for passing canoes. Nonetheless, Rug and especially Peach with his stern will make every effort to stay to the inside half of this, the last channel. Pillows, you see, not only cushion against hard places; they can also smother, which is a form of drowning. Waves rebounding off a vertical sidewall collide with other oncoming waves to create an irregular pattern. The river's neat procession of crest and trough disintegrates. While not particularly dangerous to stray swimmers, this confusion of onrush and backwash will smother open canoes. There is another reason to hug the middle rock rather than the outside one. The largest haystacks of the whole rapids form below this chute, for this is where the most water is funneled into the smallest space. The way to miss the biggest of them is to stick right along the border of the eddy line below the mid-lying rock. Rug has to be careful not to insert the bow into the eddy itself or the whole boat will spin. But if Peach draws the *stern* into the slack water, the current will straighten the boat nicely. At the bottom of this eddy, the currents from the two chutes converge, and in so doing, some waves will cancel out others and thus provide the smoothest run-out.

What if somebody, say Jim and Joe, were to pioneer another route, one out of the mainstream? One candidate is the little alley between the ledge and the nest of rocks on the right side of the river. Like any possibility, it should be scouted and may turn out to be runnable. The ledge, however, surely hides trouble along its border. Even if there is room to ride the shoulder alongside the end of the ledge, the man paddling on the left will find no water to put a brace, only a deep hole with a few bubbles at the bottom. And what if a team tries the middle, right over the ledge? In high water, they should hunt for a tongue of black water which may indicate a break in the dike. And wherever they try to run it, they should hit it absolutely straight. If the canoe broaches, the water coming over the ledge will pour over the upstream gunwale and flip the boat instantly. Unlike running standing waves, the canoeists should go over the ledge at three-quarter or even full speed in an effort to fly the bow over the foam at the base of the falls and to avoid being sucked back under by the hydraulic trap. Of course, if anybody tries this ledge in low water, they will end up wading across it, red-faced.

We have said nothing about whirlpools. Let us make amends. Avoid whirlpools.

Finally, we should report that on our trip we ran across a wave formation that none of us had ever seen before, though we wouldn't presume it unique to the Moisie. In several places where the river necked down tight and speeded up accordingly, the current would run along remarkably smoothly. For maybe ten seconds. Then suddenly all her frustration would boil up into a series of snagtooths—sharp jagged clumps of green water that would break and topple on one another, then disappear for another ten seconds or so. We were intrigued, but never made good sense of them—though we did have the sense to resolve never to let the Moisie play roulette with us. We wanted to play nine-of-ten on our terms, not hers.

19. A Disquisition on Some (Justly) Unsung Creatures of the Woods

Bugs.

Believe us, the itch to head north is nothing compared with the itch of being there. If you're a veteran wilderness paddler, you know what we mean; if you're not, listen to Horace Kephart, who wrote a guidebook in 1916. "In Alaska," he says,

> all animals leave for the snow-line as soon as the mosquito pest appears, but the enemy follows them even to the mountain tops above timber-line. Deer and moose are killed by mosquitoes, which settle upon them in such amazing swarms that the unfortunate beasts succumb from literally having the blood sucked out of their bodies. Bears are driven frantic, are totally blinded, mire in the mud, and starve to death. Animals that survive have their flesh discolored all through, and even their marrow is reduced to the consistency of blood and water. The men who penetrate such regions are not the kind that would allow toil or privation to break their spirit, but they become so unstrung . . . that they become savage, desperate, and sometimes even weep in sheer helpless anger.

It is a subject to be taken seriously. When we took it up, we meant to do just that—take it seriously, logically, rationally. A lot of good it did us.

Serious Research

We turned to Science to solve the problem of bugs, and discovered we should have known better. Think about it. Science is still looking for ways to cure cancer, leukemia, and muscular dystrophy; all the money for lasers, electron microscopes, and other sophisticated equipment gets funneled into these areas. The mosquito researchers get a few leftover Bunsen burners and some out-of-date Venus's-flytraps. And to be frank, who can blame the big charity drives for taking their money elsewhere? How generous would *you* be with some lady soliciting for the Mosquito March of Dimes?

Well, the bug researchers have been doing the best they can. They have caught plenty of mosquitoes, and made up some good names for their equipment (a sweat tester is called a Dual Port Air Stream Olfactometer). We discovered over fifty highly technical articles on our subject, not to mention the many books in related fields. You will be relieved to learn that we are passing along almost none of that information, since most of it is virtually useless. For example: scientists have discovered that people who sweat less attract fewer bugs. Ah, they say, that must mean bugs like sweat. But some other scientists begin to wonder: is it the *sweat* they like or the *body odors?* This is just the sort of thing scientists are always wondering. Immediately a seed of doubt is planted and everyone runs into print with experiments proving what mosquitoes like more. Hundreds of poor subjects have their body odors gathered by passing compressed nitrogen over their forearms. Hundreds more are inveigled into giant plastic bags and left in sauna baths to provide sweat. (Undoubtedly you think we are stretching a point. We are not. For proof, see H. I. Maibach et al., "Human Skin in Relationship to Mosquito Attraction and Repulsion," especially the section entitled "In Search of Odor Attractive to Mosquitoes," in *Connecticut Medicine* 33:1, 23.) And what are the results? The scientists get into a great debate over what attracts mosquitoes. Everyone has his own ideas. Goeldi thinks sweat does it, but maybe also warmth and humidity. Wright and Kellogg and Dakin think only heat and moisture is attractive. Rudolphs proposes sweat or sebaceous secretion as "somewhat attractive." Brown and Carmichael think lysine and alanine do it. Roessler and Brown think sex hormones are behind everything.

Roessler and Brown are probably right.

To their credit, the scientists have made some useful contributions. One is a study of effects colors have on insects. They discovered orange repels mosquitoes more than anything else. Then comes yellow and green, followed by white, blue-purple, and finally red-purple at the other end of the scale. Research also indicates that the more intense the color, the more bugs disliked it. So when you choose your clothes, prefer bright yellow to a dull tan, bright green to an olive drab, and so forth.

The most dramatic breakthrough in entomological research came in the 1940's when researchers discovered that insects do not like N, N diethyl metatoluamide. This chemical is now available in most repellents on the market; of the major brands, Off and Cutter's seem the most popular among our friends. Liquid formulations tend to have a higher percentage of active ingredients than aerosols and they take up less space in your pack. Our own favorite brand is Ol' Time Woodsman's Fly Dope, a remedy which, in addition to the metatoluamide, includes pennyroyal, citronella, and oil of tar. In polite circles, the tar smell repels more than flies, but in the woods, it is a positive advantage. Scientists say that none of the pungent ingredients do any good and therefore just use the antiseptic metatoluamide. But the extras can't hurt, and their fragrance provides the psychological conviction of effective power, regardless of whether it works.

There is also some effective, foul-smelling stuff available cheap at surplus stores. The army's standard line, a yellow liquid in glass bottles, is an extremely versatile potion. Aside from repelling bugs, it will remove paint, take pine pitch off your hands, and start fires. The other surplus repellent is a new one, in plastic bottles, with the usual additives. But the new version is still in the good army tradition. Rug and Peach made the mistake of consolidating several bottles into one large one, and unfortunately their new jug was a different kind of plastic. By a week into the trip, the army juice had dissolved the container into a melty mess at the bottom of Rug's pack. The army is also working on an internal repellent to be taken just like aspirin. This would be a significant improvement, since exterior applications generally last only a few hours. (Cut the effective time to as little as half an hour during periods of activity, since perspiration and evaporation disperse the repellent quickly.) The army has as yet had no success with their idea, which is easy to understand if they are using the same juice that takes off paint, starts fires, and dissolves plastic.

In addition to fortifying yourself with repellents, you may want to make adjustments in your wardrobe. Short-sleeved button-collar shirts are not as good as the long-sleeved variety. You may want to sew the opening above the cuffs shut, or at least take along a sewing kit that will allow you to repent your mistake later. High turtlenecks provide good protection under the chin, and even better are bandanas saturated with repellent. When things get really bad, a pair of cheap working gloves and a mosquito head net make the outfit complete. The head net should have reinforced rings to keep the netting away from the face. The gloves should be long enough to reach the shirt sleeves with a tight seal. Joe sewed some homemade elasticized cuffs to his gloves so that he didn't have to worry about sewing up his shirt cuffs. He also protected the vulnerable borderline between pants and shoes with similarly fashioned anklets. Pants tucked into calf-length wool socks will do equally well, so long as you saturate the borderline with insect repellent. Black flies will otherwise burrow under the sock to the flesh.

You may begin to wonder how the old pioneers made it without any of the modern conveniences of insect repellent and army bug nets. They had their own tricks—a bit more primitive maybe—but not very different from today's schemes. Peter Kalm, a Swede who traveled through the English colonies in 1750, reported:

> The vast woods and uninhabited grounds between Albany and Canada contain immense swarms of gnats [mosquitoes] which annoy the travellers. To be in some measure secured against these insects some besmear their face with butter or grease, for the gnats do not like to settle on greasy places. The great heat makes boots very uncomfortable; but to prevent the gnats from stinging the legs they wrap some paper round them, under the stockings. Some travellers wear caps which cover the whole face, and some have gauze over their eyes. At night they lie in tents, if they can carry any with them, and make a great fire at the entrance so that smoke will drive them away.

Nonetheless, you are likely to think yourself better equipped than the pioneers. And no doubt when you have gotten your outfit together, the temptation to put it all on will be irresistible. Go ahead; indulge yourself. Strut around a bit in front of the mirror, netted, gaitered, and gloved. You will feel and look impregnable. You will think that Science and the army surplus have given you a veritable safe-conduct pass through the woods. On that point, you are dead wrong.

Sure, the outfit looks good in the comfort of your back porch. But get out in the wilds and see what happens. Your campfire seems to be dying out, so you hunch down to blow some life into it. Absorbed in the task, you fail to notice the back of your shirt has come untucked. Twenty flies nudge their way in there. Or you are careless about keeping the bottom of your head net tight. Before you know it, the entire North Country is piloting a tight traffic pattern around the lee end of your nose. Now the net keeps them in, and you couldn't have done better if you had invited them to dinner personally.

Or speaking of dinner: have you ever tried to eat beef stew through a head net? Those swarms of flies may drive you to a subtle form of treachery: using one of your comrades as a fly decoy. Bugs, you see, prefer the easy mark—a standing target rather than a moving one. When you notice that one of your camping partners is sitting over by that log doing his best to finish the beef stew, you may not be able to resist the temptation of ambling over his way, leaning slightly in his direction (as unobtrusively as possible) and shagging your flies off onto him. If the other members of your party pull the same trick, it will not be long before that poor devil by the log will hardly be able to see the landscape.

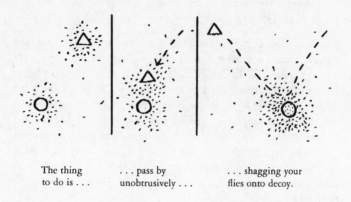

| The thing to do is . . . | . . . pass by unobtrusively . . . | . . . shagging your flies onto decoy. |

Now, you may be lucky and not ever need to use this insidious strategy. We would not stoop so low, and Joe never noticed anyway. But almost surely there will come a time when the mere presence of those swarms seems insufferable. And neither the powers of Science nor the woodlore of yesteryear can match the fecund powers of the insect world. The strongest repellent known to man is no protection against the psychological torment of constant harassment. On this matter the Approved Guidebooks maintain a stony silence. They conceive of the problem in terms of getting away from the bugs, a solution which overlooks one fact: *you cannot get away from them.*

Know Your Enemy

To go any further, you have to abandon your anthropocentrism. Forget your own problems for a moment and get to know the bugs. Don't worry; we are not about to start a preachy lecture along the lines of Our Friends the Woodland Creatures. Nor do we intend to water your stock with a lot of pantheistic ecology: every creature having his own little niche; who are we as men, latecomers on the scene, to wish to displace these fellows; in the eyes of the Oversoul the gnat runs as big a race as *Homo sapiens,* etc. Nonsense. One little niche is one big itch, to our way of thinking. When we say know the bugs, we mean know your enemy. This can have great though intangible consequences.

In the first place, knowing things about something is always reassuring, however impractical that knowledge may seem. Take the simplest bit of knowledge: names. Primitive natives always set a lot of stock in these. If they had your real name, they had power over you. If they had your real name, they knew just where you stopped and the rest of the nameless world began. They knew your inner mainspring, your essence; and knowing that, they could control you. Leaving your name off with that variety of person is as bad as giving him a little pile of your old fingernail clippings and a lock of hair; he will be off in a trice to his dark corner to conjure your body and soul into doing things you would not wish upon your little sister.

Whimsical superstition of a bygone day, eh, friend? Just don't poor-mouth it too much. No doubt there are a few men in their own dark corners behind the computer banks at Master Charge who you would just as soon didn't have *your* real name. And maybe that savage is full of delusions when it comes to the connections between body, soul, and fingernail parings; but he sleeps a little better nights. If you want protection from the hordes of insects you can't get away from, seek their real names. Seek their essences. Collect the bits and pieces of their perverted psyches as if they were as valuable as fingernail parings. When you know their devious ways, when you have their true names and mainsprings, then you have power over them and can fight back in ways more courageous and deadly than smearing yourself with repulsive odorants.

The Psychology of Balance

The mosquito is an insect of balance and humming. Since you are likely already quite familiar with the sound, begin by humming to yourself. This should be a falsetto nasal sound, thin and light, yet full-bodied. You will probably not achieve the desired quality at first. It will sound flat and uninspired. That is when you begin to realize how much a part of humming the balance is. This humming is a circular humming, a rotational humming. It is much like the faintly audible sound the spin of a gyroscope gives out. Thus although the tone is uneven, it cannot be a quaver, since quavering connotes instability. It must fairly *pulsate* with the confidence of balance achieved, like the gyroscope spinning at the tip of your finger.

Balance, you see, is the key to the mosquito's attitude. Take a moment and study, calmly, the flight and landing pattern of one of those creatures as she surveys the territory. Resist the temptation to slap wildly at her: you are winning the first battle already. Remember, you have long sleeves, gloves, and anklets on. There are plenty of harmless places where she can land. Control your emotions as she controls hers. That high humming reflects a mental as well as an aeronautical balance. Watch her hover—calmly.

Calmly you must watch her hover. . . .
    nnnnnnnnnnnnnnnnnnnnnnnnnnnnnnnnnnnnnn
  now you've got it nnnnnnnnnn
    the balance nnnnnnnnnnnnnnnnnnn the balance
      the little what have we heeeeeere investigative balance
nnnnnnnn light on the Bean's Wool Shirt nnnnnnnnnnn
  nnnnnnnnnnn not the desired eats nnnnnnnnn $n_{n_{n_{n_{n_{n_{n_{n_{n}}}}}}}}$

    light a little farther down the sleeve nnnnnnnn
   nnnnnnnn what have we heeeeeeeere nnnnnnnnnnnnn
    Hmmmmmmmmnnnnnn the balance
      the balance nnnnnnnnnnnn always the balance

See what we mean? Note the slow hover as she closes in for a perfect touchdown; sometimes to land, sometimes just for a tentative probe and a light push back off, with ever so slight an emphasis, for grace, on the rebound. If you have the patience (and you should be getting it, if you don't) you will notice that the calmness and balance make up for the mosquito's lack of intelligence. She will just as soon perch on your shirt as on your hand, and only by process of elimination—that graceful rebounding about—will she finally alight on flesh rather than wool.

But by process of elimination, she will get to your skin eventually. And if you have a thin cotton shirt, or even tight blue jeans, you will be surprised to find that her proboscis can go straight through. Look closely as your winged investigator makes ready to begin supper, and you will discover that her needle is in fact protected by a covering sheath with a split down the front. This opens to let the real tube do its work, while the sheath acts as a support and guide.

In goes the tube—the fascicle they call it—and probes around. You might think it would settle for whatever meal it could find below the surface.

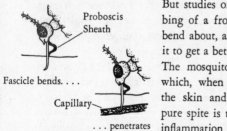

Proboscis
Sheath

Fascicle bends. . . .

Capillary

. . . penetrates

But studies of fascicle action in transparent webbing of a frog's foot reveal that the fascicle can bend about, and if it finds a small capillary, enter it to get a better meal. Now the itch goes to work. The mosquito's salivary glands secrete a liquid which, when injected, irritates the tissue below the skin and causes inflammation. Not out of pure spite is this done; just simple necessity. The inflammation involves the dilation of the capillary blood vessels in the area, and hence an increase in blood. At the same time, the saliva adds chemicals to the blood which prevent it from clotting, another necessity if the mosquito is to eat.

No doubt you are irritated at the subtle apparatus the *Aëdes* family use to get their meals; no doubt it would be nice if mosquitoes didn't bother you at all. But you have to admit, blood is what the creature is after, and this is not a bad way to get it when the only available source is six feet tall and an unwilling donor. Twelve millimeters is by and large not a profitable size for an extortioner.

Mosquitoes are creatures of moisture. They breed in swamps, lay eggs in moist depressions, and crave warm, humid days. Thus you are less likely to encounter them in windy, sunny environs; more likely in the oppressive calm just before a rain. When the sun goes down, so does the temperature; but the key factor—relative humidity—increases. Hence the mosquito's prevalence at dusk and throughout a relatively mild night.

But by now you should be prepared. You have adopted the steely calm of the sort you learned from them, so that hearing the evening filled with the balancing hum of their little gnat voices, you do not feel dread in the pit of your stomach. As they rappel by invisible ropes up and down your Bean's wool shirt, with their nnnnnn what have we heeeere investigative balance, you too have balance—your own sangfroid. The ultimate test of your will is this: watch one of them descend gracefully to your bared arm; watch her unsheath her proboscis, penetrate, strike pay dirt. No flinching of nerves now. Gently take your free hand, and with thumb and forefinger pinch together the skin on either side of the mosquito. Do not hurt the unsuspecting creature; don't even touch her. The pressure you exert will keep that proboscis of hers unsheathed, the fascicle stuck in your skin. And that mosquito, finding herself unable to remove it, is so calm and levelheaded that she does not panic. There is nothing for her to do, she concludes, but keep on drinking, which she does until her engorged body explodes. If you can sit by and watch that, you are sufficiently protected against the subtle forms of violence the mosquito is capable of perpetrating.

The Maddening Sleep of the Undead

Fortifying yourself with the psychologies of bugs is something to be done slowly, and in little bites. As a change of pace, try imagining you are Dirty Rug, something much easier than imagining you are a mosquito. Furthermore, imagine it is ten-thirty late one night in God's Country, the midst of the High Moisie. This particular corner of God's Country happens to be a little one—a jagged outcrop above the river which is short on space and long on underbrush and jack pine. But it is a sheltered nook, and plenty good enough for us, considering that three hours earlier and three hundred yards upstream dusk was coming on with us trying to negotiate Igloo Rock, a hellacious set of rapids which nearly terminated a few illustrious careers, you might say, in midstream. (That's another story, though. We're saving it for later.) It had been no time to run rapids, and when we finally got up on shore, the only place at all suitable for camping was a jagged but sheltered promontory. So we put up the fire tarp and laid into our spaghetti. By the time we were ready to retire, the slow northern dusk had turned to dark.

So here you are, imagining you are Dirty Rug: tired at the end of a long day, lethargic with the weight of that spaghetti, and wanting nothing more than a comfortable sleep. Yet the tents remain to be pitched, and as your canny eyes survey the cramped surroundings, you do not see a great deal of free flat ground. That means there's negotiating to be done. Rug's tent, being thirty dollars cheap, does not have a rain fly. True, it's equipped with a top whose bright orange fabric contrasts nicely with the blue bottom, and is sewn to *look* like a rain fly; but this is small consolation when the atmospherics are hinting at precipitation. So Dirty Rug steels himself to fight for the right to pitch his leaky model under the protection of the fire tarp. This also happens to be the flattest spot at the campsite—right, of course, where Peach is now assiduously pounding in the pegs of *his* tent.

We need not belabor here the temps and contretemps of the delicate parley which ensued. If you are imagining Dirty Rug well enough, you will be summoning up the eloquence of desperation for your re-enactment. Righteous indignation parading back and forth; touching stories of wet, cold sleeping bags; noble appeals to altruism; veiled threats of tent stakes untimely ripp'd from their earthly wombs, etc., etc. By ten fifty-seven, you will have gotten the orange-and-blue special pitched dead center under the sheltered tarp space. Not without concessions, mind you. Peach has demanded and gotten the right to pitch his own tent inches away from the front door, and there are guy ropes strung about the environs with wild abandon; but it is a passable spot under the circumstances. Rug (you will imagine) is so tired and satisfied that he passes up the usual nightly washcloth and toothbrush; strips off his shirts; crawls through the narrow tent opening; zips up the mosquito netting; and settles back, half out of his down bag, ready to meet bare-chested the embrace of Morpheus.

Next to him, Jim has retired more fully into his own bag. It is not meant for winter camping, and so not as hot as Rug's. From inside, as he is drifting off to sleep, Jim can hear Rug sigh contentedly, then shift his position slightly to obtain the maximum of comfort. There is silence for a while, then Rug once again shifting a bit. More silence. Then a little cough from Rug, and another minor adjustment. Then a slightly more energetic shuffle. Jim is only subliminally aware of these, buried in his bag and sleepy. Then some scratching from Rug. A sudden and more violent pitching about, back to the original position with a hopeful air of finality. This momentarily rouses Jim, who listens to see what's up. More silence for another six, maybe seven seconds. Then renewed and desperate scratching from Rug. "Oh, *Jesus*," he mutters to himself.

The terrible Sleep of the Undead. Jim recognizes it immediately from Rug's clearly audible whisper. It is a forlorn cry for help, whether Rug knows it or not. He is dearly hoping that Jim will roll over and ask him what the matter is. Then Rug will tell him how he can't for the life of him seem to get to sleep. But Jim knows it is the Sleep of the Undead, and burrows deeper into his bag. If he is foolish enough to start talking to Rug, whatever it is he has might be catching. Jim is himself on the verge of sleep, and if he begins to think of the cramps, itches, bumpy roots, or whatever it is ails Rug, he will soon spot enough of the same variety in his own site to keep the both of them insane all night. So he dives for cover.

But no use. Rug is out there flailing about even worse, scratching like a windmill, keeping the night air humming with his low curses. Finally he rouses himself from his bag, grabs the nearest article of clothing, which is his wool shirt, and worms his way outside the tent. Jim has his eyes open now, looking about him in the dark. Suddenly the entire tent quakes and sags, followed by a verbal fusillade from Rug, who has lost his balance and nearly castrated himself trying to step over one of those innumerable guy ropes. Then there is some huffing and puffing, and the campfire which had died down is crackling again. Jim hears Rug fussing around with the pots and pans. A longer silence, and then water sloshing around. After a few more seismic tremors from the tent ropes, Rug is back inside again, looking disconsolate as ever.

Jim decides that human decency demands he take some kind of notice, and hence groans and rolls over as if himself in sleepless agony.

"Psssst," says Rug hoarsely. "You can't sleep either?"

Jim's head appears for the first time. "No," he says. "Can't seem to drift off."

"I know! I know! You itch like fire all over, right? Can't stop itching, and scratching makes it worse, right?"

Jim says no, he's been bothered by some strange, weird noises outside.

"Noises?" says Rug, squinting, cocking his ear, and missing the point entirely. "Don't you mean itching? I've been going wild ever since I got in bed. You don't itch all over?"

Jim says he doesn't itch all over.

Rug looks sort of rueful, and says, "I think I've got biliary cirrhosis." Jim gives him the once-over. He is not at all convinced that his tentmate has biliary cirrhosis, but since he has no idea what it is in the first place, his opinion is not worth much. Besides, Rug is a med student, trained in this sort of thing.

"I figured first it had to be lice or something, since I haven't washed that much. But I went out and heated up some water and scrubbed with soap, and I'm worse than ever. So it must be biliary cirrhosis."

Jim is beginning to get worried. If a fourth-year med student says he has biliary cirrhosis with that degree of conviction, then there may be a chance he is right. And while Jim is still not clear how serious a thing that is, the name certainly sounds fearsome enough, and Rug is looking pretty mournful. To top everything off, Jim's face is beginning to itch as if on fire. He asks Rug if pillory cirocious is catching. Rug says he thinks it might be, under the right circumstances. Jim is about to ask what are the right circumstances, but fortunately his last vestige of sanity saves him from a night of Undead Sleep. He takes his pocket flash and shines it for a moment up toward the top of the tent. There is a bit of squinting around, and then he turns to Rug with a triumphant smirk. "Pillorary cycrosis, my eye," he says. "Punkies is more like it."

Punkies. Maybe you know them by the name of midges, gnats, or no-see-ums. Maybe you have never made their acquaintance at all. No matter; the roundabout purpose of this digression is to warn you about them before you spend the misery of the Undead Sleep finding out in person. For you are likely to encounter them in much the same way as we did. Like mosquitoes, their bodies are sensitive to the loss of moisture, and evening presents the best conditions for them to take the wing. Which they will do in fierce numbers: a light trap set up in the Adirondacks can collect more than 15,000 females on a good night. Or consider the case of a cold-blooded scientist who one evening clinically pulled back his long sleeve to the elbow and counted more than 300 punkies landing on that one arm *within the space of two minutes.*

Now you may be wondering how Rug was obtuse enough not to notice some 300 ravenous insects taking their ease amongst his head, arms, and torso. There are a number of good reasons for his oversight. First, punkies are small. Attach a tiny pair of wings to the dot on this "i" and you have some idea of the quantity you are dealing with: one twentieth of an inch by one sixtieth. Anyone this small has no trouble penetrating mosquito netting. Secondly, punkies are silent. You won't hear them unless they land right on your ear, and even then, it will be only the tiniest "nnnnnt" as they settle in. Lastly, their bite is stealthy. The initial prick often goes unnoticed, and only slowly—imperceptibly—will a burning itch creep across the skin. That's how punkies got their name. Algonquin Indians called them "Ponk," which was their word for "living ashes," and the Delawares called them "Punk." Dutch settlers changed that to "Punki."

Only a modicum of ratiocination is needed to discover the mainspring psychology of these insects. Consider: They are creatures of infinitesimal size. They come only at night and only together in great numbers. They proceed with silence and stealth. The evidence strongly suggests that they are plagued by an overwhelming sense of *anomie,* that sociological affliction Emile Durkheim has delineated so well in his justly famous treatise. The punkies' environment, after all, is populated by immense trees, gargantuan mammals, giant frogs and toads. Imagine what your own feelings would be were you forced to cope in a world where mosquitoes were three times your full-grown height. Now you begin to get an idea of the rootless malaise which haunts these creatures; the overawed insignificance they harbor within themselves. You can begin to see why they travel stealthily and only at night, and why they dare attack only when their massive numbers imbue them with the confidence of the common lynch mob.

Knowing the kind of courage they possess, it becomes a simple matter to deal with them. The bravado of a lynch mob amounts to a mere surface coating of brass. Mark Twain correctly described the situation, although not with the rigor of M. Durkheim, when he noted that "no mob has any sand in the presence of a man known to be splendidly brave. . . . A lynching mob would *like* to be scattered, for of a certainty there are never ten men in it who would not prefer to be somewhere else—and would be if they but had the courage to go." The obvious tactic, then, is to shower the punkies with the contempt which underneath they know they deserve. As soon as you detect the burning itch which is the hallmark of their presence, put them on peremptory notice by uncorking your bottle of repellent. This is one time when the metatoluamide really works. A volatile potion like Ol' Time Woodsman's quickly spreads its scent to all parts of a tent, giving fair warning.

Then simply ignore the pests. The punkies will be seized by the cold hand of despair and retire directly into the faceless night from whence they came. And the next time a medical student tells you he has biliary cirrhosis, silence him with the accompanying table on pruritis (the fancy word for itching).

Modifying Factors in Pruritus

(from William Stewart et al., *Synopsis of Dermatology,* St. Louis, 1970, p. 317.)

The Wisdom of Medical Science		*The Woodcraft of Dirty Rug*
FACTORS REDUCING AN ITCH	FACTORS INTENSIFY-ING AN ITCH	
1. Cold and cool compresses.	1. Heat and warmth.	Rug was nestled among the feathers of his goose-down bag, meant for winter warmth.

The Wisdom of Medical Science	The Woodcraft of Dirty Rug	
2. Scratching (mechanism unexplained), which is best performed by moderate, firm stroking with hand or brush over a wide area.	2. Rubbing and friction of clothing.	He was constantly shifting positions, rolling over, contorting one way and then the other.
3. Counterirritant or painful stimulus (for example, pin prick).	3. Wool clothing.	The first thing he did when he got up was to put on his wool shirt.
4. Avoidance of overheating.	4. Perspiration.	All that shuffling, moaning, shifting, left Rug sweating freely.
5. Physical or mental occupation (taking one's mind off it).	5. Inactivity and relaxation (sharpens the consciousness of itch).	He kept thinking to himself over and over, "Why do I itch? Why do I itch? Why do I itch?"
6. Constant moderate temperature.	6. Alternation of environmental temperature by heat or cold.	He crawled from the hot, stuffy bag into the cool evening air.
7. Reduction of inflammation.	7. Inflammation of the part (external irritants, soaps, etc.).	His remedy was to hunt up some soap and scrub the affected parts with it.
8. Presence of a lubricating layer such as sebum on the surface of the skin.	8. Reduction of surface oily layer.	This, of course, got rid of the oily film that had been clinging to him for days.

Venom and a Vaccine

Our instructions thus far have been relatively straightforward: outsangfroid the mosquitoes, cold-shoulder the punkies. Unfortunately, there are greater perils in the woods. Mosquitoes and punkies are nothing when compared with the Simuliidae. Quite frankly, some people simply cannot tolerate black flies and should thus avoid the height of the fly season. Those who lack this sense at least ought to venture into the woods forearmed with some basic knowledge.

Black flies multiply in swiftly flowing streams rather than the stagnant pools mosquitoes and many other kinds of flies prefer. Generally the breeding cycle works to make June and early July the worst time of year, with the population thinning out later in the summer. There are a number of variable factors that can change the picture, however. If the weather is warmer than usual, conditions in the streams may permit the flies to go through two generations in one season. That means the end of the summer is likely to be as bad as the beginning. But as a rule, plan your trip to avoid the early months. Of course, the start of the season varies with the latitude: the Barren Grounds has a canoeing season which lasts about three or four weeks, and that coincides with the worst of the flies. But by checking with natives in the area where you're heading, you may be able to save your party a lot of unnecessary grief.

Most of the time, you won't have to fight off black flies and mosquitoes at the same time. Flies like sunlight and dry, windy days, and generally give way to the mosquitoes as dusk falls and the humidity increases. We've seen times when the shift from one insect to the other takes place in as little as ten minutes. The flies are not out at all after dark, and much to our surprise, they did not bother us when we were swimming. Apparently something about the wet surface of the skin repelled them.

As for biting habits. Unlike mosquitoes, black flies do not mind rummaging around under clothes, and will home in on snug places, such as underneath wool socks. Their bite is often stealthy and painless; once they begin to feed, they won't disengage even when touched. There is nothing more irritating than portaging a canoe through the woods, both hands occupied, and seeing a couple flies dug in on your arm. With mosquitoes, if you blow at them hard, they will take off; no such luck with the flies. The bites may bleed for a while, and then swell up and itch for several days more. Try to avoid scratching them. They form ugly scabs, which in turn become prime targets for returning flies.

Having said that, we've covered just about all the rational things that can be said about black flies. Yet we have to warn you. The truth about them is something which apparently flatly contradicts all the advice we've given thus far. *The calm, rational approach is utterly useless when attempting to combat an attack of black flies.* Sure, it's good medicine against the mosquitoes. But rationality has nothing to do with the black fly's temperament, which is at one and the same time obsessive, perverted, suicidal, malicious, bloodlusty, and inconsiderate of others. You remember the serenity of the mosquito; none of that belongs to the black fly. Instead of the delicateness of a hummingbird's hover, you find the insane dive of the kamikaze. Watch, if you can bear it, the landing of one of these wretches. Here is no delicate bound.

More likely the creature has literally run into you headfirst as if he was so nearsighted he had missed seeing you in the first place. Although there is absolutely no scientific evidence to prove it, we are convinced the black fly is congenitally cross-eyed, and can only focus a mere centimeter in front of him.

At the same time, there is that damn throaty rasp of his. Much worse than the tentative probing hum of the mosquito. This one surges with a driven compulsion. The black fly has no more control over it than you or I, and the rasp forces its way out of God knows whatever buzzing voice box or wing vibrator was created for such perverse purposes. This is the mainspring which unhinges the little wretch—this insane mainspring of a voice box. We should really have pity on him since he has no will, no autonomy, no maliciousness (properly speaking), not even the cold-blooded deliberation of the mosquito.

You really ought to pity him, see, be rational about it. He can't help the buzz at all. It just keeps rasping away at you. A million of them out there just keep rasping away at you, see. Not his fault at all. But then he bites you, which is the rub. There's the rub, see. The black fly is mad and driven; he *has* to bite you. The madness is a contagion, spread as venom in the bite. And his biting compulsion drives out any pity you can muster for him.

A million psychotics on the wing! Jesus, an army of psychotics after you and you're being rational! Clouds of them in the air, crazy, cross-eyed, and blind! They can't fly a straight course, just watch them. Not a one in a straight course, see. But they'll get you in the end, don't worry. Plenty of them will get you. Each one of those million is lusting after your blood, each one doesn't care what the others are doing, just driven by that voice box to fly blind for your blood. Get the blood, leave his venom, that's all.

In comes the rasping monster, crashes into your arm, tangles in your hair. He plans no attack, no calm mosquito siege; instead mutters and rasps to himself over and over, mustmustmust. Don't ask must *what;* none of your business, must *what;* none of *his* business. God, *he* doesn't know, just mustmustmust until his little sucking parts claw past all the hairs and get at your skin to inject the venom. He'll crawl on your glasses, in your ear. Get in your ear with his mussmussmuss, mussing away his little itches, his little venoms. Play rational with him, will you? Try it with a canoe on your head and him mussing itches in your ear. On your *glasses,* by God—parading his muss-mussmuss in front of your eyeball! You'll play rational ten feet straight up the next *tree* is what you'll do.

This bug will put his juice into you, see, *unless you beat him to it.* You got to fight fire with fire, give yourself a little dose of the toxin so your body can make antitoxin before he starts to drive you. Like with the smallpox, and Pasteur. That's what you did against the mosquito, right? Put your calmness against his, your steel against his. But don't try switching serums, it won't work. Black fly vaccine for the black flies, see. You have to master the madness without avoiding it. No guidebook tells you this, because no guidebook knows the vaccine. But Peach knows the vaccine. He taught it to us on the Moisie just after the long six-hour portage around the mile-and-a-half set of water-falls—the one we had to go behind the hill. He told us this song, called it Little Black Flies. Maybe that's the name of the song, we don't know; Peach said it was. It makes no difference, the words are immaterial. Peach remem-bered only a few of them, and mumbled a couple more in the blank spaces.

The thing is not the words but the song. You have to rumble it in a raspy voice. It goes

> *Black flies, little black flies*
> *Rum bum umble dum little black flies.*
>
> *(This is the chorus. Repeat.)*
>
> *Oh way up in Ontario . . .*
> *(Rumbly umble dum dum.)*
>
> *(This is the first verse.*
> *Peach forgot the rest of it.)*

The music is extremely simple, in a minor key. If you have a guitar, all you have to know are two chords. The first is a C minor, which you use all the time except for the one bar when you play a G major. You should strum the guitar as fast and heavy as you can. Avoid any semblance of good tech-nique. You will probably be better off without the guitar. The music is simple, but the copy Peach made for us was small and crabbed. Not small for saving space, see, but more for the aesthetics, which are of the stifling and driven variety. He put in the guitar part too, and made us memorize it off that scrap of journal paper. We were cross-eyed at the end of the trail, easy.

You probably think all this business we have been telling you—all this talk of songs as antitoxins, the need to have a raspy voice—is the sheerest hogwash, entertaining enough perhaps for the stay-at-home armchair, but useless when the going gets tough. You are the kind of person that will

revert to the platitudes of the approved guidebooks, take yourself up to the north woods with a little repellent, and go stark raving mad when you find that the swarms of flies pay no attention to the worthless baubles and trinkets that have been pawned off on you as sound remedies. But by God, friend, you would know how well our remedy works had you been on that six-hour portage with those flies—hundreds of them—swarming around you. You would have seen Peach get out that raspy old voice of his, screw up his face into the driven look all black flies have. Complete it with that intense cross-eyed expression. You would have seen him rip off "Little Black Flies," rum bumble um and all; and you would have laughed until the tears came.

We started this disquisition with the intent of treating the bug problem in a logical, rational manner; and maybe we should have stuck with it. Watching someone else play at being an insane and driven black fly is not the kind of madness you would expect *any* guidebook to peddle as a nostrum. But it is a catching kind of madness, and you may find yourself playing the same game. Don't be afraid of acting a bit insane. Like we said, a little toxin to make the antitoxin. Sanity is maintained only by healthy and regular promenades around its border.

20. Mouthwatering

The river goes on unfolding itself as it always has, irrespective of our portages and tracking around its banks. And now we are shut of those damn alder-bushes for a time, so we can unfold ourselves along with it. We like to think it's an even deal, taken all in all; the river winds out its character for us on its way to the sea, and we, like the fiddleheads stretching in late spring, un-wind ourselves to the river. Down at the next leisurely bend there is a boulder garden just off shore, big twenty- and thirty-foot chunks from some past un-winding. We have a story about them to tell you, with our own reasons for the telling. We'll get to those soon enough; for now take our story as it is—the simple tale of lunch on a twenty-foot cube.

The river slips its way around this stand of boulders, giving us easy pas-sage among them. Rug and Peach let the current drift them down onto our target, and then Peach stops the boat with a hand against the rough rock. Joe draws the other canoe to the far side. There at the back a fissure provides the route we need to the platform above. It is a ridiculous, impractical place to stop, since the mooring is precarious and the way to the top a matter of chimney-climbing the fissure. But Joe scrambles up, catches the bow line tossed him from Peach's canoe, and awaits further developments on the lunch.

Rug is busy in that department, scrounging around in the duffel for the jars of peanut butter and jelly, the hard-cased cheese, the Civil Defense biscuits, the chocolate bits. One by one he hefts them up to Joe, with a care that shows he values these lifelines far above the mooring rope tossed before. Up above, Joe cradles the cheese in his lap, doing his usual meticulous job of measuring the proper proportions to be chipped off the hunk for the day's ration. Jim's head appears at the top of the chimney crack, and then the rest of him; more scruffling of jeans in the crevice as Peach follows; and finally Rug, an evident lust for jelly and biscuit in his eye. Peach stacks the crackers in four neat piles—that's his routine job. Jim pulls out his hunting knife to donate to the peanut-butter pot. Joe glances briefly at the other three of us, a sort of unspoken grace, and the meal begins.

So far this noon, lunch is unfolding as usual: Joe with his cheese cradled, Peach with his cracker piles. But twenty feet below, still snug under the canoe seat, is the plastic water jug. Jim is the first to notice it, because he likes to eat the natural peanut butter plain, and that makes him thirsty. He debates remaining silent about the matter (after the portaging, he is too tired to fetch it himself, and figures it will sound impolite to suggest someone else get it). He has just decided to speak up anyway, when he notices Rug casting his eyes about the rock. Quickly Jim averts his glance, feigns absorption in his peanut-butter biscuit. Rug clears his throat.

"Where's the lemonade?" he says. "Could somebody pass it this way?"

Rug knows very well where the lemonade is—or isn't, to be more precise. Jim would have taken this bait immediately, had he not glanced up before and saved himself. But Peach. Peach is over there polishing off some jelly, and beginning to feel a bit dry himself.

Joe, innocent as ever, allows as how he doesn't think anybody's made the lemonade yet. That makes it Peach's move.

"The powder's in my pack," he says. "Right in the top pocket if you want to get it." Peach has started his own maneuver here, but Dirty Rug knows these tactics inside and out, and reaches to outflank him. In fact, Peach has just committed the cardinal sin: indicating some actual interest in having the lemonade. Rug now knows he has a mark to work on.

"No, that's O.K.," he says. "I was just curious, is all. It's probably better to save it for tonight. Tart, cold lemonade would go well with the spaghetti."

A fine example of the double-reverse tactic. Rug fakes disinterest, but at the same time slides the adjectives "tart" and "cold" into the conversation. Peach shifts uneasily, restless at the prospect of a lunch without tart, cold lemonade.

"I think it would go better now," he says. "It's a hot day and we're more thirsty than at dinner."

"Well, the river water's good enough for me. I don't seem to be that dry anyway."

"Sure," says Joe hopefully. "Let's just lower the jug with a rope and forget the lemonade."

"The jug's down under the seat," says Peach, glummer than ever. He lets out a sigh which sounds to Rug entirely too much like resignation. Perhaps he's not taking the bait after all. Jim is secretly watching, trying to figure out whether this is genuine or part of a countermaneuver.

Rug can't afford to take a chance. "That sharp citrus tang *would* give a nice edge to the meal," he observes. "And it sure makes a good contrast with this dry peanut butter and sticky jelly."

Peach's eyes are getting bigger.

"I don't know, I don't know," continues Rug. "When I think about the spaghetti, I'm inclined to hold on till tonight." He pauses as if ravaged by some inner battle. "Oh, *hell,* I won't object if you make it now. Really, it's O.K. by me."

Peach throws off his Baden-Powell hat in surrender, and heads for the fissure. Joe goes back to eyeing the cheese. "You like a bit more, Jawn? I think I gave myself the lion's share of this hunk."

Rug shakes his head with magisterial calm. He lies all the way back on the rock, looking up at the sky, listening to the scruffing noises of Peach in the chimney.

Jim can only marvel at Rug's virtuosity, thankful *he* was not the one caught in a duel of wits. You almost took the bait, he says to himself. Then you'd have had to fight back by out-mouthwatering him. Would have needed to get your own set of tasty metaphors moving. But God, what a superb show of disinterest! There would have been nothing left to do but try and top it. And *then* what?

21. A Day Off

Travel posters, you may have noticed, invariably bask in the gold of late-afternoon sunlight, while wilderness albums, a more interesting and honest medium, contain a fairer share of drizzles and thundershowers. Look into the accounts of exploration and you will learn something of the storms that break out among expeditioners themselves. History is cluttered with the wreckage. Remember Henry Hudson in his shallop. Or Howland, Howland, and Dunn, who deserted John Wesley Powell at Separation Rapids on the Colorado to be killed by Indians in the canyon lands. Or Thomas Simpson driven to suicide by his men in the Barren Grounds. Or Charles Hall dead of arsenic in the arctic in 1871. Not that deadly wilderness storms happen only to famous explorers. We have seen a report of a North Country trapper who shared a winter cabin with his partner and eventually murdered him for whistling the same tune day in, day out. A dozen sourdoughs acquitted the avenger—justifiable homicide, open and shut. Pierre Berton in his history of the Klondike tells of two partners, said to be boyhood friends, splitting their outfit down the middle at the end of the Chilkoot Trail; in a rage they sawed in half every item they owned right down to individual bags of flour to deprive the other man of any chance of getting out alive.

Terrible cataclysms, these episodes, and they make us wonder about all the other wilderness manuals filled with faces that only smile. Review the literature and you will find either sunny friendships or murderous rivalries. Judging by the printed word, few wilderness trips are troubled by small conflicts that reasonable people might solve together. Is this possible?

For our part, we are still trying to write a book that is mostly true. We bet the four of us had more good times and parted better friends than most of those expeditioners who write the travel posters. But we weathered a few storms too, and unlike the others, we mean to tell you about them. Now we should say right away, we don't particularly enjoy airing our feelings or our fights. It's just we keep running up against this—what shall we say—Lyrical Thoreauvianism that pervades camping literature. A lot of people, it seems, assume that because they love nature, enjoy the company of friends, and are out for a good time, they can expect a month of spiritual uplift. We look at it this way: throw a group of people together without benefit of organization, uniforms, or the flag, deprive them of outside contact, and then put them at hard labor hauling around edibles that they have to ration among themselves. You have just rolled gunpowder. Now forbid these people the use of hot emotion—no anger, no resentment, no irritation, no conflict of any kind. You have just spiked that keg of powder. We will put the problem as directly as we know how: the rigors of a wilderness trip will draw out differences among fellow human beings, and the wilderness paddler is well advised to prepare for them.

A certain amount of insight—simply knowing how tension can grow on a trip—can help to resolve some conflicts before they even come up. It is, for example, much easier to work out a system for dividing expenses before the trip than afterward. Some people with a faint disdain for finance may just count on dividing the total cost of the trip by the number in the party. But consider: If you travel to the edge of the wilds by car, the driver and his riders will surely split the cost of gas and oil. That still leaves uncomputed the fees for general wear and tear. And who is going to pay for a dropped muffler? The best time to hit on an equitable settlement is even before you decide whose car to take; certainly before you bottom out on some overgrown logging road. Photographic expenses fall into another debatable area. Why should the whole party pay for all the shots one idiot behind the lens over-exposes? Then again, why should one person pay for all the film so that the others can pick over the results to copy and keep the best of it? On the Moisie, we worked out two different arrangements. Jim paid for all the movie film to establish a moral claim on editing rights and the master print, while Joe provided the film for the Instamatic according to an elaborate system of common and preferred stock that only Joe seemed to fully understand; fortunately, the rest of us were satisfied by the authority, if not the clarity, of his explanations. And then there's the most crucial anticipation of all: deciding in advance who's to pay for a lost or damaged canoe. Our policy is that liability belongs to whoever is paddling, not the owner alone. There are other possible arrangements but we should warn you that any attempt to assign fault for a broken canoe is the fastest way we know to warm up dunked boaters.

Friction—two sticks rubbing—creates heat, and two people rubbing will also, sooner or later, throw sparks. Working at the end of a paddle for eight, ten, twelve hours a day with only one other person to talk to can become a psychological strain after a few weeks. Put it down as a subtype of cabin fever. Small mannerisms begin to grate, and after a while seem to become a studied attempt to annoy. Two people traveling alone have to grit it out, but any larger party should reduce the pressure by rotating partners. It was by conscious design on our trip that Rug paired with Joe on the lakes and with Peach on the river itself; that we all switched tentmates every three nights; and that we never allowed canoeing partners to share tents. We even switched automobile passengers twice a day on our drive up to the railroad. This constantly changing routine may seem self-conscious at first, but remember that later in the trip your fondest wish may be to rid yourself of your best friend's tuneless "Old Man River"—and this gives you a diplomatic out.

If little things like whistling begin to rub, you can imagine how emotionally charged the really serious issues of river life can become. Issues like whether a stretch of whitewater should be run or not, who does the supper dishes on a particular night, or who gets the least burned piece of gingerbread. Every wilderness party has to deal with these problems; they go right to the heart of how people relate to one another, how they organize into a group. Different groups will work out different solutions to suit themselves, and we do not intend to prescribe our system of government for anybody else. All the same, we think it worthwhile to describe how we solved these everyday problems.

Let's take one issue at a time. First is the decision whether or not to run any particular rapids. The canoe clubs are unanimous in advocating a leadership model of decision making. One person, the most experienced and presumably the most skillful canoeist of the group, is designated leader and makes the law not only on whether to run but also on who runs and who doesn't. For many activities and many groups, this approach is fine. On the Moisie though, we had no leader, no badges, no whistles. Put it the other way: good leaders need good followers, and we were short. As regards whitewater, three of us—all except Peach—had run enough rivers to train the eye, and Peach was a quick learner and never one to hold back an opinion. Rug did most of the scouting, but his reports were only that; they never became commands. On the nip-and-tuck decisions we sought a consensus. When we couldn't get one, we took a vote. Never a show of hands or a head count, but something like an applause meter with strength of feeling counting instead of sheer loudness. An example: After the four of us scouted Rim Canyon, Rug wanted to lower the boats and run the last rapids single. Jim was dubious, but Peach was willing to turn his canoe over to Rug for the run. Then very slow, Joe said, "Jawn, for the good of the trip, don't chance it." So we portaged the extra distance and "for the good of the trip" became our language of veto.

Second issue: Who washes the dishes? Different people have different interests and in the course of a trip certain jobs will devolve on specific people. Rug, for example, is a fanatic about chopping wood. Unless restrained, he is liable to cut enough deadwood to burn the night through and still leave a bundle for the next party. Needless to say, the rest of us never needed to go out with the ax. Peach, meanwhile, became our fire starter; Joe, our baker. But we never have found anybody who enjoyed the cleanup. Of course, if everyone waits long enough, somebody (usually the hungriest guy at breakfast) will get out the dishpan. Often the same person may give in time after time; but sticking one man with a job nobody wants is a sure source of bad will. On this score, we were inflexible and, one day in four, each of us washed the pots. (We won't go into the politics of putting off spaghetti dinners, our dirtiest meal, until the next guy's turn as dishwasher.)

And who gets the best (or biggest) piece of gingerbread? Wilderness trips run on a shortage economy. By some perversity of human nature, a lack of supplies creates increased demand. Our gingerbreads were exactly the right size for four paddlers: our calorie count proved it. Although none of us ever went hungry, we never had the chance to overeat, and so took an enormous interest in our portions. Perfect equity is a rare thing in this world, and most portions are unequal, as anyone who studies them as closely as we did will realize. Our method of dividing unfairness fairly is to hold raffles. On the count of three, each person shows a number, one through five fingers at the end of a fist. Dealer adds the total and counts around clockwise. Wherever the lucky number lands, that person gets first pick of the gingerbread. The system isn't fair and doesn't pretend to be; the same person can win one raffle after another and often does. But at least the losers can only rail against their own bad luck or some impersonal fate, not against the other guy's greed or stinginess.

You are now pretty deep into our psychology and know how we rotated tents, sought a consensus on tough decisions, bartered our supplies, and generally thought about our strain on one another. You are entitled to know that we still had some squalls. By any reckoning, the most even-tempered of us is Joe. A long fuse is, we suppose, part of his natural caution. Rug, who has known him a long time, has only once seen him steaming mad—and that was after our lining capsize. We never did formulate a way for smoothing over raw spots like that one; we only note that the rough and tumble of wilderness life usually presents an outlet and makes partnership possible again. In this particular instance, we ate a somber lunch until Peach went for the water jug and found Joe's canoe drifting out of the eddy with absolutely no line fixed to shore. Joe's mortification canceled out his earlier anger. Another time, Peach began to fume on a tortuous portage over huge boulders alongside the river. The way he saw it, Rug was letting the bow end of the canoe bang too hard on the rocks. Rug, already doing the best he could, was helpless to improve on a bad job. No words were spoken, but none were needed to spoil the atmosphere. Then, on the second trip with the packs, Rug missed a handhold and fell backward eight feet into the river. He was furious and swore mightily—at the goddamn Moisie. And Peach laughed uncontrollably. The river had taken its revenge on Rug just as it was taking it on Peach's canoe, and once again we were right with one another.

If you have guessed by now that we are leading up to something, you are right. No world-shaking revelation, mind you. Just the difference between papering over small differences and telling the truth. In the preceding chapter, we told you about one of our lunches. Picked out one to give you a feel for life at midday on the Moisie. As you might suspect, our choice was not random; we selected the meal on the cubes because it stands out the most vivid. But here's the thing: the story you got was the way Jim saw it, watching the play between Peach and Rug. Joe, busy with his cheese and crackers, didn't see the mouthwatering game at all. As for whether Rug was baiting Peach or really did want to save the lemonade for supper, he's not saying. To round out the account, we have to tell you that Peach came back up from the river awfully quiet. Somewhere in the chimney, it occurred to him he was always conned into getting the lemonade. That the last time he suggested a raffle, Rug and Jim had vetoed the suggestion with uncommon heat. That another lunch when he voted to hold lemonade for dinner, Rug argued for serving it up right away. Now we don't want you to think that Peach was being small-minded or peevish. Lunch on a river trip, remember, is the one time of legitimate, maximum repose.

So Peach, when he got back up on that table, turned to us all and said, "Listen. I think we need a day off." And so doing, he committed us to the ultimate and best tension reliever that any wilderness party has—a sabbath. The simple chance to break the pattern that locks canoeists two by two is sometimes the only way to repair an endangered friendship. To be alone for a few hours is the surest method of improving the company of others.

Half a mile below the big rock cubes, we found a campsite. That afternoon, Rug went fishing, Joe collected what he called rare plants, Jim climbed eight hundred feet up the side of the canyon to get an overview of the river, and Peach built a sauna out of hot stones and the fire tarp. That evening, Joe held a dramatic reading by candlelight from Stefansson's *Unsolved Mysteries of the Arctic*, Chapter 4, which details how Captain André and his party attempted to reach the North Pole by balloon, and died on their return, the victims of carbon-monoxide poisoning.

Tomorrow we would return to the river.

22. *Canyon Rapids*

This is the High Moisie. Some sections, the river is lazy and we float along, Huckleberry style. Other places, the river pitches in as canyon digger. We quote from Jim's journal:

> The canyon rapids are spaced farther apart than on the upper river but are louder and more powerful. . . . The one this afternoon was typical except for our being able to run the whole length of it. The rapids start on a curve to the west, we on the inside of the river. Between us and the near bank is the usual picket fence line-up of boulders, and just to the outside of them, enormous standing waves. We have to keep clear of the boulders but stay out of the haystacks. Once around the bend, the waves stretch out into big rollers that we have to cross to reach the inside of the next bend. . . .

This is the finest and most demanding kind of wilderness water. Waves and rocks obstruct all but one tricky passage. The paddler who ventures it needs everything he has learned in simpler currents: the ability to turn his boat stroke by stroke, the wit to coordinate those strokes with the river's own changing currents, and the audacity to climb out on his paddle when the river is roughest. But he needs even more. Success in a complex rapids requires putting them together into a few smooth maneuvers.

RIVER CROSSINGS. In our section on riffles, we discussed the most basic kind of downriver maneuvering: pivot, paddle, and pivot again. This turn-and-shoot style of steering enables a canoe team to dodge most obstructions, but it has definite limitations. The initial pivot takes time to execute and exposes the whole side of the boat to whatever trouble lies downstream. In addition, the forward speed that carries the canoe past one rock decreases the paddlers' lead time to deal with others and can help to swamp an open canoe in heavy waves.

To demonstrate alternative maneuvers, we have Rug and Peach at the top of the canyon rapids, heading straight for a small boulder at A. Paddling left, Rug needs to pry or else crossdraw right to clear that rock. If he pivots the boat, however, the bow will slide into relatively slow water while the stern remains in the powerful main current. The result would be a dangerous broach. So Peach draws right at the same time that Rug crossdraws right. The effect is to sideslip the whole boat parallel across the current. Canoes do not shuffle sideways with agility, especially if they are weighted with packs or designed with a keel. Nonetheless, two strong paddlers using opposing draw and pry strokes can inch a boat sideways without otherwise disturbing its orientation in the current. In swift boulder gardens and man-made slalom courses, this sideslipping by inches is sometimes the perfect dodge.

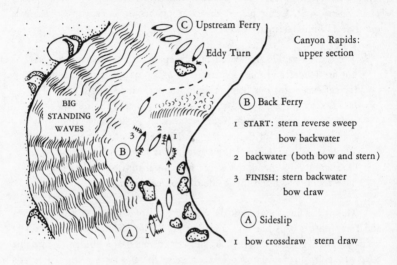

Canyon Rapids:
upper section

© Upstream Ferry

Eddy Turn

BIG STANDING WAVES

B Back Ferry

1 START: stern reverse sweep
     bow backwater

2 backwater (both bow and stern)

3 FINISH: stern backwater
     bow draw

A Sideslip

1 bow crossdraw   stern draw

At B, Rug and Peach are riding the boundary between the impassable rock garden near shore and big swamper waves in the middle. The current is pulling them so fast that they will be unable to avoid the ledge below by sideslipping, so they go one step further and do a *back ferry*. This is a maneuver used to cross rivers without slipping downstream. Both men backpaddle to stop the boat's forward motion. As they do, Peach uses a backward sweep stroke to angle his stern left toward the far shore. Since the downstream motion of the current cancels out the upstream component of the backpaddling, the boat simply ferries sideways across the river without losing ground.

That is the textbook description of the back ferry, but things get complicated when you ask just exactly what angle Peach should set the boat at to get sideways with the least amount of downstream slip. If you can backpaddle at a speed faster than the forward current, the answer is simple: Set as broad an angle as you can without slipping downstream. Keep one eye to shore as a point of reference, and if you are actually moving some upstream, broaden the angle; if you are slipping downstream, make it narrower, more parallel to the current. But what if you can't completely offset the downstream current with your paddling? Then no matter what angle you set, you're going to lose *some* ground; but either too broad or too narrow an angle will lose more ground than the optimal angle. There is always one best angle, and it can be calculated on paper the same way you do vectors in physics.

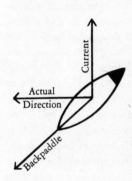

To wit: The river current is one vector, moving you downstream; the backpaddling is another, moving you upstream and across the river. The actual course the canoe takes is the combination of these two forces. Once the current's speed is greater than the speed at which you can backpaddle, the more that current increases, the broader the angle you must set your boat. Thus if the current is flowing twice the speed of what you can backpaddle, the best angle is 60° to the current. With the current three times your opposing speed, the best angle is 70°. And with the current four times as fast, the best angle is 75°. That you should *increase* your angle as the current itself increases is a notion contrary to what most expect. But the vector calculations prove it's true.* Of course, you can't

---

* We are indebted to Robert McNair's *Basic River Canoeing* for correcting our original intuitions on this point. We debated whether or not to explain the whole business of vector angles in the text and figured it was too complicated to bother with. For those still curious, we offer this short order course on the basic calculation of vectors. The canoe starts at A, is carried by the downstream current as in Vector 1; moves by way of backpaddling the amount shown as in Vector 2. The net movement (the course the canoe actually travels) is from A to B. Now suppose Vector 1 (river current) is two times the speed of Vector 2 (backpaddling) as below. 2A is the vector taken if you backpaddled with an angle of 30°; 2B, an angle of 60°; 2C, an angle of 90°. If we draw in the net directions for each possibility, and extend them to the hypothetical riverbank, we discover that both the narrower angle 2A and the broader angle 2C will land the canoe farther downstream than the optimal angle of 2B.

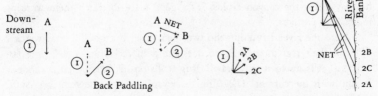

take a protractor out on the river, but at least you can learn to estimate the angles by feel. Few paddlers care to ferry a current more than four times their speed (at least in a rapids of any complexity), so you know that almost never will you have to set an angle broader than 75°. Even a current moving three times paddle speed is quite fast.

There are other factors which may affect the angle you set. A 75° course may be called for in theory, but if your line of travel runs across some sizable standing waves, you may have to trim the angle to a narrower quartering one of about 30° to keep from broaching (see pages 184–5). Furthermore, in extremely strong currents, the backpaddling stroke is not very effective. The sternman (who should be the one to fix the angle, since he can best see the boat work in the current) may decide he can control the angle better by turning the boat around and doing the ferry facing upstream. This is exactly what Peach and Rug are doing at C: an *upstream ferry*. They've turned into the eddy, so they're pointing in the right direction; then they head out of the eddy on their right side, setting an angle to the current just as they did on the back ferry. Only this time they can use the full power of the forward paddle stroke. In crossing the eddy line boundary, they paddle vigorously to keep the canoe steady, and Peach is on guard so that the bow is not whipped around broadside by the downstream current. The boat moves across the river with very little downstream slippage.

The most awkward and unnerving feature of the upstream ferry is that you are paddling forward but traveling backward and sideways. You look forward (upstream) to estimate the proper angle to the current; but you also have to look sideways to shore for a reference point. And on really fast currents where slippage is inevitable, you have to crane around and look downstream to dodge any rocks and make sure the standing waves are not so big that they're breaking over the low stern end. Our advice is to go out and run a few rapids in reverse before trying an upstream ferry in really rough water. The practice is good anyway: there are times you'll find yourself spun around in the middle of a course and have to run the rest of the set backward, rather than chance a broadside capsize trying to get pointed right again.

TEAMWORK. Peach and Rug are where we left them—out among the rollers halfway across the canyon rapids. It's a good place to watch them working together as partners.

Here the river is pulling the two men close to a granite boat wrecker (D) off their rear quarter. Peach does the dead reckoning and, at the last moment, yells up to Rug, "Draw!" Rug sculls on his left until the canoe is in line with the current. They drop backward through the midriver chute, and Rug pries into the eddy. They turn out of the eddy with Rug cross-drawing and Peach paddling straightaway, then fishtail through the next few boulders. Finally, Rug calls out to Peach, "Head into shore," and they land at E to scout the next turn.

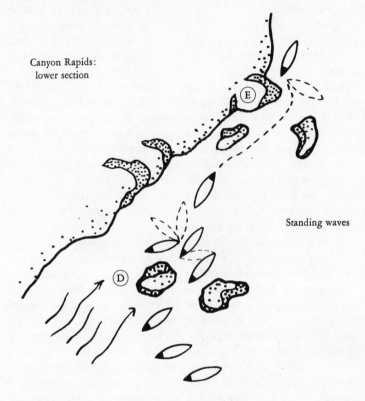

Canyon Rapids:
lower section

Standing waves

Teamwork is what makes this run sound easy, even a bit automatic. The fact is that this whole sequence from C to E was improvised. Scouting from shore, Rug had expected to ferry upstream of the "boat wrecker." That this miscalculation did not lead to frantic maneuvering or midriver name calling is a credit to a few simple principles.

The first principle is that in whitewater canoeing responsibilities are split, not shared. Route picking, for example. Nothing is more dangerous than bowman and sternman both trying to pick the course. The bowman turns toward one chute, sternman corrects him to go another way, and before long the river sends them down in pieces. Or each paddler waits for the other to decide between rock left and rock right, and the river decides by default—rock center. Every ship needs a captain, and whitewater canoes are no exception. The captain, as every sailor knows, is not necessarily the most able seaman; he or she is just the one who sits in the captain's chair. In whitewater, that chair is the bow seat. Sitting up front, the bowman can see unobstructed any trouble that is coming and how to avoid it. Thus the bowman initiates the turn, and as we've already seen (page 138), in doing so he also creates more time for turning. Meanwhile, the sternman keeps one eye on the bow and one eye on the river. He sees where the lead wants to put the bow, helps put it there, and then brings around the middle and the caboose.

The more two paddlers work together, the more sensitive they become to one another's movements. Verbal signals become less and less necessary. When they are used, spoken commands should be clear and convincing. Shouting "Rock left!" is all right, we suppose, if both partners have agreed on what this information implies (go left? or literally "rock left"?) and if both can instantaneously tell left from right (Rug, for one, cannot). We prefer utter simplicity. Peach's command to Rug ("Draw!") was ideal in that it required no thought, no interpretation, and no understanding on the part of the recipient. (Peach, you remember, was enjoying the luxury of command by virtue of cruising in reverse.)

The most important coordination that develops between paddlers is neither verbal nor cerebral. It is rather the small unconscious adaptation of one's own motions to the habits and abilities of another. Peeling out of the middle eddy in the canyon rapids, Peach threw out the rule book. Although turning out on Rug's off side, he didn't brace, but instead paddled straight-away. Two weeks earlier, this kind of sloppiness could have upended the two of them. But a hundred eddies later, in the canyon, Peach knew exactly how much weight to expect Rug to put into his downstream lean and could deduce how much he should contribute; he also knew he could trust Rug's crossdraw to absorb the initial shock of hitting the main current. And he knew that some hard forward jabs would swing the canoe through a smooth arc nicely into the river's inside alley. For his part, Rug leaned out on his paddle and noted with satisfaction that his crossdraw swung the boat through exactly the right turn, though Peach seemed a bit shaky on his brace. "Funny," Rug thought to himself. "Not like Peach to tense up in a tight spot."

CANOEING SINGLE. Now and then the wilderness paddler will come to a section of river that is best canoed solo—either a riffles too shallow to sup-port the weight of two or a set of waves too tall. Once you try it, you'll find that paddling single is a pleasure in its own right and a part of every canoeist's education.

Experiment first in flatwater and you will learn about side wheels and pinwheels all over again before you master the fine art of weaving a straight line. Out in a shallow rapids, though, you will come to appreciate the ease of turning the lightened boat and the luxury of skimming over rounders that hard knocks have taught you to detour. Paddling at midships, the single canoeist has his choice between bow and stern strokes. Say that Rug is paddling C-1 and wants to pivot to the right. He can either lean forward and do his usual crossdraw or he can lean out on his paddle side and draw the stern left—and is reminded very quickly of the difference between a bow and a stern pivot. At times, of course, the soloist misses the symmetry of two paddles and invents such new contortions as the *cross backstroke.*

This is begun like a crossdraw but carried even farther around so that the paddler eventually is scooping backward with the power face of his blade on his off side. More often, he will find that combinations of familiar strokes blend smoothly to give remarkable directional control. Thus he combines a draw at the bow with the hook of a "J" to create an *inverted sweep* and turns sharply to the paddle side.

In heavy water, the solo canoeist is glad for the extra buoyancy, but

Cross Backstroke   Inverted Sweep

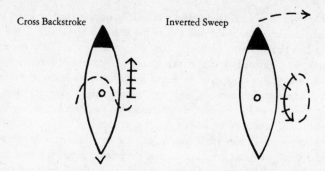

he misses the levering power of paddles at each end. In fact, the canoe will yaw in any sizable wave where the paddler is not already fighting the broach. Bracing strokes provide good stability in high waves, though some situations (such as turning out of eddies on the off side) may call for a lean against the current without benefit of a brace or else a shift in paddle sides. In the excitement of whitewater, the paddler is often happy to be alone, glad to be able to make his own mistakes and know where they come from, even more glad to have the satisfaction of bringing the boat through a tough set single-handed. But once back in the smooth flat current at the bottom, watch that paddler look around for his partner's two willing arms.

MULTIPLE BOATS. For safety's sake, no canoe should enter whitewater or wilderness waters alone. But unless you take care, a second canoe can become a dangerous missile. Allow plenty of leeway in any rapids so that if the lead canoe unexpectedly broadsides, the next boat doesn't run her over. At the same time, keep in sight of the boat behind. The reason for doing this is to ensure that a rescue party is always on the alert, although we suspect that in addition there is no more guilty pleasure than to look back on a successfully run rapids and watch the following boat flounder and capsize.

23. Igloo Rock

For all the times friends are drawn apart on a long wilderness trip, the river provides other times to bring them together: the stillness of a narrow canyon, the grandeur of a cascade, the easy acceptance of a stick thrown it one rainy night. If you ask us, though, the river is never more effective in cementing the bonds of friendship than when it obliges with a few threats of imminent disaster.

It is late afternoon deep in the canyon. In the lead boat, Rug and Peach both know that in the last short rapids Joe drew his bow a little too far to the outside curve, and now he and Jim are bailing. Rug smiles to himself, though he would be careful not to show it—not even to Peach. Serves Joe right to try a better route. If he wants to experiment, he can bail too. Rug, anyway, is tired and welcomes the chance to open up a little extra distance on the other boat. He feels the canoe surge as Peach lays extra muscle into his paddle. Peach's thoughts, meanwhile, are elsewhere; certainly he has no intention of jumping the lead. He is moving more by instinct, or at least by habit learned too well to require conscious attention.

Jim's teeth are set on edge and he bails with a furious speed. "Looks like clear water ahead," he tells Joe. "Rug and Peach are nearly around the bend already." He wants to ask Joe what the hell he had in mind running the outside of the turn and hitting the big haystack at an angle, but he doesn't—only scrapes harder with the bailer.

Peach looks back and reports to Rug. "Well, they're under power again." The two men relax into a long easy stroke.

None of us time it, but Joe and Jim take thirty or forty minutes to narrow the gap to a single canoe length. Just as they pull up, Peach and Rug cut their power and turn to the others as if waiting the whole time for the laggards to catch up.

"You should have heard Rug back at the rapids," Peach says. "He's sitting up front mumbling, 'Put in a crossdraw just past—' and I'd have to yell up that I couldn't hear a word of it. He'd mumble back, 'Never mind, we made it. Just watch the—' and I'd yell up, 'What?' Then the wind gusted up, and the next thing, clear as a bell, he's shouting, 'My hat! My hat! Hook it with your paddle! In the eddy there—grab it!' As if I hadn't smelled it going by."

Joe laughs and sets his paddle on the gunwale. Rug laughs at himself, and eyes Joe to make sure he doesn't pull ahead.

Jim interrupts, "Before you guys get carried away, you might tell me what you think about this next rapids."

A quarter mile ahead the river curves to the west; at the turn, there is a small island of rocks spread out around a little family of scrub alder. Exactly in midriver across from the island a single boulder the size of a granite igloo divides the current in half. The river itself appears smooth and black-green, but in the spaces of our conversation a properly tuned ear can pick up a soft, unobtrusive rumble. By now we know the Moisie well enough to understand her tones and see past her appearances. The sound ahead is pure. When it fades in the wind, deeper, more distant tones don't pass through, so we know the rapids are short. The rumble is low-pitched, meaning the river narrows past the island; but there is no hint of a crashing, vertical falls. That next rapids might even be runnable except that the water remains dark all the way to the horizon. Obviously, the river drops so fast that all the whitewater is below our line of sight. Probably another portage, at best a lining.

Grimmer now, we paddle to the island and walk its length. To one side, the smaller channel funnels down to a series of high roller waves, bounded by jagged rocks where we are and a steep cutbank on the shore. No eddy line to run and no footing for ropework here. The main river sweeps outside our island, divides into several chutes around the mid-lying igloo, and then a hundred yards downstream drops over a set of steep triple ledges. All three together are no more than a geologist's small fault. But even a short drop through eleven thousand years or less is enough to inspire the swollen Moisie to kick up steep waves eight and ten feet high. The time spans of our own lives are short enough without chancing a trip through there.

"Well, Rug, looks like a four-man carry down the island," says Jim. "Then ferry over to the inside bank and portage from there. You agree?"

Peach, dead-eye we would call him, chimes in. "By then it'll be dark. The sun's down already. We can shoot the top set by just skinning that huge rock in the middle there, eddy-turn below the island, and then ferry direct across to shore."

Joe scratches. "With those three ledges below, you sure don't want to miss that eddy, Jawn."

Rug looks once after the sun, once at the rock, and again at the drops below. After all, *he* wasn't the one who had to use the bailer on the last go-around! "Sounds reasonable to me, Peach," he says. "Let's go."

They point their canoe upstream and paddle thirty yards, for leeway, before swinging around toward the igloo. As soon as they pivot, Rug stands for a final look.

"Damn! The angle by the rock is too tight. There's a keeler alongside it, and we'll never make the inside turn."

Peach replies, not quite calm, "I meant to take the rock on the outside, not inside."

"Never. There's a curl on the outside would swamp us sure. Head her back upstream. We need some time to get our bearings on this one."

Both men draw the boat around, then lean on the current with hard, quick strokes. Rug counts them, four, eight, twelve, takes the next half beat to glance downstream over his shoulder and *Jesus Christ, here's the igloo not ten yards away and the canoe closing on the curl!* Rug's gaze shifts from rock to shore and he realizes too late the current is pulling them down despite all the paddling.

He shouts back to Peach, whose head is still bent to the uphill effort. He doesn't mumble. "Draw back around, the current's got us! We'll be dead in the curl but damn if we want to go down backward!"

Paddles at bow and stern stretch to their limits and the heavy boat begins to pinwheel one more time. But the river senses victory in her strength, and accelerates down into the big curl. How do we read this water? The Moisie's triumphant smile? Her own breaking point, where pure speed disintegrates into purposeless motion? A warning of the real violence below? Interpretations mean nothing as the canoe swings too slow, exactly broadside at the lip of the long wave. Then it slides down into it.

Drawing on the downstream side, Rug instinctively times his stroke to be hanging farthest out when the canoe hits the trough. At that instant, the curl breaks over the gunwale. Peach is visibly jarred as the wave hits him full force at the chest. The white bubbles topping the wave catch Rug in the face, and by instinct he holds his breath for the next act.

24. Capsizing

Never mind, for the moment, just how Rug and Peach managed to crash through that wave and arrive half sunk but safe in the eddy below the igloo rock. Every wilderness trip worth its salt ought to have a miraculous story or two, and this is ours; but we'll spare you the *mirabile dictu*'s. Right now we'd rather have you hanging on that wave with Rug for a special reason. Someday you'll be hanging on one of your own, and you'll be as sure as Rug was that your boat is heading for a dump. Sometimes, miracles notwithstanding, you are going to be right.

For we might as well face it, anybody reckless enough to paddle out to the trackless waste will capsize there sooner or later, all pious intentions to the contrary. Consequently, we're taking our literary license and asking you to think about our predicament not as it turned out but as we expected it to—with Peach and Rug tumbling out of the canoe and floating straight for the butter churn below.

First questions first: How would they tumble? The only right answer is, very reluctantly. We don't mean to be facetious, only to warn you against the natural tendency of inexperienced capsizers to give up a foundering ship too easily. You won't believe how often this happens, but there's a way to get revealing proof. Next outing bring a movie camera along and take pictures of your boats going through a few big swamper waves. Then project the results and analyze them a frame at a time. The first big wave that sends a canoe off balance is the one which separates the beginner from the veteran, for the novice invariably grabs the gunwales to steady himself. If you haven't gotten into the habit of relying on your high and low braces, you too will grab without even realizing it—our movie camera has silenced enough eloquently protesting friends to guarantee that. So we reiterate what we said earlier: get in the habit of bracing even on rapids where these strokes are not strictly needed. And when the big curlers come, lay on that paddle until you're practically drinking water. It's the only way to pull a miracle out of the bag.

If you have to go, capsizing in big waves is the way to do it in style. Unfortunately novices are equally likely to exit ignominiously in a small, relatively shallow rock garden. The classic capsize occurs when you let your boat get broadside to the current, either from misjudging the forces at an eddy line, bouncing off a rock the wrong way, or losing control of a ferry. The boat then sweeps down onto a rock. The current holds it there, sweeps by under the hull, and in doing so pushes the canoe bottom up on the rock and pulls the upstream gunwale into the water.

Quick action can save you. If the boat has stuck on a rock and is beginning to swing broadside, try to stop it. In relatively shallow water, the sternman might plant his paddle against the bottom to stop the canoe from swinging, but in anything more than a small current the boat may lever the paddle right out of your grip. In bigger water don't fight the swing—encourage it. Instead of trying to halt the boat halfway, pivot all the way around the rock and go downstream backward until you hit an eddy where you can turn around. Going backward aligned with the current is less dangerous than going broadside. If the boat does get broadside, be ready to lean downstream to offset the current's counterpressure. Also be prepared to hop out quickly if the rock or stream bed permits. The lightened boat gives the river less to work on and you can jockey the canoe free and hop back in. But *act quickly*. You usually have only a second or two before the upstream gunwale is under and the river's got what it wants.

Back to Rug and Peach. Suppose the curler had rolled them; what then? Shock, that's what. One moment you've been hanging for what seems like an eternity, fighting to keep the canoe's balance contained on the end of your blade; next, the river has you spinning in its numbing, disorienting grip. The shock comes partly for psychological reasons: up to this point on a tough set of rapids, you've been making snap decision after snap decision, which requires conscious initiative and control, of both yourself and your boat. Suddenly the tables are turned and you're in a world where you have no control. But the shock comes also for simple physiological reasons: you have caught a mouthful of water and are gasping; you are plummeted into a sea of white foam and become so unfastened you're not even sure which way is up.

With the first gasp of fresh air comes the need for a clear head. Orient yourself. Where is the near shore? The second boat? What is the river like downstream? Any holes or other trouble spots? A realistic appraisal of the situation is enough to show that capsizes are not dangerous if a boater is well prepared for them. By prepared, we mean a decent regard for safety that becomes simple routine: life jacket on as well as wool clothes (wet suit in very cold water), light sneakers (not hiking boots), no loose-fitting garments like ponchos. As for the boat, everything tied in and waterproof, no loose floating painters. Under these circumstances you are in good shape; we have heard of only one person who observed these few rules and drowned in whitewater. Freak accidents and acts of God can occur, but it is the idiots and lapsers who give us safe capsizers reputations as lunatics.

In orienting yourself, three items need checking. The ideal order would probably run: your partner, your canoe, and your paddle; but the usual experience goes in just the opposite direction. You usually find your paddle clutched in your hand. If you don't, get in the habit. To lose it is a twenty-dollar mistake plus the inconvenience of using second best the rest of the trip. (If the current does carry it away, keep an eye on either shore once you've gotten under way again. On occasion we've found paddles several bends and several miles downstream.)

Keeping the paddle in hand should be an unconscious reaction. Your check on the boat should not be, for it may be the most important thing you do. *Keep upstream of the boat at all times.* A seventeen-foot canoe filled with water weighs just about a ton, though you would never guess it from the way that ton gaily careens and spins down a rapids. Would never guess, that is, until you get pinned between its weight and some two-ton boulder. Fortunately, most capsizes tend to dump you upstream of the canoe anyway. But turbulent waters can reverse the situation in a matter of seconds, so we repeat: the cardinal rule for surviving a capsize is *keep upstream of the boat!*

Thirdly, it is nice to look around for your partner. Odds are he is somewhere close by and almost certainly in no more distress than you are. Which is a good thing, since neither will be in any position to rescue the other. If in fact one partner does need assistance, the other will likely be swept far downstream before being able to offer a helping hand. All the same, peel an eye for your friend. The sight will buck up your spirits, and when you finally reach a quiet pool, two people can manhandle a swamped canoe a lot easier than one.

Meanwhile, both of you have to decide whether to stay with the canoe or abandon it. And this decision requires that you first unlearn the usual advice for flatwater canoeing: that staying with the canoe is always the best bet. We've already seen the need for healthy respect concerning that ton of water, and there are other good reasons for leaving. A canoe may be caught in a stopper wave or below a dam, trapped to stay right where it is. Staying invites danger of being pinned there yourself. In a cold-water capsize without the protection of a wet suit, the wisest move is to strike for shore immediately. Finally, the currents in very large, deep rapids may take the canoe on a submarine ride, and you do not want to follow the canoe on its undersea excursion.

With all this said, many situations remain where staying with the canoe is not dangerous and can be of some use. Maneuvering is all but impossible, but by hanging on to the upstream end of the boat, maybe doing a slight frog kick to retard motion, you act more or less like a sea anchor to help keep the boat parallel with the current, which is the most effective way of preventing the canoe from being destroyed by the rocks. If your boat does stick momentarily to a rock, try to keep the open face from turning toward the oncoming current.

Whether you elect to hang with the boat or bounce through the waves solo, the technique of floating remains the same. Don't waste energy fighting currents which will overpower you anyway. (Rug doesn't worry much about being a weak swimmer because no one can actually swim in heavy white-water, and lacking the ability removes the temptation to try.) The trick is to lie on your back with legs extended downstream to cushion any crash landings against rocks. Keep your feet near the surface to prevent trapping them in underwater crevices. Be wary of trying to stand in any fast current that is more than knee high. To put your feet down, lose your balance, wash downstream, and find one foot still wedged between two rocks is a scenario for a broken leg and worse. Otherwise a person can fully expect to float safely through any rapids that is even remotely canoeable.

SALVAGE OPERATIONS. For all practical purposes, the only way to deal with an overturned canoe is to get it to shore. With the proper combination of lurching and cussing, it is possible to board a swamped canoe in midstream and bail it—but that's only in calm water, where it's just as easy to dog-paddle the boat to shore. While still in the rapids, try to edge the boat as much as possible toward the bank, and then reach under the deck, free the coiled painter, and swim with the end to shore. Sometimes a small island or boulder in midstream offers an opportunity for snubbing the boat's down-river progress until other boats in your party can come to assist recovery.

We should say a word about painters. Some people argue that they ought to lie uncoiled in the bottom of the boat so that they fall free in a spill. This arrangement has definite advantages so long as the painter is less than about ten feet. A rope is easier to lay your hands on if you don't have to search to pull it free. On the other hand, ten feet of rope isn't much good for lining boats, and you can do little with it while in the drink. The longer ropes make it possible to strike out for shore, but when allowed to drift free, they become dangerous. We've tried it and had several unpleasant tangles, the worst being when Rug had to cut himself out of a noose in the middle of a swim. If you do stow your painters, make sure they are coiled neatly and can be pulled free easily. Our system is described on page 110.

If shore is not within reach, another boat may be. Two people paddling can handle a painter better than two people swimming. Yet your rescuers have only to anticipate the fantastic drag imposed by a seventeen-foot sea anchor to realize they must never tie the two boats together; the penalty is to find the second boat and two more canoeists in need of rescue. (If the capsized boaters are themselves near exhaustion, the second team must of course forget the canoe and save their friends. More on this in the next chapter.) The most helpful salvage technique is to paddle an upstream ferry toward the nearest shore, one person holding the rope as he paddles, once again creating a drag which helps to keep the swamped canoe parallel with the current. Another strategy is to nudge and bump the boat toward the bank. Throughout, keep the priorities in proper order: personal safety first, keeping upright boats upright next, rescue of the swamped boat last. The only thing more demoralizing than one capsize is two.

By the time you catch up to your canoe, it may be ingloriously bent around a midstream boulder. The more time the waves have a chance to work on it, the less it stands to look like a canoe, so act quickly but calmly. Usually two people in an empty canoe can paddle into the eddy below the scene of the accident, though on one or two occasions we have had to let someone swim down from upstream. Upon arrival, extract the packs and get them safely to shore. The rescue boat may ferry the goods, but if the rapids are dangerously rough, have someone haul the gear in with a rope from the riverbank. (Attach it well to the frame or duffel—you don't want to swim after your equipment and food.) For more precise control, tie a rope to a tree and to the sunken canoe; then a second rope can be used to pull each pack along the tightrope.

Once the canoe is lightened one or two people can sometimes lift it off the rock. Equally often the current will hold it fast and you will have to resort to rope hauling. Attach the rope securely: hitched around the whole canoe (not just one of its struts), snubbed on a tree or rock to prevent backsliding, and firmly anchored at the end to prevent the canoe from floating on to more mayhem once it's freed. As to specific hauling strategies, each new debacle will call forth new techniques. The chief general principle to remember is to fight the current as little as possible. The rope should pull so as to rotate the hull upward with a revolving circular motion. Do your pulling on the end of the boat that is highest out of the water, in order to free the rest of it from the current's pressure.

Sad to say, you may not always succeed in coaxing the canoe back from the river. In a populous area, you can attach a rope, leave your name and claim of ownership nearby, and fetch the ruin when the water level drops. Where the canoe itself is your link to the outside, such an adventure contains the seeds of disaster.

25. Disasters

If you are bored with life, the cynic says, risk it. We are not bored with life and certainly had no intention of putting it in jeopardy on any back-water in Quebec. Sure, we like having a few good stories to tell and a few feet of film to put to drums and bugles. But we are sensible adventurers. Wherever the Moisie dropped in cascades, we kept a safe distance on the portage trails. When the calls on the rapids got tough, we had our safely drawn lines "for the good of the trip." No wonder we felt stunned when the goddamn river nearly shoveled our lead boat backward over a vicious little drop at nightfall. Watching Peach dry out his stowaway issue of the *New England Journal of Medicine* that night, we had a lot to think about.

There are so many possible disasters on any wilderness trip that if you let them obsess you, they'll make you completely unfit for the job. Afflictions range from abasia (an inability to walk: not unlikely after long portages) to zymonematosis (a fungal infection: not likely at all). Injuries from hostile moose tramplings (canoes sometimes annoy them) to black-widow bites (mostly confined to the near wilderness, specifically the underside of out-house seats) and the usual capsizes and shipwrecks. The imaginable bad ends are innumerable.

Fretting doesn't help, yet there's no way to memorize the right remedy for every ailment and misfortune. On any wilderness trip, a certain irreducible risk of serious trouble remains, and the best a man can do is develop an intelligent approach to problem solving. Though he can't know everything, he has to be *ready* for anything. To wit: He should know a true medical emergency when he sees one and be able to act on it. He should study and learn to manage any special trauma that he may be chancing (for the canoeist, river thrashings). What information he doesn't know but might need, he should carry with him between two covers. And he had better make some plans against the day that he loses the very supplies and gear that he is depending on for survival.

Wilderness Medicine

Every long wilderness trip needs a doctor, whether or not he has an M.D. Preparing and providing for medical needs requires leadership and some expertise. Somebody has to compile a medical kit either from his own experience or from the lists available in almost any guidebook. You can find our own in the outfitting appendix along with comments on specific items. If you are heading out on anything more than a casual outing, do *not* rely on the prepackaged kits available in the outdoor shops. You will need analgesics, antibiotics, and anti-emetics (to mention the top of the alphabet) that can be obtained only by prescription from a physician. These days, it should not be hard to find a doctor willing to be helpful. If you repackage your medications, keep evidence that it has been legally obtained. Passing through customs, Jim and Joe had visions of being nabbed with syringes and two duffels full of white "powder."

Assembling medical and surgical supplies is not cookbook simple. Before presenting your list to the local pharmacist, make sure that you know whether any members of your party are allergic to any drugs. Also check everybody for allergies to bee stings, chronic or recurring illnesses (e.g., epilepsy or colitis), and any current medications. Everyone should have received a tetanus booster within the last five years.

Few laymen and not every physician will know all the medicine that might be needed in the backwoods. We recommend you do as we did. Buy a first-aid manual, read it through a couple of times, and pack it in. Most trips, you will never turn to it, but someday you just may appreciate a short refresher course before manipulating your bowman's dislocated shoulder. (Rug says this with feeling; he has popped out both of his, though never far from home.) Unfortunately, the medical literature for wilderness canoe-ists is not extensive. Many of the best first-aid manuals suffer from two deficiencies. First of all, they devote many pages to topics of marginal to zero benefit to hikers and canoeists. *Advanced First Aid and Emergency Care* by the American Red Cross includes a chapter on precipitous childbirth and another on extricating accident victims from an automobile. We don't mind carrying around the information, but the paper is heavy. Secondly, the au-thors of these manuals are strict constructionists in their interpretation of "first aid." They concentrate exclusively on preparing the patient for the trip to the doctor, thirty minutes away. Thus, the Red Cross handbook, though excellent on its own terms, tells nothing at all about how to suture a lacera-tion. On a thirty-day expedition or even a seven-day cruise, you may need some advice not as first-aider but as field surgeon. Along these lines, there are several authoritative manuals prepared for mountaineers, both long and short versions;* but these are naturally oriented to the special demands and hazards of alpine conditions. For canoeing, we take along *Being Your Own Wilderness Doctor* by E. Russel Kodet (M.D.) and Bradford Angier. It is a small book, but comprehensive and comprehensible. Kodet's information is accurate, and Angier shows his usual knack for a title.

Whatever book you select as a reference, in a genuine emergency it will be the second thing you need, not the first. The first requirement is a set of reflexes. An emergency, by our definition, is a crisis requiring immediate life-saving intervention. And a reflex is an automatic response. We are born with some of them (like the knee jerk), but others come only with training and practice. Behind the practice is knowledge, but we stress: knowing isn't the same as doing. Rug found that out as a third-year medical student. He was on rounds during his first hospital clerkship when the attending physician, Dr. Pincus, a neurologist, was called to the Emergency Room to evaluate a comatose child. The whole group tagged along, Rug last. Everyone squeezed into the little girl's cubicle and Rug, to be helpful, pulled the curtain. The attending physician looked across the row of heads and said, "John, would you examine the patient for us?"

Rug was stunned helpless. Finally, he tapped the girl's knees with his hammer, then shone a light to look at her pupils. This was neurology.

Thirty seconds was all the professor could allow.

"John," he said, "nobody ever died with normal vital signs."

Even if you don't have a dozen of your betters watching you struggle with your first medical crisis, you will feel just like Rug did—overwhelmed. The only way to overcome the initial paralysis and the subsequent trivial, wasted motions is by developing a systematic approach to the injured patient and by practice, practice, practice. For both the drillwork and the practical demonstration of basic emergency procedures, attend a Red Cross or other first-aid course. Either that or go to medical school. All we can do in this book is outline our own system—how we have learned to assess an emergency and to organize our efforts to help. The nuts and bolts of what really is *first* aid you will have to learn one on one.

Let's say you have just pulled Peach off the rocks somewhere below the big curl; he's not talking and he looks sick. Common sense tells you first to evaluate the total situation. Are you in a position to help him? Never delay giving assistance for the sake of more comfortable work space and never move an injured man needlessly, but it's impossible to set a leg in the

---

* See James A. Wilkerson, M.D., ed., *Medicine for Mountaineering* (The Mountaineers, Seattle, 1968); Dick Mitchell, *Mountaineering First Aid* (The Mountaineers, Seattle, 1972); or the shorter *Mountaineering Medicine* by Fred T. Darville, Jr., M.D. (Skagit Mountain Rescue Unit, Mount Vernon, Wash., 1969).

middle of a rockslide—or a rapids. Next give him a quick once-over. Concentrate on getting one good look. Is he conscious? Does he move spontaneously? All extremities? Are there any abnormal movements (posturing or convulsions)? Is he pink or blue? As you look, run your hands over the length of his body head to toe. Is there any blood? A person can exsanguinate (bleed to death) in less than a minute from a large artery. If you see blood spurting, lots of it, this is an emergency and the wound must be compressed immediately. Use your hat.

Once you have gone over your patient (so far you've spent about five seconds), you need to collect some technical information. Remember what Dr. Pincus told Rug and do it systematically. Nobody has ever died with normal vital signs. Respiration, pulse, blood pressure, temperature. Put them to memory and learn to evaluate each one in order.

Respiration. As always, first questions first: Is Peach breathing at all? He almost certainly is if he is still pink, but check anyway. If you can't see his chest move, put your ear to his mouth and listen. Even if he isn't breathing, don't stop in the middle of your evaluation. You've got three more vitals to check and what you can learn from them in the next ten seconds could change your treatment and save Peach's life. If he is breathing, what is the quality of his respirations? Shallow or deep, quiet or noisy, regular or not? Make a mental note even if you are not sure of the significance. A change in vital signs over the next few minutes may carry more significance than his present condition; the only way to notice a change is to establish a baseline.

Pulse. The radial pulse at the wrist is often difficult to locate and may disappear even when cardiac function remains adequate. Learn to check instead the carotids in the neck or the femorals in the groin. With a little practice, you can pick up the knack of estimating the pulse rate without bothering to count on a watch. Rug does this even in the hospital. Is the pulse regular or not? Is it present at all? If it is absent or uncertain, put your ear to the person's chest to listen for a heartbeat, unless there are too many layers of clothing to remove. (This is nineteenth-century medicine but it works; the stethoscope does not amplify heart sounds, only puts an aesthetically acceptable distance between doctor and patient.) Absent pulse together with absent heartbeat indicates cardiac arrest. Corroborating evidence includes preceding respiratory failure, blue skin, and (after two minutes) dilated, fixed pupils.

Blood pressure. You will have to estimate by palpation of the pulse. A weak, thready pulse may indicate low and inadequate pressure; that is, acute circulatory failure—shock.

Temperature. If Peach's heart has stopped or if he clearly has a broken leg, it may seem stupid to check his temperature. Wrong. Check it every time (with the back of your hand, which is more sensitive to temperature than the fingertips) both at an extremity (hands, feet) and at the neck or trunk. If the heart has stopped, a running estimate of body temperature will provide an indicator of success or failure during resuscitation. If the leg is broken, cold skin together with a faint pulse warns you of shock. If on a hot humid day your partner suddenly becomes delirious or simply collapses, hot dry skin will give you the diagnosis—heat stroke, a definite life-threatening emergency.

In thirty seconds, no more than twenty with practice, you have learned everything you need to know about Peach's condition to begin rational and effective emergency care. To initiate treatment, follow the same outline and *keep thinking.* The sequence comes by rote; the thinking doesn't.

If your friend is bleeding, stop it. Use a compress, elevation, cold pack. For desperate cases, pinch off a bleeding artery with your mosquito clamp (see Kodet, *Being Your Own Wilderness Doctor*) or your fingers, or press on a pressure point. If you decide to sacrifice the limb to save the life, apply a tourniquet. If your friend is convulsing, protect him from danger and wedge a stick between his teeth to save his tongue.

Respiration. In the absence of effective respiration, first clear the airway— the mouth and throat. Turn the head to one side and wipe out any water, mucus, vomitus, teeth. If the tongue is at the back of the throat, hook it forward with your finger, but again wedge the teeth and save your finger. To keep the tongue from blocking the pharynx, tilt the head way back and pull the jaw forward by lifting at the angle of the mandible (jawbone). Now re-evaluate your friend's breathing. If it is still ineffective, proceed with mouth-to-mouth respiration. Kneel at the victim's head, pinch his nostrils, and exhale sharply through his mouth about fifteen times a minute. Make sure that the chest rises and falls normally. The most common mistake of the inexperienced is to overbreathe in the excitement. If you start getting dizzy or feel tingles around your lips, slow down. Most important of all is knowing when to quit. Stop whenever the patient recovers sufficiently to breathe for himself. But *never stop until then so long as his heart is still beating.*

Pulse. What if his heart has stopped? Until recently, this was the very definition of death, but not now. Begin extrathoracic cardiac massage— chest thumping. You or better yet another helper should first strike the central chest with a sharp blow. This maneuver sometimes reorganizes the electrical rhythm of a failing heart. Next place the heel of one hand on the lower sternum, the other hand over the first. About sixty times a minute (and estimating takes practice), depress the bony cage of the chest about two inches. This massage should be alternated with the artificial respiration, four pumps on the chest for each breath. Properly done, this technique of total resuscitation will provide adequate oxygenation and perfusion of the brain and other vital organs by compressing the heart against the spine. In the hospital with the help of nurses and medications, it often succeeds but more often fails. Out on the riverbank, the statistics, if any were to be had, would surely be dismal, but a healthy person cut down in an accident certainly deserves the benefit of a potentially lifesaving technique. A number of cases have been reported of persons recovering without any disability whatsoever after two and three hours of cardiac massage. If you ever have to use it, you will likely have to decide to quit eventually. But take it from two guys who have seen a couple dozen people come back from the dead: keep pumping long after you have given up all "reasonable" hope.

Blood pressure. There are many causes of falling blood pressure, including blood loss, heart failure, exposure to cold, or simply the "shock" of injury. The best treatment is often to attend to the underlying cause, but in addition the patient should be laid flat with his legs elevated. He should be covered with dry clothing or blankets but generally not actively warmed unless the underlying problem is hypothermia. Heating from the inside with warm fluids, salted and sugared, should be encouraged so long as the victim is conscious and has not just vomited. Optimism and reassurance are also indicated in liberal doses, although blatant lies, cheerful idiocy, and other confederates are worse than a simple, even glum businesslike approach. Peach may be sick, but he isn't stupid.

Temperature. If heat stroke is the problem, throw the victim in the river immediately. Hypothermia, the result of cold exposure, is a more likely danger on a river trip, as we shall see. Priority goes to warming up. Remove any wet garments and replace them with dry clothing or a sleeping bag. If the person is cold but not shivering, another friend should strip down and crawl inside with him. Build a roaring fire or two roaring fires, and again encourage intake of the standard drink—warm water with a half teaspoon of salt and a handful of sugar added to every quart.

Notice that by monitoring vital signs and understanding their significance you are already treating Peach without even having to understand what's happened to him. If you can keep his vitals going, you will keep him alive. Nobody has ever died with normal vital signs. But of course we know very well what's wrong with Peach. He was keel-hauled down some prehistoric drop on the Moisie River and has almost drowned.

Well, the truth is, as we've said before, drowning is a very rare accident among canoeists who follow the simplest safety precautions—wool clothing or wet suit, life jacket, no free painters, keep upstream of the boat. Actually, even on a tough whitewater trip, drowning may be less likely than a moose trampling. We know of four men who died at the hoofs of moose on the Albany River, Ontario, fifteen years ago, and the closest we've ever had anybody come to drowning was pretty outlandish. Rug's father was nearly choked to death once by a self-inflatable life vest. Nearly done in by Mae West. Still, drowning does represent ultimate failure in technique, and every serious paddler should know something about it.

Common intuition seems to grasp easily why prolonged submersion in water leads to deleterious consequences: it prevents a person from breathing. In fact, only a minority of drowning victims, about one in ten, dies simply from lack of air. Examination of these people shows that their epiglottis, the valve of the windpipe, goes into spasm and blocks any inspiration of air —or, for that matter, water, which is why they are called victims of "dry drownings." Survivors may report inappropriate feelings of detachment or even euphoria and experience the panorama of their life passing before them. If rescued and resuscitated in time (up to twenty or more minutes after going down the last time in cold water), these people may recover without suffering any further medical complications of the drowning itself. In this sense dry drowning carries a good prognosis.

Although the majority of drowning victims hold their breath as long as possible, rising levels of carbon dioxide cause the lower control centers of the brain to overcome all voluntary effort and initiate a succession of desperate agonal gasps. "Wet drowning" is the result. The aspiration of fresh water not only fails to supply oxygen but also leads to other, equally detrimental effects. Large volumes of water are absorbed into the bloodstream, resulting in a sudden violent overload of the circulation. (Never waste time trying to empty a person's lungs of fresh water. By the time you reach him, all the water will have escaped into the blood.) Red blood cells burst in this new hypotonic environment and serum salts are thrown into disequilibrium. The dilution of serum sodium is specifically thought to throw the heart into ventricular fibrillation, a fatal disturbance of its rhythm. To add injury to more injury, there is shunting of blood within the lungs themselves, damage to the lining of the alveoli, and frequently the superimposition of a chemical pneumonia. The electrolyte disorder can cause cerebral changes and the hemoglobin of broken red cells can clog the kidneys. No one finds wet drowning pleasant and survivors may complain of severe central chest pain. Even with expert emergency care, the patient may show signs of full recovery only to relapse and die hours later. Therefore, any victim of near drowning should be evacuated and hospitalized immediately if this is at all possible.

How is it that Peach, an excellent swimmer, is drowning with his life jacket on? The answer of course is that the Moisie is not only wet; it is also cold. Man is a warm-blooded animal and he has to stay that way to survive. Over the last several million years, he has developed a number of ways to produce body heat and preserve it. To create heat, he digests food and, lacking that, metabolizes his own stores of glucose and fat. To increase heat production, he releases adrenaline and thyroxine, and he initiates muscular exercise, either voluntary or involuntary (shivering). To conserve warmth, he comes lined with subcutaneous fat and is equipped with a thermostat that can shut down circulation to nonvital organs, the skin and extremities.

Nonetheless, life is endangered when heat loss exceeds heat production. At core (that is, central body) temperatures between 95° and 91°, normal compensatory mechanisms begin to fail; shivering begins to *decrease,* and both activity and thinking become sluggish. Below 90°, muscular incoordination causes jerky movements, and general comprehension declines, even to the point of total amnesia. Below 85°, muscles become rigid; thought, irrational and unrealistic; pulse and respiration as well as temperature, notably depressed. Around 80° consciousness is lost and at about 75° death ensues.*

A fatal drop in body temperature can occur at temperatures well above freezing. An environmental reading of 50° is, after all, 48.6° lower than normal physiological temperature; the crucial factor is whether heat loss is outpacing heat production. Unfortunately for the canoeist, cold water (with the exception of supercooled petroleum products) dissipates heat faster than any other commonly encountered substance. Not even wind chill can compare with water chill. Water conducts heat 240 times faster than still air— faster than gale-force winds. Thus an unprotected swimmer cannot survive indefinitely in water colder than 70°. In arctic waters at temperatures of 29° or 30°, survival time is shortened to three minutes or less. In the more usual range for a springtime canoeing, 40° to 50°, a person can count on a grace period of thirty to sixty minutes. Mitigating factors are just what you would expect from a knowledge of the physiology of temperature control— namely, good nutritional status, physical conditioning, generous stores of body fat, and warm clothing.

Scientific observation tends to support our own subjective experience that the cold-water swimmer believes he is doing all right and then suddenly becomes weak and helpless. A British investigator, credited by the medical journals for recruiting "some of the most enthusiastic colleagues in the world," induced four volunteers to jump into a pool refrigerated to about 40°. One man suddenly stopped swimming and sank without making any effort at all to reach the pool side just three feet away. The lesson is that if you are only marginally dressed for the water temperature, strike out for shore; don't wait to feel cold or tired. For canoeing rivers colder than about 60° we try to wear some wool covering; for water below 45° we wear wet suits.

* We are using the figures of Theodore G. Lathrop, M.D., from his excellent monograph, *Hypothermia: Killer of the Unprepared* (The Mazamas, 909 N.W. Nineteenth Avenue, Portland, Ore. 97209).

If you pull an exhausted boater from the dip, evaluate him closely. This means a routine emergency examination. Do *not* rely simply on his word that he is O.K. Remember that irrationality and unwarranted optimism can be a part of hypothermia. And if the case is serious, your friend will *not* be shivering. As we said earlier, exchange wet clothing for dry and actively warm the victim with body heat, a blazing fire, and warm fluids. Make a special effort to cover the head and neck. The blood vessels there do not constrict, and most of the body's loss of heat will occur here by radiation if left exposed. Once again, evacuate the victim if possible; if not, stop for the day and keep him flat, warm, and at rest. As with drownings, people can die from exposure hours after apparent initial recovery.

Survival Tactics

Disasters have a way of happening in batches. The time that a person is sick or injured is just when you are most likely to soak your perishables, lose your gear, and wreck a boat. There are so many possible contingencies that there is no way of divining the best specific plan of action ahead of time. Nonetheless, some general preparations are important.

Above all, make absolutely sure that you never lose *everything*. Everyone should at all times wear a personal survival kit. Tied to the belt should be a knife, some waterproofed matches, and a compass; a waterproof watch rounds out the list. The knife and matches will, with the exercise of a little woodsmanship, provide warmth, shelter, and a means of sending signals. The compass and watch will indicate which direction to head and how far. So long as the separated or stranded paddler is left with a whole body, keeping alive is possible with these basic utensils.

Most disasters will leave you better equipped, but at least you now have the right attitude. Whatever is lost, you can do without, and whatever is damaged you will try to repair.

Damage on a river trip usually refers to boats. Most gashes, rips, and holes can be fixed with a temporary patch of plastic or silver duct tape. In case of major fractures, however, both aluminum and fiber-glass canoes may need the help of sapling splints along the gunwales and some fiber glass over the break in the skin. Take epoxy since it binds more strongly to cured glass than does polyester. Fiber glass, polypropylene, and nylon all serve well as patching material, though fiber glass wears the smoothest. With a fiber-glass boat, scrape away any loose flakes and sand the surrounding area. You probably won't have brought any sandpaper but the stuff that lies around on beaches works as well. Thoroughly dry the area around the hole and then cut a number of patches, the smallest just big enough to cover the hole and the largest allowing four or five inches of overlap. Mix resin and hardener; more hardener on a cold day, and a blazing fire to raise the temperature of the working area. You are now ready to lay on the patches. Put the largest one closest to the hull so that the repair work will roughly match the rest of the boat in flexibility. Fiber-glass repairs on aluminum craft usually have to be applied to the inside of the boat after the metal has been stomped back into shape. Not all epoxies will bind to aluminum; inquire to make sure that yours does before you buy it. If you break an ABS canoe in pieces, you're ahead of us. The manufacturers sell ABS repair kits but we don't know much about them. As a matter of fact, whenever we've needed epoxy on a river trip, we haven't had it along. More than once, we've resorted to spruce-gum plugs; they work middling well but, believe us, the taste is stronger than the patch.

If a canoe is damaged beyond repair or a person is too sick to be moved, a party has several alternatives. One is to stay put and wait for help. This is a hard decision for a group of wilderness nomads, but it is often the safest. If food is short, camp life requires the least expenditure of energy and offers the best chance for successful foraging. Anxiety is kept to a minimum since you can reasonably expect to be rescued within a few days of your pre-arranged search. If only a canoe is ailing and the party is large, it may be possible to distribute the extra gear and crew members among the remaining boats. Smaller parties may instead have to consider splitting up, but one canoe should never go on alone unless the run to the outside is known to be easy. Dividing the party carries the disadvantage of having to divide the remaining supplies. If there is a shortage of community property such as matches or of important items like sleeping bags, you may need to seek safety and comfort in numbers. The final possibility is to hike out. Riverbanks make for difficult terrain but bushwhacking is often no better. It is a good idea to carry maps not only of your intended route but also of the country you would choose to hike if the necessity arose. Of course, disasters are no respecters of maps. Partly out of prudence but mostly because we enjoyed the game, our evening ritual included going over the next day's maps—including the "hike out" maps.

As the river and the maps unfolded, we came to develop the concept of "maximum remoteness." Remoteness, we began to realize, depends on much more than where the railroad swings farthest from the river. As we calculated it, our maximum isolation came about three quarters of the way down the Moisie at a spot where the Quebec North Shore and Labrador was only forty miles to the east. But walking east from that bend in the river would lead 1600 feet straight up over the cliffs and twenty miles farther on would bring us to the middle of a long lake running sixty miles north to south. On that stretch of river, we solemnly vowed to tread extra light and careful. And we made it without a hitch, except for one little incident maybe half a mile from our point of maximum remoteness—the place we call Igloo Rock.

26. Feel of the River

"Maybe it's just the letdown of the trip coming to an end," Rug says.

Jim gives the breakfast coals a kick and shakes his head. "I don't think so."

"I dunno," says Peach. "The last day and all. I'm sorry to see it too."

"Bull," says Jim. "The only reason Joe's so down is the scouting report you guys gave us, and you know it. You should've known better than to pull that 'Harry's Last Chance' stuff. He takes it to heart."

Rug and Peach grin at each other with the delight that belongs to secret knowledge. Then Rug goes poker-faced. "I swear it's as bad as we say. Maybe worse. Harry's probably booked the train from Oreway to watch."

Peach does the mimicry: "Ye see, there wasn't no way ye was ever gonna make it."

"All right," says Jim. "Maybe you're joking and maybe not. All I'm saying is, we got ourselves a reluctant paddler." And having spoken his piece, he walks off to find Joe. As he leaves, the second train of the morning rumbles along the upgrade high above our camp.

Your expedition, if you run it according to the Ideal, should end with a final bursting out of the pristine wilderness back to the world of men and machines. Unfortunately, men and machines usually have little respect for the pristine. On our trip we ran into them soon after we left the High Moisie. First day beyond, we saw a salmon fisherman and his two guides; next day it was an airplane that came at us waving his wings. Day after, we passed the mouth of the Nipissis and started down the home stretch where the railroad follows the river. For once, Peach wanted to skip an early camp and push ahead to the campground and the cars. But three of the remaining eight miles were covered by hatch marks on the topos and the rest of us voted, for the good of the trip, to spend one last night on the river.

We pulled into shore and made camp with the railroad tracks a hundred feet above—thinking we had a leisurely evening ahead of us, thinking rather sadly how much tamer civilization seemed, not suspecting in the least what was coming the next morning. That is why we are hesitant about tendering advice on how to bring your trip to an end. Every canoeing expedition has its universal problems—running rapids, scouting portages, navigating big lakes; but every expedition, thank God, has its own unique ending. We will be happy if this guidebook has given you some help with the universal problems; we will be even happier if your story finishes differently from ours—and with as much of a surprise as Peach and Rug got that afternoon when they hiked the railroad two miles down to the trestle in hopes of scouting the next morning's run.

The trestle lay about six miles upstream of the St. Lawrence and is where the railroad crosses the Moisie. Even in this low country, the riverbanks are four, five hundred feet high and have forced the railroaders to accommodate. They dug a tunnel a mile and a half long to get to the river, then built the trestle a hundred feet high to get to the east side of the valley. There they laid their tracks on one of the terraces that slopes up from the river.

Peach and Rug came back from that walk bursting with the anticipation of a good story, but also decidedly edgy. As usual, Rug did the calling.

"The river stays necked down all the way to the trestle and past," he says. "Current is really fast. There must be big waves in the middle, but you know what you can see from a hundred fifty feet up."

"They're big waves," says Peach. "You can see them."

"My guess is we can sneak through on the right bank. There's definitely no way on shore this side."

"They're big waves," says Peach. "No way even on the right side."

"Maybe line, then. Anyway, the drops along there aren't the main problem. Past the really narrow stuff is a more bouldery set that runs all the way down to the trestle. We figure still stay right. Then the river turns sharp left at the trestle cliff. We crossed the bridge and the railroad people have a set of ladders rigged down the cliff to the bottom, so we got a chance to look at the outside of the bend from up close."

"Listen to this," says Peach.

"It didn't seem so bad. The river was coming right down into the cliff at the outside of the turn—and the cliff's straight up, by the way. Just upstream of it is a big bay which in this kind of water is one huge eddy. You'd think with all that current piling onto the cliff wall, there'd be a hell of a mess. But we looked at it and there wasn't. Good current moving through, and a few haystacks out to the middle, but nothing to worry about."

"Yeah, it was just a couple of rollers," says Peach. "Now listen to this."

"Right as we're sitting there working a course through it, these big mother of God waves rise up, right where the little rollers were before. It was the damnedest thing I ever saw."

"*Nothing,*" says Peach. "And then these big irregular waves. We couldn't figure it."

"No question we got to ferry over to the left side somewhere above the big eddy, take the trestle water way over left side. I just wish we could've gotten a better view of *that.* But there's no ladders down, so we came back."

Thus the scouting report of Rug and Peach. They ran it through a second time right away, with Joe asking a lot of questions and Jim following up a few points. Then at dinner Jim asked a lot of questions and Joe followed up a few points. At the popcorn session before bed, Jim told it back to see if he had it right and Joe said nothing.

But it's only at breakfast we notice that Rug runs the scouting report through right and Peach runs it through right and Jim runs it through right and Joe says nothing again and goes to do the dishes.

Jim works his way around the bend of boulders toward the rattle of pots. Just before he clears the last rock he hesitates. The rattle continues, and then stops. On the heels of this silence comes some unaccustomed language from Joe.

"Christ Almighty! *Hey!*"

Jim rounds the bend at full tilt.

"Look! Look at that!"

"What?"

"The stick! Hey, the stick!"

"What stick?"

"The stick you threw that night in the rain! I can't believe it!"

"You're kidding!"

"No, look! About a third of the way out, just past that riffle. See the yellow tape?"

"Well, I'll be damned!"

"I just can't believe it! What in the world were the odds of ever seeing that again?"

Jim laughs. "As I remember it, *you* were the one said we'd beat it to the end of the river."

Joe pockets the soap and bundles up the dishes. "Well, hold on," he says. "It hasn't won yet by any means."

Both of them return to the campsite. Jim carries back the two big pots full of water and throws both pailfuls on the fire's embers. He walks through the billowing cloud of steam, bends over his pack, and slips back into the side pocket his little roll of bright yellow utility tape.

We load up our boats as we always do, except that we don't look around for deadwood to lay on the bottom. For once, it won't matter if the packs soak up a little splash water. Rug and Peach are ready first and head out of our cove toward the main current. The river is smooth, and since their boat is crossing currents at a small angle running downstream, neither Peach nor Rug bother with a brace as the canoe descends a constriction between two boulders. At the bottom of the drop, the river unexpectedly pulls the boat off on a wide arc to the left, sounding a deeper repetition of the sucking noise we heard a few times up in the canyon. By the time Joe and Jim respectfully veer way over right, Peach and Rug have gone one full circle around the arc and fully halfway into a second go-around.

"What the hell are you guys doing?" calls Jim.

"I don't know," says Peach, a little puzzled. "We'll be with you in a minute." Three times through 360 degrees the Moisie takes the boat, and slowly—very carefully—Rug and Peach edge it to the outside of the whirlpool.

As the gorge closes in, our usual banter comes to a stop. The reverberation off the valley walls amplifies the roar of the rapids, and with it, our astonishment. We had, like always, allowed for a little surprise between the scout and the run, but we have never seen a river so powerful. The waves are no higher than in many of the upper rapids, but they seem almost vertical, they are so steep. Each of the little drops we had hoped to run (but expected to line) turns out to be a definite portage. We try to convince ourselves it is only the acoustics of the gorge that are putting us on edge. But deep down we know the noise is not what's frightening us; it's the knowledge that in this water there will be no way of crossing the river to get left above the trestle.

Just past noon, we reach the big eddy bay and our fears are confirmed: open canoes do not attempt ferries through seven-foot waves. All four of us work our way along the cliffs and spend two hours studying the currents on the right side beneath the trestle. We try to time the intervals between the upsurges of turbulence, but they conform to no pattern we can decipher. So we have two choices. To start down the slot and hope to slip through when the river is quiet, or to hike out with the hope of returning for our boats and gear when the river level drops. The cliffs eliminate any portage to the trestle. We calculate that we have a thousand dollars, tops, invested in the entire outfit, and at this point any one of us would be willing to pay the whole ransom to avoid this game of roulette. But a certain amount of honor is at stake. We started out to run a river from headwaters to the mouth, and six miles before the end seems an unconscionable time to quit. The rapids below the trestle run solid, large, and bouldery for a mile. We decide that nobody would drown in case of a capsize, though we'd probably lose the boats and get a good bouncing ourselves.

So we go for the run. Although the cycles of turbulence are obviously impossible to plot, we can't resist trying. Peach leaves Rug, Jim, and Joe at the trestle and goes back to the canoes. At the top of the eddy, he throws a chunk of deadwood out into the river just as the spit of the waves is most violent. By the time the driftwood gets to the trestle, the water has quieted down.

"That settles it," says Rug. "You guys signal to us when the waves come up the biggest. That's when we'll leave the eddy."

Jim is doubtful. "I don't see how that's going to improve the odds. You can't predict the river, and besides, how do you know you'll catch the same current as the stick?"

Rug is adamant. Jim shrugs his shoulders and says he'll give a wave, then tries to convince Rug to give him time to fetch the camera for movies of them coming through. Rug is too taut to bide time and heads upriver towards Peach and the boat.

"Let's cut the eddy line good," he tells Peach. "We want to miss that cliff."

"Hah," says Peach.

They work their canoe up the eddy and hold it there until Jim gives the high sign. They can see Joe pacing the ledge. The boat crosses the current boundary smartly, but once in the main flow, Rug calls, "Back!" The canoe continues to speed up despite both men backpaddling. Rug is surprised at how the current is sliding the boat toward the big waves in the middle. "Back ferry!" he yells, and draws his bow farther midriver to help set the angle. Peach worries about a broach; these waves are already four feet.

Slowly the boat edges back outside right, toward the planned slot. Rug looks downstream: the breakers at the trestle are still up. Passing the first massive abutment (what are those engineers trying to do, hold the cliff up?) a gust of wind blows Rug's hat off. Peach is not even tempted to try to retrieve it and keeps hanging on his brace. As the boat closes with the slot, the irregular waves along the cliffs suddenly smooth down. Rug's bow slaps one final time and enters green water, twisty but easy rolling. Two canoe lengths below, the long regular waves pick up again. Rug and Peach ride them out and head into shore.

Rug hops out and tells Peach, "Snub the boat. I've got to catch the others." Peach wonders what there is to tell them. Just run it the same as us. Rug reaches the other two as they are getting into their canoe. "Give me the camera and wait for us to get set up," he says, and is taken aback by how tense they look. "No problems," he says. "The current's shifty, but a good brace'll get you through."

"You caught it when it was flat," says Joe.

"So will you—just go when Peach waves. Now how about the camera? It'll be safer with me anyway."

Jim seems willing but Joe is uneasy. Rug does some quick bartering and extracts fifteen minutes' preparation time in return for his life preserver, which Joe puts on under his own. Rug returns to the trestle and finds a ledge to lie on about twenty feet above the river. Then he pulls the tripod out of the ammo box, screws the three tiny legs into place and the camera into its seat. Sighting through the lens, Joe and Jim appear small against the expanse of roiling river, and he shifts the zoom to telephoto. The long lens zeroes in, and catches both men staring glumly at the river. Rug smiles, satisfied with the view. It is like looking through a long, narrow tube, the central focus of action surrounded by darkness. "Wave them on whenever the waves are right," he calls to Peach, who is below on the ladder.

Half a minute passes, the turbulence reappears, and Peach waves his arm. At the end of the lens, Rug searches, finds the canoe caught in what seems to be vicious boiling current. Both men are paddling hard, quick strokes; yet the canoe makes no progress. Rug thinks at first this is the deception of the long lens, but Joe and Jim keep paddling and move nowhere. Rug turns the camera aside and watches them swing back to shore. They had tried to avoid getting sucked toward the middle like the first boat, but the upstream currents of the eddy overpowered them. They drift back around the eddy and make ready for another try.

"Switch sides," says Jim. "Then you can draw left to get us out center a bit more."

"Wait for Peach?" Joe asks.

Jim is not accustomed to being bullied by backwaters, doesn't like it a bit, and so says nothing and points the canoe back toward the downstream currents. They are calm and rolling. The boat hits the eddy line again, and this time it clears along Rug's route. But the river, instead of carrying them toward the middle, pulls more toward the wash against the cliff. Peach's arm wavers in the air a moment, then frantically waves them away from the trestle: he sees the black rolling turbulence which the river spreads before rearing up.

Joe doesn't know what to do. The river, thank God, still looks flat but Peach says to go more middle. How? Can't back ferry or Jim's stern will spin out. No time to sideslip. Hell with it, just move her through and keep some momentum against the twisty, broaching currents. "Paddle!" he yells, and lays into his own.

The bow hits the trestle water while it is still fairly calm, but Joe is abruptly buoyed up by a huge surf. As the canoe begins to slide sideways, he lays out on his longest draw. Jim pries hard to straighten the angle and then braces himself. The wave keeps climbing. Joe concedes the point and pulls his paddle in; he can no longer reach water in the trough, and leaning on air means a sure capsize. Peering down the other side of the breaker, he thinks, "We're in."

Rug listens to the tick-tick of the footage counter and watches the boat lift. Hard to tell how rough the water is through the long lens. He keeps the trigger tight as the boat plunges and submarines. Looking through the camera's tunnel, he sees two heads, no boat, and assumes it has swamped. He forgets he can be of no immediate help and slams the camera down, only to see that one great wave has carried Jim, Joe, and half a boatload of water past the trestle onto the regular rollers.

"Eddy! Shore eddy!" Joe yells, and shifts his paddle over to a crossdraw. Jim pries; works to swing the sluggish stern around with his hips. As the canoe pivots, the water in the boat sloshes to the outside of the turn and the left gunwale yaws dangerously. Jim's paddle is jerked out of the water half a second by the imbalance, but Joe holds the pivot long enough to stop the roll and then paddles for shore like a man possessed. The boat slews around the rest of the turn and bangs unceremoniously into the cliff wall with a jolt that pitches Jim right onto the duffels.

Not a textbook landing, but it will have to do. Downstream lie a few smaller rapids; then five or six miles to big water of another sort, stretching beyond sight of land. This is how our trip unwinds with the river.

Rug and Peach work their way from ledge to ledge, tossing the ammo box back and forth when balance necessitates. As they reach the boats, Jim is bailing. Joe takes the box of camera and film, ties it back in the boat, but never takes his eyes off the stern. Smiling now, he is counting Jim's strokes, measuring the swamp water half a gallon at a time—for the record.

"You guys are going to love it," Rug says. "Wait'll you see it! Two heads and a paddle. Boat just disappeared, and that was looking almost straight down!"

A thousand miles and some time have passed, but the memories stick. And four states—Maine, Massachusetts, New York, Oregon—contain within their borders, one each, a reel of celluloid that proves it happened the way we say. (Any one of us, given the chance, will unwind it for you.) That film proves that ice covered the big lakes in June, proves that we crossed them without a prop. Proves that the portage trail to the river started with a Coke bottle

(Jim never did get it dated). Proves that we portaged thirty-two rapids, lined another eight, and ran—well, rapids *run* are not the sort of things you quantify. Our film also proves that our trip ended with two heads sitting very unnatural-like on a sizable wave—though the wave is shrunken some by the perspective. Some people, our families for instance, might say that the trip ended elsewhere. But we like to think it ends with the two heads because that's where the next trip seems most likely to begin. Our trip, your trip—anybody's trip. With some recruit watching Joe and Jim still stroking to get out of the eddy bay, still drawing hard to pull out middle, still bracing when the river boils up and sends them scuttling down the turn with half a boat-load of water.

And you ask, "Was it really that tough?"

And we say, "Worse than it looks. Not one in a thousand would chance it."

Appendix I

A Review of Strokes
(Including Some Useless Ones)

We do not intend to duplicate here the more detailed treatment of paddling techniques found in the body of the book. But we have several reasons for summarizing in one place the basic strokes used in flatwater and whitewater paddling. For one, the story of our trip has been used to introduce new paddlers to the sport a step at a time, rather than confront them right off with a list of strokes they could not possibly remember or absorb at one sitting. It may help now to have a summary of the various paddling techniques, available for reviewing or reference. Secondly, since our text emphasizes actual river situations to demonstrate strokes, this appendix focuses on the subject in terms of general principles. The two methods of presentation are different, but the connection between them is close. Our concrete examples were picked to be typical of situations encountered on a lake or river; thus the general principles are illustrated by the more specific discussions in the text. We have indicated under each stroke the page numbers where these discussions can be found. For further references, check the appropriate headings in our index, for instance "crossdraw," "brace," and so on.

A word about the canoe diagrams. In this appendix (and throughout the book) the bow of the boat is always marked by a dark triangle. Arrows indicate the direction of the paddle stroke; dotted lines, when they appear, indicate the paddle is out of the water. The hatch marks show the angle of the paddle blade. If the canoe is generally leaned during a particular stroke, that too is indicated. In descriptions of strokes, when we talk about the "power" face of the blade, we mean the side facing the stern during a forward stroke. That is called the power face even when it is not the side pushing the water (which it is not during the stern pry and some other strokes).

Moving

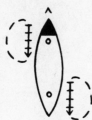

FORWARD STROKE (page 84)

Purpose: For straightaway paddling.

Comments: Comes about as naturally as walking. (Remember, it took you a year to learn to walk.)

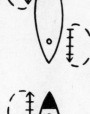

BACKSTROKE (page 85)

Purpose: For moving in reverse, checking speed, or stopping.

Comments: Rarely necessary in flatwater, but you'll use it as much as the forward stroke in whitewater.

CROSS BACKSTROKE (page 219)

Purpose: Same as the backstroke.

Comments: Used mostly when paddling single, for fine control in whitewater. The ordinary backstroke tends to move the bow toward the side of the paddle; the cross backstroke does the same on the other side of the boat.

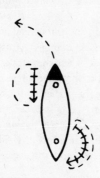

Turning

SWEEP (page 86)

Purpose: To turn the canoe away from the side of the paddle.

Comments: Used in both bow and stern, but works slowly and in long arcs. The aptly named "reverse sweep" is the sweep in reverse

STERN RUDDER (page 87)

Purpose: To turn the canoe toward the side of the paddle.

Comments: Only effective when the canoe has forward momentum. Basically, a flatwater stroke for correcting course and making gradual turns.

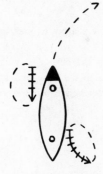

J STROKE (page 87)

Purpose: Also to turn the canoe toward the side of the paddle.

Comments: A weak stroke used only by the sternman for correcting course in flatwater paddling.

STERN PRY (OR PUSH) (page 87)

Purpose: To turn the canoe sharply toward the side of the paddle.

Comments: For the pry, the paddler locks the paddle shaft to the gunwale, like an oar. What we call the "push stroke" is identical, except that the shaft as well as the blade is pushed away from the canoe. Both variations are useful on lakes and indispensable in whitewater (see page 134).

BOW PRY (page 134)

Purpose: To push the canoe sharply away from the side of the paddle.

Comments: Note that, unlike the stern pry, the paddle is held vertical to the water. The bow pry is the trickiest and least stable stroke of all. Be especially careful not to catch your paddle on a rock.

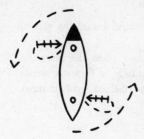

DRAW (page 132)

Purpose: To pull the paddler's end of the boat toward the side of his paddle.

Comments: A powerful stroke equally important in the bow and stern. To appreciate the difference between a draw pivoting the canoe from the bow vs. a draw pivoting the canoe from the stern, see page 138.

CROSSDRAW (page 135)

Purpose: To turn the bow sharply to the paddler's off side.

Comments: Used only in the bow. The crossdraw is a useful alternative to the bow pry. For our discussion of relative merits, see pages 136–7.

INVERTED SWEEP (page 219)

Purpose: To turn the canoe sharply toward the side of the paddle.

Comments: This is actually the draw stroke, forward stroke, and push stroke done in a single smooth motion by a solo paddler. Most effective and most necessary in highly rockered canoes.

Bracing

LOW BRACE (page 181)

Purpose: To steady the paddler in the direction of his lean.

Comments: Used by either bowman or sternman to provide stability in twisting currents. It blends easily with the backstroke, the reverse sweep, and the stern pry (see page 185).

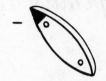

HIGH BRACE (page 179)

Purpose: Again to steady the paddler in the direction of his lean.

Comments: A radical version of the draw, useful to both bow and stern. Good for stability (see page 179) or for turning (e.g., into or out of eddies; see pages 141 and 177).

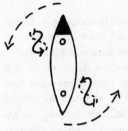

SCULLING DRAW (page 185)

Purpose: Same as the draw.

Comments: Provides bracing support as well as turning power in heavy water. It increases the power of the draw by minimizing the recovery phase of the stroke.

USELESS STROKES
(which certain Official Guidebooks continue to foist shamelessly upon an unsuspecting public)

JAM: A fanciful stroke used to stop the canoe. The author advises holding the paddle "with the thumb and fingers of your lower hand locked securely against the gunwale." The paddlers in the author's photographs ignore this advice and use a backstroke, as well they should.

OUT-DRAW: As near as we can figure, the draw in reverse. A misdesigned stroke which lacks the leverage of the pry.

BOW-RUDDER: Slow for one, awkward for another, and needs a second man to provide the power for the turn. Besides, when was the last time you saw a sailboat with a rudder in the front?

CROSSBOW RUDDER: Misery compounded. Use a crossdraw or pry.

THE "FLAM": The boating editor of a major sporting magazine has this advice on handling big haystacks: "If the bowman is a real expert, he will lean forward and slap his paddle from side to side to 'flam' an open path through the frothy wave . . ." Best trick since Moses parted the Red Sea.

Appendix II

An Outfit Checklist

This outfit list is a historical document, not an exhaustive catalogue. Except for some revisions Rug has made to keep the first-aid items up to date, our list is the same one that got handed to Peach after dinner one fine spring evening. We have not attempted to be comprehensive down to the last knife and fork because different people take different kinds of trips and have different tastes. (And we never take forks.) Besides, although we've read many guidebooks on backpacking, canoeing, and wilderness camping, we are always too bored to read their outfit lists. Our advice is to ignore this one, make up your own, and afterward come back if you want and see if you've missed anything.

I. PERSONAL GEAR

    A. *Clothing*

        Hat
        Head net
        Gloves
        Raincoat/rain gear
        Jacket
        Shirts (2)
        T shirts (2)
        Sweater or wool undershirt
        Pants (2)
        Long underpants (wool)
        Short underpants (army uses drawers style: supposedly better insulation)
        Ankle guards (homemade, for bugs)
        Socks (4 pairs, at least 2 wool)
        Wet-suit booties (optional)
        Sneakers
        Hiking boots

B. *Hygiene*

> Toothbrush
> Toothpaste
> Soap
> Nail clipper
> Toilet paper
> Towel (washcloth will do as well)

C. *Survival*

> Bug dope
> Match case
> Sunglasses (polarized)
> Whistle (for bushwhacking)
> Watch
> Knife
> Compass

II. TRANSPORTATION

A. *Land*

> Packs
> Duffels
> Extra pack frame(s)
> Day pack

B. *Water*

> Paddles
> Life jacket
> Rope
> Knee pads (optional)
> Bailers

III. THE ROUTE

> Maps
> Compasses
> Map case
> Binoculars

IV. CAMP

A. *Shelter and Sleep*

Tents
Tarp, 9 by 12 plastic
Sleeping bags
Foam pads (closed-cell)

B. *Fire and Cooking*

Matches (500)
Ax
Folding saw
Mess kit (frying pans, pots, cups, plates)
Spatula
Wooden spoon
Grill
Dish scrubber
Salt shaker

C. *Light*

Candles
Flashlight
Batteries

D. *Photography*

Camera
Film
Ammo box
Extra batteries
Polaroid filter (to cut sun's reflection on water)

E. *Fishing Gear*

F. *Education and Entertainment*

Harmonica
Books (survival manual; identification of fish, flora, and fauna;
    arctic adventures, etc.)
Playing cards

V. EMERGENCY, REPAIR, AND STORAGE

A. *Medical*

Handbook: We used Kodet and Angier (see Appendix III). Make sure that whatever book you carry tells exactly when and how to use the drugs and equipment you carry. If it doesn't, write the information down inside the book so every member of the party will have explicit instructions to follow should he need them. Many of the drugs listed below are obtainable by prescription only. You should consult with your physician about them before leaving on an extended trip.

Pain relief: We took aspirin, codeine, and morphine. To administer morphine we carried several small (1 cc.) syringes with 22-gauge needles. We repeat: learn doses, indications, and contraindications from your physician before you leave home.

Wound repair: Debriding (cleaning the wound) is crucial. We carried a couple of disposable sterile scrub brushes saturated with Betadine. Also: 3-0 chromic and 4-0 nylon sutures; sterile gloves; scalpel, a mosquito clamp, surgical gauze dressing, Adaptic non-adherent dressing, and 1-inch adhesive tape. Toting local anesthetics is scorned by tough-minded woodsmen, who know that taking a stitch is hardly painful at all; we took Novocain (2% without epinephrine).

Sprains: Ace bandage and more adhesive tape. Plastic finger splints are also worth their weight.

Antibiotic: Systemic (i.e., either oral or injectable antibiotics) are needed most often for infected wounds. We took decloxicillin, a new improved penicillin. Since a ten-day supply costs upward of twenty dollars, you might prefer the cheap, brand-X penicillin if you can't borrow a free supply the way Rug did. Again, check for allergies. Topical antibiotics for direct application on infected wounds may be worthwhile. We took Neosporin.

Eye: The most common affliction here is a stray twig. Ophthane, an anesthetic solution, makes removal of such a foreign body easier on the victim and the search party alike. If the cornea is scratched or conjunctivitis is the problem, you'll need an ophthalmological antibiotic such as Sodium Sulamyd.

Gastrointestinal upsets: Phenergan for vomiting. Either an injection or a suppository is necessary for severe cases when tablets won't stay down. Suppositories melt on hot days. Lomotil stops diarrhea.

Overheating: Chapstick for dry lips. A sunscreen such as Presun or zinc oxide for exposed skin. Salt tablets to replace salt loss in perspiration.

Snake country: suction cup and an antivenin kit.

B. *Other*

Plastic tape (waterproof)
Sewing kit
Space blanket
Grindstones (carborundum, soft Arkansas)
Sno-proof (for boots)
Plastic bags (spares)
Nuts and bolts
Wire
Aluminum tape
Nylon cord (plenty)
Patching cement/seam sealant for rain gear

ADDENDUM: Canoes

Appendix III

Selected Bibliography of River Guides and Other Various and Sundry Literature

We admit to presenting this list with trepidation. First, because of the ambivalence which must infect all writers of wilderness books: the love of the wilds and hence the wish to share that pleasure with others; yet the knowledge that in publicizing the activity, more and more wilderness will be tamed by the growing numbers who use it. We have salved our consciences along the usual lines, by claiming that this is a guidebook of methods, not a gilt-edged passport to a particular river (or rivers) described and catalogued down to the last riffle and bend. (Although our own book has used the Moisie River to tell a story, it is emphatically not a guide to the Moisie itself—as anyone who got near the river would soon realize. Had we been doing a guide, the number of pages devoted to portages would have been close to 200, to cite only one difference.)

The logic of that last paragraph appears to put those of us writing about wilderness *techniques* in the category of saints, while the *river* guide writers are left somewhere on the lower circles of Dante's Inferno. Yet these authors have their workable rationalizations, just like we do, and some of them hold as much water as ours. For one, rivers that are used by whitewater boaters fall prey to the designs of the Army Corps of Engineers. The theory of river guide writers is that the more people who see and enjoy the beauty of whitewater, the more political clout we wilderness types will wield in our battles to save what wildness remains. That makes some sense, and so we list a sampling here of guides to canoeing around the United States.

Yet our trepidation persists, for a second reason. Descriptions of particular rivers are only as good as the folks who write them. Guides may be helpful in getting you started, but you should run any river as if you had no idea what lay around the bend. All the normal rules of scouting we have outlined will apply, no matter how detailed your catalogue. Do not continue around the bend merely because you have been informed that Bear's Head rapids is only Class II all the way to the bottom. The best policy, if you're going to make mistakes, is to make your own.

Having spoken our piece, we present a selected bibliography. Because so many guidebooks are published by small presses and go in and out of print, we suggest writing the American Canoe Association Book Service, P.O. Box 248, Lorton, VA 22079 for a current list of their titles. They carry a good, up-to-date selection. In addition, two books deserve special note as basic sourcebooks for other materials. One is *The Canoeist's Catalog* by Bill and Fern Stearns (International Marine Publishing Company, Camden, ME 04843), a fascinating compendium produced in the *Whole Earth* style; and Val Landi, *The Bantam Great Outdoors Guide* (Bantam Books, New York), an 800-page encyclopedia of canoeing, fishing, and hunting literature, guide services, charter air companies, and map information for all fifty states and Canada. Between these two publications, paddlers should find the necessary leads they need to begin planning a wilderness canoe trip.

Adney, Edwin Tappan, and Chapelle, Howard I. *The Bark Canoes and Skin Boats of North America* (U.S. Government Printing Office, Washington, D.C. 20402).

A.M.C. New England Canoeing Guide (Appalachian Mountain Club, 5 Joy Street, Boston, Mass. 02108).

Arighi, Scott and Margaret. *Wildwater Touring* (Macmillan, New York). Includes river tours in Oregon and Idaho.

Beletz, Al, Syl, and Frank. *Canoe Poling* (A. C. Mackenzie Press, Box 9301, Richmond Heights Station, St. Louis, Mo. 63117).

Burmeister, Walter. *Appalachian Waters 1: The Delaware and Its Tributaries.*

———. *Appalachian Waters 2: The Hudson River and Its Tributaries.*

———. *Appalachian Waters 3: The Susquahanna River and Its Tributaries* (Appalachian Books, Oakton, Va. 22134).

Burrell, Bob, and Davidson, Paul. *Wild Water West Virginia* (McClain Printing Company, Parsons, W.Va. 26287).

A Canoe Trip Manual for British Columbia (Canoe B.C., 4022 West 27th Avenue, Vancouver, B.C.).

Carter, Randy. *Canoeing Whitewater: River Guide* (Appalachian Books, Oakton, Va. 22134). Covers Virginia, Eastern West Virginia, and North Carolina Great Smoky Mountain area.

Cawley, James and Margaret. *Exploring the Little Rivers of New Jersey* (Rutgers University Press, New Brunswick, N.J. 08903).

Denis, Keith. *Canoe Trails through Quetico* (University of Toronto Press, U.S. Branch, 33 East Tupper Street, Buffalo, N.Y. 14203).

Gabler, Ray. New England White Water River Guide (Appalachian Mountain Club, 5 Joy Street, Boston, MA 02108).

Grinell, Lawrence. *Canoeable Waterways of New York* (Pageant Press, New York).

Hawksley, Oz. *Missouri Ozark Waterways* (Missouri Conservation Commission, Jefferson City, Mo. 65101).

Kodet, E. Russel, and Angier, Bradford. *Being Your Own Wilderness Doctor* (Pocket Books, New York).

Martin, Charles. *Sierra Whitewater.* (Fiddleneck Press, P.O. 114, Sunnyvale, Ca. 94088).

Mayfield, Michael. *Tennessee Whitewater* (Southern Brochure and Book Press, Knoxville, TN).

McNair, Robert. *Basic River Canoeing* (American Camping Association, Bradford Woods, Martinsville, Ind. 46151).

Nickels, Nick. *Canoe Canada* (Van Nostrand, New York). A veteran paddler with plenty of good wilderness trips.

Peekna, Andres. *Guide to White Water in the Wisconsin Area* (Hoofers Outing Club, Wisconsin Union, University of Wisconsin, Madison, Wis. 53706).

Proskine, Alex. *No Two Rivers Alike* (The Crossing Press, Trumansburg, NY). Fifty streams in New York and Pennsylvania.

Riviere, Bill. *Pole, Paddle and Portage* (Van Nostrand, New York).

Rutstrum, Calvin. *North American Canoe Country* (Macmillan, New York).

Satterfield, Archie. *The Yukon River Trail Book* (Stackpole Books, Harrisburg, Pa. 17105).

Schwind, Dick. *West Coast River Touring* (Touchstone Press, Beaverton, OR).

Sehlinger, Bob and Lance, Bob. *A Canoeing and Kayaking Guide to the Streams of Tennessee* (Thomas Press, Box 2210, Ann Arbor, MI 48106).

Thomas, Eben. *No Horns Blowing* (Hallowell Printing Company, Hallowell, Me. 04347). Guide to ten rivers in Maine.

Urban, John and Williams, T. Wally. *White Water Handbook for Canoe and Kayak* (Appalachian Mountain Club, 5 Joy Street, Boston, Mass. 02108).

Walbridge, Charles. *Boatbuilder's Manual* (Wildwater Designs, Inc., Penllyn Pike and Morris Road, Penllyn, Pa. 19422).

INDEX

A NOTE ABOUT THE AUTHORS

Both Davidson and Rugge have canoed for many years throughout the northeastern United States, from Maine to West Virginia, and in the Canadian North, from Hudson's Bay to Goose Bay, Labrador.

James West Davidson was born in Rochester, New York, in 1946 and now lives in Boston. He was educated at Haverford College and Yale University (Ph.D.). He is a writer with a special interest in Colonial American history. John Rugge was born in Little Falls, New York, in 1944 and was educated at Williams College, Harvard University, and Yale University (M.D.). He currently practices medicine in the Adirondacks.